Mr. and Mrs. Robinson,

I thought you would enjoy a
bit of Richmond history
especially since you have
some family roots here!

With best wishes,
Virginia   December 2011

RICHMOND'S MONUMENT AVENUE

MONUMENT AVENUE

Sarah Shields Driggs, Richard Guy Wilson, and Robert P. Winthrop

The Historic Monument Avenue and Fan District Foundation

ORIGINAL PHOTOGRAPHY BY JOHN O. PETERS

The University of North Carolina Press

Chapel Hill and London

Designed by April Leidig-Higgins

Set in Carter & Cone Galliard by Eric M. Brooks

Manufactured in China

The paper in this book meets the guidelines for permanence and durability of the Committee

on Production Guidelines for Book Longevity of the Council on Library Resources.

Library of Congress Cataloging-in-Publication Data

Driggs, Sarah Shields. Richmond's Monument Avenue / by Sarah Shields Driggs, Richard

Guy Wilson, and Robert P. Winthrop; original photography by John O. Peters.

p. cm. Includes index. ISBN 978-0-8078-2607-2 (alk. paper)

1. Monument Avenue (Richmond, Va.)—History. 2. Monument Avenue (Richmond, Va.)—

Pictorial works. 3. Richmond (Va.)—History. 4. Richmond (Va.)—Pictorial works.

5. Richmond (Va.)—Buildings, structures, etc. 6. Architecture—Virginia—Richmond.

7. Monuments—Virginia—Richmond. 8. Historic buildings—Virginia—Richmond.

I. Wilson, Richard Guy, 1940– II. Winthrop, Robert P. III. Title.

F234.R58 D75 2001   975.5'451—dc21   00-064878

12 11 10 09 08   7 6 5 4 3

This book is dedicated to the citizens of Richmond and
all those who have cared for Monument Avenue
and worked toward its preservation.

CONTENTS

ACKNOWLEDGMENTS

From its very inception, when Otway Allen proposed that an enormous statue of Robert E. Lee be placed next to a baseball field in the countryside west of Richmond, Monument Avenue has engendered controversy and fascination. Although buildings, like many other things, are not usually venerated by Virginians until considerable time has passed, this street was different. The grand boulevard layout, complete with large and opulent houses, became an advertising card for the city's business interests, anxious to have Richmond anointed the capital of the New South. For others, especially those in the African American community, the street and its statues were a reminder of an unfortunate past. To this day, they recall Richmond's central role in our country's tragic civil war.

Monument Avenue is perhaps Richmond's most complex—and contested—enigma. Volumes of information and opinion have been written about its history and meaning, and discussions of Monument Avenue can become passionate and argumentative. As historians, we are only too aware that we are treading on what some see as sacred ground, and we know that we cannot please everyone. We have tried to address both fact and emotion, but Monument Avenue is history and, as such, it is open to interpretation. This book is our attempt to illuminate some of the motives and meanings that lie behind its origins and subsequent history.

The authors wish to acknowledge the contributions of the many authors, historians, and residents whose work and information has informed our understanding of Monument Avenue. We need to recognize those who have worked to preserve the street and to applaud the groups that use it to educate all of us about history, politics, and preservation.

The Historic Monument Avenue and Fan District Foundation and the Monument Avenue Preservation Society celebrate Monument Avenue's unique place in the city of Richmond. Activists in the neighborhood made this book and the centennial celebration happen. Many worked behind the scenes providing support, but those who met frequently with the authors to prod this book along include Sylvia Summers, Ceci Amrhein-Gallasch, Drew Carneal, Millie Jones, Calder Loth, George Wickham, and Gail Zwirner. Sylvia Summers's extraordinary dedication to the project led her to continue participating in the process of this book's gestation even after her term as president of the foundation ended.

Some of the information we have used in this book was first uncovered as part of a study of downtown Richmond's architecture commissioned by the city and prepared by three

University of Virginia students—Carden McGehee, Mary Watson, and Timothy Bishop—under the direction of John G. Zehmer. McGehee, Watson, and Bishop discovered the names and commissions of previously unknown architects who played a major role in shaping downtown Richmond as well as Monument Avenue. McGehee's 1980 thesis in architectural history, "The Planning, Sculpture, and Architecture of Monument Avenue," offered us several important insights into the development of the street.

In 1985 three undergraduate students at Virginia Commonwealth University—Ashley Neville, Diane C. James, and John Garcia—developed further information that we found valuable. They identified architects and owners of properties on Monument Avenue for papers written for a class on the history of Richmond architecture.

Several books have been indispensable for us. The comprehensive 1992 study *Monument Avenue: History and Architecture*, published by the Historic American Buildings Survey and authored by Kathy Edwards, Esme Howard, and Toni Prawl, was essential in the development of this book. It was sponsored by the Historic Monument Avenue and Fan District Foundation and provides exhaustive detail about the street's early residents and their relationships, as well as its architecture and real estate. One of the most insightful studies of the street is Jay Killian Bowman Williams's *Changed Views and Unforeseen Prosperity: Richmond of 1890 Gets a Monument to Lee*, which was written as an undergraduate paper in 1969 and then privately printed.

Our ideas about Monument Avenue evolved during work on earlier projects. Bob Winthrop taught a course on the history of Richmond architecture for several years at Virginia Commonwealth University. Richard Wilson wrote a chapter on Monument Avenue in *The Grand American Avenue: 1850–1920*, edited by Jan Cigliano and Sarah Bradford Landau and published in 1994 by the Octagon, the Museum of the American Architectural Foundation. Sarah Driggs coordinated a survey of Virginia sculpture for the Save Outdoor Sculpture! project in the mid-1990s and then wrote the National Historic Landmark nomination for Monument Avenue in 1998.

Richmond is blessed with several insightful architectural historians. Calder Loth and Drew Carneal have been particularly helpful and generous with information. Drew Carneal wrote a full and detailed history of Richmond's Fan District, published as *Richmond's Fan District* by the Historic Richmond Foundation in 1996, which provided impeccable background material. Drew also read the manuscript for us. Also, it is hard to write about architecture in Virginia without consulting *The Virginia Architects, 1835–1955: A Biographical Dictionary* by John E. Wells and Robert E. Dalton.

For help with various questions, illustrations, or ideas, we would like to thank Steven Bedford; Drew Carneal; Jane Cecil; Pierre Courtois, Gregg Kimball, Selden Richardson, and Mark Fagerburg of the Library of Virginia; Paul DiPasquale; Paul Dolinsky and Martin Perschler of the Historic American Buildings Survey; Zayde Dotts; Susan Eckis; Barbara Groseclose of Ohio State University; Calder Loth; Ann Hunter McLean; Carden McGehee; Howell Perkins of the Virginia Museum of Fine Arts; Dean Simpson; Pamela Simpson of Washington and Lee University; and Bob Tingle. For their interest and hard work, Brian Green of the Virginia Historical Society and Teresa Roane of the Valentine Museum need to be singled out, as does Liz Gushee of the Library of Virginia, who jumped through hoops to help. Indexers Monica Rumsey and Emily Salmon deftly sifted through the text to create a useful guide for readers and scholars. We would also like to thank Sian Hunter and all those who helped us at the University of North Carolina Press. Their guidance led to a much better book.

The photographer and the authors would like to thank the following people and institutions who made the beautiful photographs taken for the book possible: Beverley Aldredge and Heartfields, Whit Baldwin, Mason and Wyatt Beazley, Ann and Drew Carneal, Carole and Doug Conner, James DeJarnette, Zayde Dotts, Joni and Mark Dray, Rita Earl, Susan and Tom Eckis, Kenny and Bill Garbee, Grace Covenant Presbyterian Church, Austin and Billy Hancock, Joe Hill and Jim Gunn, Mary Anne and Walter Hooker, Mary and Tom Horton, Gary Inman, Todd Jenkins, Millie and Tom Jones, Keith Kissee, Frances Lewis, Bob Pogue, the Polish American String Band, Kay and Ray Ramming, Deborah and Edgar Roach, St. James's Episcopal Church, Rodney Shortell and the Martin Agency, Mary and Jack Spain, Sylvia and Dick Summers, Helen Marie Taylor, David Tolman, Wilson Trice, Ian Wallace and Bon Secours Stuart Circle Hospital, Del and George Warthen, Jim Whiting, Mr. and Mrs. David Wilson, Cindy and David Wofford, and Lindsay and Coley Wortham.

In addition, the authors would like to thank their families for their love and support. In particular, Abigail Elisabeth Victoria Wilson deserves special mention. Sarah Driggs would like to recognize Peggy Shields for her ceaseless encouragement and for sharing her love of good design, and—always and most importantly—to thank Frank, Katie, and Clare, who waited.

This book is for and about Monument Avenue. The residents have done more than anyone else to preserve and enhance the street. Without them, this would have been just a history book, not the story of a living neighborhood.

RICHMOND'S MONUMENT AVENUE

INTRODUCTION

The creation of a great avenue or street of power transformed many American cities during the nineteenth and early twentieth centuries. Across the country, broad, grand boulevards appeared. Boston's elite had Commonwealth Avenue; Chicago's wealthy lived along Prairie Avenue; and in Los Angeles the celebrated address was Wilshire Boulevard. Smaller towns also felt the need for a great street, as evidenced by Washington Avenue in Fredericksburg, Virginia; Bellevue Avenue in Newport, Rhode Island; and Magnolia Avenue in Riverside, California. Here lived the wealthy in large and impressive houses along a street that gained a special character through landscaping and decorative features. The forces that made these streets lay with real estate speculation, transportation changes, the growth of wealth, and the need to express identity and power. Monument Avenue in Richmond is one of these grand American avenues.

The character of each of America's great avenues is unique, but Richmond's Monument Avenue, as its name implies, has its own distinction. A place of beauty and a successful example of city planning, the long parade of houses and trees frames a sequence of statues unique not just along American streets, but in American cities. The meaning or iconography of these statues is complex, for most of the statues relate to the Civil War, and, depending on the viewer, offer different interpretations of that cataclysmic event. More recent additions represent attempts to either reconcile different versions or provide an alternative view of the South's past.

The Monument Avenue historic section, a renowned example of urban design, is lined with impressive houses and churches and punctuated by six statues dedicated to different heroes. Richmond is known as a city obsessed with its past, and Monument Avenue serves as a shrine to that obsession. It infuses the city with a mythology and demonstrates how history and perceptions of the past change, and how new meanings are created.

Monument Avenue marches out from Richmond's old city limits for one and a half miles, a grand avenue laid out with a dual purpose. Proposed in 1887 to provide an appropriate setting for a major memorial to Robert E. Lee in the former capital of the Confederacy, the broad, tree-lined boulevard embodied the growing City Beautiful movement of the turn of the century. Lee's statue was unveiled in 1890, and in time other statues were added and houses were built further west as the street was extended. Here Richmond's wealthy and prominent citizens chose to construct houses, apartments, and churches. The

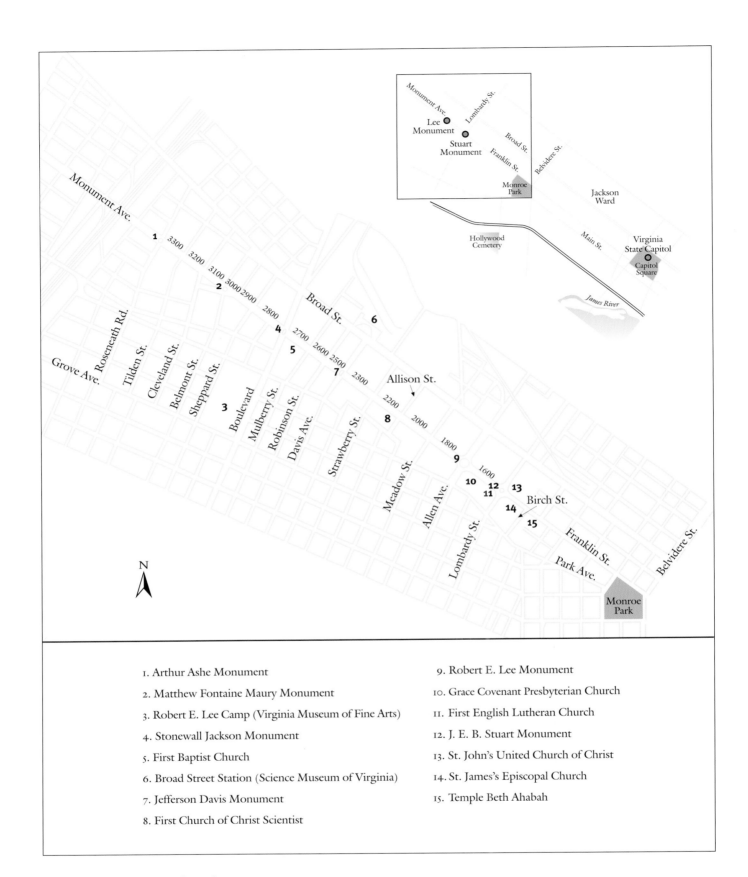

1. Arthur Ashe Monument

2. Matthew Fontaine Maury Monument

3. Robert E. Lee Camp (Virginia Museum of Fine Arts)

4. Stonewall Jackson Monument

5. First Baptist Church

6. Broad Street Station (Science Museum of Virginia)

7. Jefferson Davis Monument

8. First Church of Christ Scientist

9. Robert E. Lee Monument

10. Grace Covenant Presbyterian Church

11. First English Lutheran Church

12. J. E. B. Stuart Monument

13. St. John's United Church of Christ

14. St. James's Episcopal Church

15. Temple Beth Ahabah

Monument Avenue and Environs

The Jenkins house,
1839 Monument Avenue,
1908, M. J. Dimmock
and W. Duncan Lee,
architects.

result is a panoply of the architectural styles by which Americans defined themselves between the 1890s and the 1920s.

But the roots of Monument Avenue go back much earlier. In a large sense, the street was a response to the new wealth of post–Civil War America. Monument Avenue simultaneously symbolized Richmond's rising from the ashes of defeat and celebrated the past embodied in that defeat. As the avenue grew, it became the centerpiece for a specific interpretation of Virginia history, a memorial to the "Lost Cause" and the particularized white Southern view of the Civil War. The statues of J. E. B. Stuart and Jefferson Davis (both erected in 1907) and Stonewall Jackson (1919) that followed Lee's demonstrate the power of this myth. A statue to the navigator Matthew Fontaine Maury, unveiled in 1929, began to shift the focus and meaning of the street away from the Confederacy alone. Then in the 1990s, after considerable controversy, a statue dedicated to Arthur Ashe, the great tennis

ABOVE: *The Lee Monument, Monument Avenue at Allen Avenue, 1890, Marius-Jean-Antonin Mercié, sculptor. Spectacular houses form an impressive backdrop for the row of sculptures along Monument Avenue.*

RIGHT: *Unveiling the Lee Monument,* Harper's Weekly, *June 14, 1890. The huge extravaganzas staged for the unveiling ceremonies drew crowds from across the South, with parades, bazaars, balls, and speeches. (The Library of Virginia)*

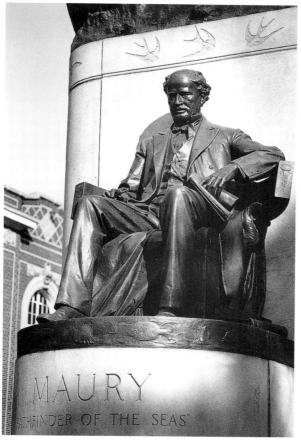

ABOVE: *3100 Monument Avenue, 1926, W. Duncan Lee, architect (right); 3102 Monument Avenue, 1931, Carl Lindner, architect (center); and 3104 Monument Avenue, 1928, Davis Brothers, Inc., designers and builders (left). Monument Avenue boasts a wide variety of architectural styles, contrary to stereotypes about the colossal white columns that adorn all important houses in the South.*

LEFT: *The Matthew Fontaine Maury Monument, Monument Avenue at Belmont, 1929, F. William Sievers, sculptor. The impetus to raise statues on Monument Avenue was not always motivated by reverence for the Confederacy. Matthew Fontaine Maury, the father of oceanography, inspired twentieth-century Richmonders with his considerable scientific achievements.*

South side of the 2200 block, Monument Avenue. The repetition of scale, form, materials, cornice, roofline, and setback contrive to project a perception of architectural harmony along the street.

star and champion of African American achievement, was added at Roseneath Road, further redefining the avenue as a parade of heroes, and not a testament to a single cause.

Monument Avenue is also a neighborhood of 263 houses and apartment buildings and 6 places of worship. The churches and residences display aspiration, competition, and achievement. Monument Avenue shares a common characteristic with other great American residential avenues from the turn of the century: many of the buildings are not architecturally distinguished themselves, but gain their significance from the impact of the harmony of scale, form, materials, cornice, roofline, and setback. The perception of unity is deceiving, for great variety exists among the buildings, since the street grew piecemeal over a period of forty years. The avenue becomes a virtual catalogue of the stylistic interests of early twentieth-century Americans, as the buildings compete with their facades ranging from prim James River Georgian to giant Southern Colonial columnar and more eccentric Spanish and Jacobean.

By the Depression, most of the avenue was built up as far as Roseneath Road to the west, for a total length from Stuart Circle of a mile and a half, or fourteen blocks. The infill of a few buildings added after World War II for the most part followed earlier examples. The historic area begins with two great circles that surround the Lee and Stuart Monuments; the intersecting streets gently curve into the traffic pattern. Asphalt paving blocks still remain in portions of the avenue. Eventually Henrico County extended the avenue to the west, creating a boulevard of more than five miles.

Monument Avenue incorporates many stories, but the main plot involves the statues

and the various memories they impose upon the viewer. Statues attempt to shape a collective memory, to give legitimacy to a point of view. Statues and monuments—and those on Monument Avenue are both—speak to those who see them, or convey meanings, some obvious, others submerged. The initial statues on Monument Avenue attempted to convey the nobility of martial exploits and vindicate the Confederate cause. Symbolism and validation underlay the creation of Monument Avenue, for its location at the end of Franklin Street created an alignment with Capitol Square and two powerful statues there, Houdon's Washington inside the Capitol, and Crawford and Rogers's equestrian Washington on the Capitol grounds. Certainly political motives underlay the erection of these statues, and for Richmond's African American population, the statues symbolized decades of disenfranchisement. Many years later the political roles were reversed, and the decision to place the Arthur Ashe statue on Monument Avenue gave the street a new meaning.

The controversy surrounding the Ashe statue is indicative of the still unfinished nature of the armed conflict that divided our nation some 120 years ago. The nature of the Civil War—whether it was a contest between slavery and freedom, or a defense of states' rights—will forever be debated. And while militarily, and to a large degree legislatively and legally, the issues arising from the Civil War have been settled, still in many places, especially in the South, they arouse deep passions.

The focus of this book is the historic core of Monument Avenue, why and how it was created, and the statues and houses that line it. Many different individuals, with a variety of motives, created Monument Avenue. The statuary committees, including the various

2307 Monument Avenue, the MacLean house, 1916, W. Duncan Lee, architect; 2309 Monument Avenue, the Golsan house, 1917, William Lawrence Bottomley, architect; 2315 Monument Avenue, the Parrish house, 1924, William Lawrence Bottomley, architect. Contrary to first impressions, the great variety of houses along the avenue creates a virtual catalogue of early twentieth-century styles in America.

ABOVE: *The J. E. B. Stuart Monument, Monument Avenue at Stuart Circle, 1907, Frederick Moynihan, sculptor. The drama of the Stuart Monument emphasizes the martial aspects of heroism.*

OPPOSITE: *The Arthur Ashe Monument, Monument Avenue at Roseneath Road, 1996, Paul DiPasquale, sculptor. As politics evolve, so do the messages conveyed in public sculpture. The siting of the Ashe Monument asserted that the heroes of all Richmonders have a place on Monument Avenue.*

INTRODUCTION

ABOVE: *Civil War reenactors at the base of the Lee Monument on the anniversary of Lee's birthday.*

RIGHT: *Crowds line the street surrounding the Davis Monument, Easter, 1997. Parades and festivities launched Monument Avenue, and various events ensure that it will continue as the city's gathering place.*

Runners passing the Lee Monument in the Richmond Marathon, 1997.

backers and sculptors, seldom if ever lived on the avenue, but they gave it one aspect of its character. Very different were the concerns of the merchants, doctors, and architects and builders who created the street's houses and churches. For them it was a neighborhood. The story of the avenue involves the history of the city in which it is located and the varying politics that held sway there. To tell that story in the following pages, the plan for the street is first considered, followed by the statues and then the buildings. The story also involves the personalities, the spaces and gardens, and the stories of both individuals who lived on the avenue and those who, though they never lived on the avenue, are commemorated there.

In a sense Monument Avenue represents a saga, one that is very American and yet unique to Richmond and its own long, and still ongoing, history. That the avenue still exists nearly intact is an important story of preservation. Monument Avenue embodies recovery and reconciliation.

ORIGINS

Beginning at the Stuart Monument two miles west of downtown Richmond, Monument Avenue lies in direct alignment with Franklin Street and the Virginia State Capitol at Capitol Square. The story of Monument Avenue traditionally begins in the 1880s with the selection of a site for the Robert E. Lee statue, but the origins of that selection lie within the origins of the city.

Richmond derives its name from the similarity of a view overlooking the James River with one over the Thames in the London borough of Richmond. William Byrd I, who owned the land in the area, established a post near the falls of the James River in the seventeenth century. In 1737 his son, William Byrd II, commissioned Colonel William Mayo to lay out the town in a grid of square blocks on the eastern, hilly side of Shockoe Creek, where it emptied into the James. The younger Byrd had warehouses built for the tobacco trade, and a small settlement grew up along the James River. In 1752 the General Assembly moved the Henrico County seat to Richmond, and by the Revolution about 600 persons lived in the port. Change came in 1779, when, under the leadership of Governor Thomas Jefferson, the state legislature voted to move the capital from Williamsburg to Richmond, which was more centrally located and easier to defend from British forces. The General Assembly first met there in a rented frame building in May 1780. The assembly decreed that Richmond would be expanded by 200 squares, or city blocks, located on the western side of Shockoe Creek, with six of these blocks reserved for the state government. That year Governor Jefferson selected the six blocks that would become Capitol Square.

Richmond was transformed overnight from an insignificant tobacco port to the capital of the largest and most populous state of the new United States. Instead of provincial, it became cosmopolitan, attracting a varied and talented population of artisans, lawyers, businessmen, actors, and architects. Centered around the capitol building designed by Jefferson, the city grew. Initially commerce and industry located generally to the south, along the riverfront, while residential areas grew up around the Capitol. In the 1840s the western section of Franklin Street, which began at Capitol Square, assumed the mantle of most prestigious residential street in Richmond.[1]

Lee statue, in Lee Circle, at the intersection of Monument Avenue and Allen Avenue.

In the nineteenth century, and the greater portion of the twentieth, Richmond expanded mostly toward the west and north. Periods of intense real estate speculation and development occurred nearly every decade, each followed by the inevitable downfall. The city's location at the fall line made Richmond a logical center for the processing and transshipment of agricultural products. In the three decades before 1860, Richmond became the tobacco manufacturing center of the United States and one of the great flour processing cities. The iron industry, led by Tredegar Iron Works, boomed in Richmond, and the city became known for the production of cannon, rails for railroads, and iron porches. In the late 1840s John Notman of Philadelphia laid out Hollywood, a rural cemetery, and in 1851 the City of Richmond acquired three park sites.

At the outbreak of the Civil War in 1861, Richmond had an area of two and one-half square miles and a population of 38,000, of which 14,275 were slaves and free blacks. The third-largest city in the South, Richmond ranked twenty-fifth in size among American cities and thirteenth in manufactures. Home to four banks, fifty-two tobacco factories, reputedly the largest flour mill in the world, and the largest iron foundry in the South—and served by five railroad lines—Richmond was essential to the Confederate cause. Between May 29, 1861, when Jefferson Davis arrived in the city, and April 3, 1865, when he hastily departed, Richmond, the capital of the Confederate States of America, became a much sought-after prize for the North. The Union believed that capturing Richmond would end the war, and the city's defense by the Army of Northern Virginia, under the leadership of General Robert E. Lee, eventually became the all-consuming task of the struggling Con-

View of Richmond, frontispiece, Letters of a British Spy *by William Wirt, 6th ed. (Baltimore: Fielding Lewis, 1817). (The Library of Virginia)*

federacy. When the Confederates were forced to abandon the city, they set fire to warehouses containing cotton and tobacco. Because of wind and explosions the fires spread and destroyed much of Richmond's industrial base and twenty blocks of the commercial district.

Post–Civil War Richmond recovered with amazing speed. Accounts of Reconstruction hardships in other areas of the South have to be tempered with the example of Richmond. The commercial section along Main Street rebounded rapidly—ironically, with significant Northern investment in larger brick and cast-iron-fronted buildings. The population grew, and by 1870 Richmond was the second-largest city of the South. The city recovered industrially with the reopening of the Tredegar Iron Works and the founding of a number of new companies, among them the Albemarle Paper Company, Old Dominion Nail Works, and Belle Isle granite quarries. The tremendous wealth that arose in the North after the Civil War, ushering in the so-called Gilded Age, could also be found in selected areas of the South, such as Richmond. Richmond's economy changed, and in the 1870s—and then increasingly in succeeding decades—industry gave way to finance, insurance, banking, and large-scale retail operations. At the same time, the old social order of landed families gave way to a new class. As the *Richmond Whig and Advertiser* reported in 1876,

> A new race of rich people have been gradually springing up among us, who owe their wealth to successful trade and especially to manufactures. . . . They are taking the leading place not only in our political and financial affairs, but are pressing to the front for social recognition. . . . We no longer condemn the filthy lucre. . . . Our provincial characteristics are fast disappearing, and we are not only advancing toward metropolitan development, but are losing our petty, narrow prejudices and becoming truly cosmopolitan. . . . We are no longer a village but a city.[2]

Amid Richmond's newfound prosperity, tensions with the freedmen and the question of political representation for the city's blacks emerged as a problem. Reconstruction had allowed some blacks and laboring whites into governmental positions of power, but, by the mid-1870s, the resurgent white Democratic Party wrested control from them. A split in the Democratic Party in the 1880s reversed the trend briefly, giving more representation on the

Richmond, ca. 1870. This view appeared in several publications in slightly different forms over a period of about twenty years. This example was taken from R. A. Brock, Hardesty's Historical and Geographical Encyclopedia Illustrated *(New York and Richmond: H. H. Hardesty, 1885). (The Library of Virginia)*

Richmond, 1890. (Valentine Museum)

city council to blacks and white labor interests. But by the late 1880s, at the instigation of a newly united Democratic Party under the leadership of Fitzhugh Lee, the tide began to shift again toward exclusion of blacks and labor. The Virginia Constitutional Convention of 1901–2, dominated by the Democrats, effectively disenfranchised blacks and working-class whites. In Richmond, the city council redistricted historically black Jackson Ward out of existence in 1904.

Economic depressions affected Richmond, just as they did other cities, in the late nineteenth century. In particular, the big slump of 1873 halted growth for most of the decade, and then no building activity occurred in the city between the Panic of 1893 and the end of the century. But, in time, prosperity returned after each of these economic downturns, and the city continued to grow and modernize. Until the 1870s, Richmond had been a walking city, but this changed as horse trolleys began tentatively pushing development to the west. In 1888 Richmond introduced the world's first successful electric streetcar system, and the urban area exploded with developments such as the Fan District, Ginter Park, Forest Hill, Woodland Heights, and the West End. By 1890 the population stood at 81,388; and, although it stagnated in the following decade, growing to only 85,050 in 1900, in the next twenty years it more than doubled, to 171,667 in 1920.

The origins of Monument Avenue can be found in the diverse attributes of this growing urban population: new wealth and the desire to express it in the form of impressive residences, the will to erect monuments to the recently vanquished of the Civil War, and belief in the concept of a "New South." The Richmond that built Monument Avenue found itself in the 1880s being challenged by newer Southern cities, such as Atlanta, for the distinction of being the "first" city of the New South. Beginning in the late 1880s, and extending well into the early twentieth century, many Southern leaders argued that the South could no longer afford to be tied to its agrarian, hence poverty-stricken, past. Instead, they contended, the South had the natural and human resources to establish a great industrial, commercial, and financial empire, complete with the requisite cultural emblems, to rival the North. According to these progressive leaders, the South should become modern. For it to do so, urban rivalry among Southern cities, and especially with Northern cities, was paramount.[3] Nowhere was this attitude more prominent than among many of Richmond's citizens, who continued to view their home as the first city of the South, and its cultural and financial center. Richmond was the only Southern city that came close to the national mean of males employed in manufacturing in 1890. But Richmond was slipping, and in the next several decades it would lose its economic leadership. Other Southern cities—Atlanta, Birmingham, and New Orleans—would eclipse it. Although Virginia lost the distinction of being "first among equals," Richmonders never lost a feeling of having special significance.

City Planning

Richmond's urban plan and development in many ways mirrored those of other American cities. Beginning with an initial grid superimposed over uneven topography, the checkerboard pattern would be extended as the city grew. Also in common with other cities, these extensions did not always align; developers would alter the grid and hence the street alignment. The reasons may have been topographical, but the results were separate neighborhoods with slightly different street patterns from those of the original city. In Richmond, the roads running west from downtown shifted direction at Monroe Park, and a new grid appeared, creating a distinctly different district known as the West End.

In the nineteenth century, Richmond expanded its formal open spaces beyond Capitol Square and St. John's churchyard. Cemeteries segregated by religion appeared north of downtown in 1816 and 1825. The Northern fad for rural cemeteries arrived in Richmond in 1847, when a group of businessmen hired the Philadelphia-based architect John Notman to lay out Hollywood Cemetery. Located on a bluff overlooking the James River, Hollywood, with its curving streets, had some of the characteristics of an urban park. In 1851 the City of Richmond established a number of green spaces at the city's edges to ensure "in-

2340 Monument Avenue, the McClellan house, 1910, Scarborough and Howell, architects. Impressive residences boast of thriving business climates. Chamber of commerce publications often picture dwellings like the McClellan house to promote a city's reputation. (Valentine Museum)

vigorating air" for its citizens. The one at the western edge, known as Western Square, was soon renamed Monroe Square because it abutted Monroe Ward, and then finally was called Monroe Park. Initially it served as a space for cattle and agricultural shows; during the Civil War, it first served as a drill ground and then hospitals and barracks were built upon it. Not until 1871 did it become what might be called a public park, when, at the request of nearby homeowners, the city graded it, laid out pathways, and planted trees. More park land was acquired in 1875 in the East End. The introduction of urban transit allowed the development of amusement parks such as Forest Hill Park across the James River in Manchester (later incorporated into the city). Beginning in 1874, the city engineer, Wilfred E. Cutshaw, began acquiring land around the city reservoir and designed, over the years, what later became Byrd Park.[4]

Richmond, in common with several other Southern cities, differed from Northern cities in its pattern of development. Although larger houses were located on generous sites beyond the city limits, Richmond had no real suburban development until the 1880s. Whereas New York had a Llewellyn Park in the 1850s, and Chicago had a Riverside in the late 1860s, Richmond remained tightly bound. In 1888 Forest Hill and Woodland Heights were laid out south of the James River. Ginter Park, located northwest of downtown, was laid out beginning in 1893. The areas south of the James River loosely followed the curvilinear picturesque aesthetic, whereas Ginter Park followed the grid. Richmond witnessed no attempts at elite private residential squares such as New York's Gramercy Park, Boston's South End, or the various private streets of St. Louis.

The other, more common, elite housing option in most American cities became the grand avenue. Although there were earlier predecessors, it was in the 1850s, and especially in the decades after the Civil War, that ostentatious displays of financial success began to appear on streets such as Fifth Avenue in New York, Euclid Avenue in Cleveland, and Prairie Avenue in Chicago. Along Fifth Avenue, rich families such as the Vanderbilts erected versions of Italian palazzos and French châteaus. Influenced by a new cosmopolitan vision that came from increased foreign travel, wealthy Americans sought to emulate cities such as Paris, when they saw the rebuilding and extension carried out by Baron Haussmann in the French capital in the 1850s and 1860s. The tree-lined boulevard, viewed initially as very much a French-inspired urban garden, began to appear in America tentatively in the 1850s, and with increasing frequency in the 1860s and thereafter. Frederick Law Olmsted and Calvert Vaux employed boulevard schemes, for example, for an extension of Delaware Avenue in Buffalo in 1870 and for Eastern Parkway, as part of the Prospect Park design, in Brooklyn in 1865.

The most famous of the American boulevard schemes, and one intimately connected to Monument Avenue, is Commonwealth Avenue in Boston. A 240-foot-wide divided boulevard eight blocks in length, with a central walkway planted with trees, Commonwealth Avenue became the elite residential street for Bostonians after the Civil War. Several statues were placed in the median, and some of the most substantial houses in Boston were erected along the street. Part of the great landfill scheme of Back Bay Boston that began in 1857 and concluded in 1880, Commonwealth Avenue announced a bold new vision of the

Commonwealth Avenue, Boston. (Boston Athenaeum)

future expansion of the American city. Instead of being the usual piecemeal development that tended to focus inward, Commonwealth Avenue was very much envisioned as urban fabric and part of the city's sequence of public spaces. On another section of the Back Bay landfill Copley Square was laid out; envisioned as the cultural and spiritual center of the new Boston, it was the site of several major churches, a public library, and a museum.[5]

Richmond's entry into the grand street tradition began tentatively in the 1840s along Franklin Street, running west from Capitol Square. Prior to this, the city's primary elite housing area had been near the Capitol in Court End and on Church Hill. The establishment of St. Paul's Episcopal Church in 1845 at the corner of Grace Street and Capitol Square helped provide impetus for the elite and those who aspired to that status to construct substantial houses on Franklin Street. Houses in the Greek Revival, then Italianate, and, after the Civil War, Second Empire and Queen Anne styles, among others, appeared as building moved westward. Both along the street and adjacent to it were erected substantial churches, such as Second Presbyterian (1847), by Brooklyn architect Minard Lefever. Two of Richmond's elite men's organizations, the Richmond Club and the Commonwealth Club, also located on Franklin. In 1893–95, Major Lewis Ginter had Richmond's grand hotel showplace, the Jefferson, erected on Franklin Street, after designs by the New York architects Carrère and Hastings, and then between 1889 and 1892 he erected his own elegant mansion a few blocks further west. Franklin Street ends two miles west of Capitol Square, where it becomes Monument Avenue at what is now Stuart Circle.

Monumental Statuary

The initial statues erected on Monument Avenue grew out of a small, yet significant, American tradition, which in a sense began in Richmond. A few monumental statues, such as those to Lord Botetourt in Williamsburg and George III in New York, had existed prior to the Revolution, but Richmond is the site of the first major American monumental sculpture, Jean Antoine Houdon's *George Washington*. Commissioned by the Virginia General Assembly in 1784–85, it was installed in the rotunda of the State Capitol in 1796. Based upon a life mask and measurements Houdon had undertaken at Mount Vernon, the statue portrays Washington life-sized, dressed in his Revolutionary army garb, his sword hung on a bundle of thirteen fasces, with a plow at his feet. The later events surrounding Secession that took place in the Capitol lend an air of irony to Houdon's Washington, since the sculptor portrays Washington as employing his sword in the cause of freedom and then sheathing it when the unity of the thirteen colonies was settled. Following this initial foray into the monumental genre, other sculptors, both foreign and native-born, created personifications of American deities. Although there are exceptions, such as Clark Mills's equestrian *Andrew Jackson* (1848–51), most American monumental sculpture prior to the Civil War focused on the father of the country. The Philadelphian William Rush carved a Washington in pine (1814); Horatio Greenough sculpted an infamous Zeus-like *Washington* out of marble (1832–41) for the United States Capitol; and Henry Kirke Brown created an equestrian *Washington* in bronze (1853–56) for Union Square in New York. And in Richmond, beside the Capitol and on the axis of Franklin Street, stood a monument to Washington (1850–69), by Thomas Crawford and Randolph Rogers. An iconographically

complex composition, the monument features an equestrian Washington riding on top of a high pedestal, while around the base stand six of Virginia's favorite sons and several allegorical figures. Crawford died in 1857, having completed only Washington and the smaller statues of Patrick Henry and Thomas Jefferson. Randolph Rogers received the commission to finish the complex design, and contributed—after designs left by Crawford—the figures of George Mason, John Marshall, Thomas Nelson, and Meriwether Lewis. The unveiling of the equestrian Washington took place in 1858, and other statues were added in 1867 and 1869.

At the base of the Washington statue, on February 22, 1862, Washington's birthday, the official founding of the Confederacy was marked, when Jefferson Davis took the inaugural oath as president of the Confederate States of America. The obvious symbolism was further reinforced with the selection of a bas-relief of Crawford and Rogers's Washington Monument as the central image of the Great Seal of the Confederate States of America. Washington as Founding Father, warrior, and protector of liberty was appropriated by the Confederate States.[6]

Crawford and Rogers's Washington Monument in Richmond actually represented the culmination of a process begun in 1815–18 when the Virginia General Assembly and the

900 Block of West Franklin Street, ca. 1890. Franklin Street's distinction as the most fashionable address in Richmond began as early as the 1850s. Throughout the nineteenth century the construction of elegant residences moved further west. This view shows the handsome houses that faced Monroe Park. (Virginia Historical Society)

LEFT: George Washington, *Virginia State Capitol, 1788, Jean Antoine Houdon, sculptor. With this statue, Virginia claimed one of the earliest monumental sculptures in the United States. The General Assembly commissioned Houdon to model this famous marble portrait from life, expressing profound respect for a living hero. (Valentine Museum)*

RIGHT: *Washington Monument, Capitol Square, Richmond, 1850–69, Thomas Crawford and Randolph Rogers, sculptors. An even more elaborate tribute to Washington was undertaken several decades later when erection of the equestrian Washington Monument was begun in Capitol Square. The Confederacy appropriated this image of Washington in its Great Seal to symbolize what it saw as its fight for freedom. (Valentine Museum)*

state's governor announced a competition for a Washington monument, very much in response to the 1814 Washington monument competition in Baltimore. Robert Mills had won the earlier competition (though work on Baltimore's monument was not completed until 1842) with a design featuring a large, 178-foot-tall Doric column, following the form of Trajan's Column in Rome, crowned by a statue of Washington. Mills followed this with the Washington obelisk in Washington, D.C., a commission won in competition in 1845 but not completed until 1884. These various statues and monuments played a significant role in the developing American city. Intended to commemorate and instruct, they were to teach both history and values to future generations, of the native-born as well as the swelling tide of immigrants. They also functioned as urban landmarks, as generative ele-

View of Baltimore City, ca. 1862. The desire to commemorate Washington also struck Baltimore, where Robert Mills designed a Washington Monument (completed in 1842) that anticipated his later obelisk for Washington, D.C. The wide, tree-lined median and elegant houses of Mount Vernon Square, the neighborhood that developed around the monument, influenced Otway Allen's scheme for Monument Avenue. (Maryland Historical Society)

ments in the planning and development of a city, such as Baltimore, where around the Washington Monument tree-lined squares appeared. Elite citizens of Baltimore built their houses on Mount Vernon Square, and in time it became the city's cultural acropolis, home to the Peabody School of Music and the Walters Art Gallery.

These earlier monuments and sculptures provide the backdrop for the sculptural program that lies at the heart of Monument Avenue and also for the sculpture wave that occurred after the Civil War and into the 1930s. Monument Avenue is part of the transformation of America into a great outdoor sculpture gallery. Beginning the trend was the commemoration of the Civil War, which had several phases and was marked by a variety of sculptural and monumental types. As the victorious side, the North led the way. One of the first commemorative monuments is the Union Henry Hill Monument, dedicated June 13, 1865, on the Manassas battlefield. A stumpy central obelisk with four short piers at the corners, each topped by a howitzer shell, it is typical of the nonsculptural battlefield monuments. On July 4, 1865, the cornerstone of the Soldiers' National Monument was laid at the Gettysburg battlefield cemetery, and work on the monument was completed in 1869. A central column with eighteen stars for the Union states carried Victory, and at the base of the monument sat four allegorical figures, including a personification of a Union soldier. One of the first monuments located in a city is a standing Victory figure in Lowell, Massachusetts, which dates from 1867. Who created the first statue of a standing Yankee soldier is unclear; the Boston sculptor Martin Milmore produced one example by 1868 for a Boston cemetery and copied it for other locations.[7] These were early efforts, for the major flurry of ubiquitous Civil War "Yanks," or commemorative monuments, came in the period after 1880, and most intensely in the 1890s and 1900s, as nearly every Northeastern and Midwestern town and city erected some sort of a monument. They could be statues or obelisks and could be constructed out of granite, marble, or bronze. Companies such as the American Bronze Foundry, the New England Monument Company, the Monumental Bronze Company, the Maurice Powers National Fine Arts Foundry, and the McGibbon and Curry Company specialized in supplying these generic types. Large commemorative statues and monuments for individuals and events begin in the North in the 1870s with Thomas Ball's *Emancipation Group* (1869–76) in Washington, D.C., which shows Lincoln freeing a slave. John Quincy Adams Ward, a leading sculptor, produced a standing *General John F. Reynolds* (1871) for the Gettysburg battlefield and one of the first equestrian Union statues, *General George H. Thomas* (1878), for Washington, D.C. Momentum grew in the 1880s: Augustus Saint-Gaudens's Admiral Farragut Memorial, with its base by Stanford White, was unveiled on Madison Square in New York in 1881; Vinnie Ream's *Admiral Farragut* in Washington, D.C., was also completed in 1881; the arch at the Grand Army of the Republic Plaza in Brooklyn was proposed in 1885 and erected (without the sculptural embellishments) in 1892; and Grant's Tomb in New York was announced in 1885, though it was not completed until 1897.[8]

In the former Confederate states, a similar, though initially slower, commemorative and sculptural program took place, and out of it came the Lee statue and Monument Avenue. In 1866 the federal government announced that it would not bury Confederate soldiers in national cemeteries. Partly in reaction to this announcement, Richmond's Hollywood Memorial Association commissioned former Confederate officer, local architect, and city engineer Charles H. Dimmock to design a pyramid for Hollywood Cemetery, where many Confederate dead had been placed. A rough granite pyramid met the financial limitations of the immediate postwar era. The cornerstone was laid in December 1868, and nearly a year later, on November 6, 1869, a convict from the nearby penitentiary guided the pyramid's capstone into place as a crowd cheered. In 1872 the Hollywood Memorial Association reinterred some of the Southern dead from the battle of Gettysburg. The association also organized one of the first Confederate Memorial Day celebrations on May 31, 1866. (Although the North traditionally celebrated Memorial Day on the 30th, the date varied widely throughout the South.) At such an observance in Virginia's Middle Peninsula, in front of the Lancaster County Courthouse in 1872, the local Ladies' Memorial Association erected reputedly the earliest noncemetery Confederate monument in the state. A marble obelisk, it is inscribed with names and bears a small sculpted plaque. The ubiquitous "Johnny Reb," or Confederate soldier, standing in front of a courthouse or in a cemetery is often indistinguishable from his Yankee counterpart except for his belt buckle and hat, and in many cases the statues were made by the same company. Most date to the 1890s or later. The first statue dedicated to a specific Confederate came as a gift from a group of Englishmen who in 1875 presented the state of Virginia with a statue of Thomas J. "Stonewall" Jackson. Depicting the general standing in uniform, the Jackson statue was unveiled on Capitol Square in Richmond during a ceremony attended by a crowd estimated at 40,000.[9]

Although the first specific Confederate statuary monument honored Jackson, Robert E. Lee received most of the recognition. His death, while serving as president of Washington College in Lexington, Virginia, in 1870 sparked several campaigns to erect monuments in his memory. Edward Valentine, a sculptor from Richmond, received the commission to create Lee's tomb sculpture for Lexington, the so-called Recumbent Lee. He completed it in 1875, but it was not unveiled at the renamed Washington and Lee University in Lexington until June 28, 1883.[10] In New Orleans a large traffic circle was renamed Lee Circle, and

LEFT: *Confederate Memorial, Hollywood Cemetery, Richmond, 1868–69, Charles H. Dimmock, designer. This massive pyramid, a monument to the Confederate dead, was partly underwritten by a gala bazaar at which raffles and sales of donated souvenirs, crafts, food, and drink raised more than $18,000. (Valentine Museum)*

RIGHT: Thomas Jonathan Jackson, *Capitol Square, Richmond, 1875, John Henry Foley, sculptor. As early as 1863, a group of Englishmen discussed raising a monument to Stonewall Jackson, the first Confederate to be honored individually. They donated this statue to the state of Virginia more than a decade later. (Valentine Museum)*

a tall Doric column pedestal was built in 1877, after designs by John Ray. The statue of a standing Lee by Alexander Doyle was not installed atop the column until 1884. And in Richmond two groups—one composed of former soldiers, the other of women—which soon became rivals were formed in 1870 to erect a monument to Lee. From these two groups sprang, in 1887, the decision to erect the Lee statue that would lead to the creation of Monument Avenue.

The American Renaissance

That Richmond, one of the leaders of the New South of economic and industrial expansion—this self-declared modern South—would create an immense statuary program commemorating a war it lost a quarter of a century earlier attests to the paradoxical elements in American culture in the period from 1870 to 1930. Throughout the United States, industrial and financial expansion created great fortunes, and yet the dominant artistic expression of this new wealth took on not a modern cast but a retrospective searching of the American and European past for the reassurance of tradition that was known at the time as the American Renaissance. The alternative, known as the Arts and Crafts movement and personified by Gustav Stickley or Frank Lloyd Wright, played a very minor role in the American South. Americans there, especially those with money, instead looked either to the American past or abroad, especially to France.

Historians have noted that in the nineteenth century bourgeois Americans began to identify with the cosmopolitan style of Napoleon III and Empress Eugénie, and, even after their fall in 1870, France remained the touchstone for the arts in America. Although many Americans recognized Italy as the fountainhead of the arts, the source of the Renaissance and many of the great art traditions, they perceived Italy through a French haze, as American painters, sculptors, and architects flocked to Paris to study at the École des Beaux-Arts, or in other ateliers and schools. Prior to the Civil War, English taste had largely dominated American art, but afterward—while some elements of British influence remained—France became the interpreter of art for America.

Beginning in the 1870s and continuing into the 1930s, many artists, critics, and commentators employed the term "American Renaissance" to define the artistic and cultural changes taking place in the United States. The lavishly decorated monumental governmental and commercial buildings, along with much of the sculpture, painting, landscape design, and city planning of the period, were viewed as signaling a renewal of art equivalent to that of the Renaissance in Italy. This American Renaissance drew upon European precedent but attempted to give it an American cast.[11] In a sense a hegemonic cultural system, the American Renaissance provided a means of self-identification and fully reflected the nation's aspirations. Americans from all walks of life and every social status, from artists to politicians, financiers, and shopkeepers, believed that American culture—including the arts—would not only draw sustenance from the past to create an American Renaissance, but that through the remaking of the physical landscape with statues, buildings, and murals, the civic life and values of Americans would be improved. Coinciding with increased immigration from Europe and the new freedom of the African American community, the outpouring of art in the American Renaissance would create shared values and impose a collective memory on all classes.

The American Renaissance was idealistic, nationalistic, and cosmopolitan all at the same time. It was the primary expression of the new wealth in the United States, of the vast industrial and commercial expansion that permitted individuals and families to construct and furnish large houses, collect old masters, contribute to sculptural programs, support American artists, and endow museums, libraries, symphonies, and universities.

Not specifically a style, the American Renaissance embodied a consciousness of the United States as the heir of the Old World, and especially of European art traditions. Through the visual arts—painting, sculpture, and architecture—and by the collecting of great examples of European art, the United States would create a great civilization. To that end, the sculpture of the post–Civil War years often embodied a continuing commemora-

The Minute Man, *Concord, Massachusetts, 1875, Daniel Chester French, sculptor. Interest in our national history provoked by the American Renaissance led to the erection of various statues to the Founding Fathers and to anonymous heroes of the past. (Concord Free Public Library)*

tion of the Founding Fathers, but it also included statues like that of the anonymous Minute Man at Concord, Massachusetts (1875), by Daniel Chester French, and *Pocahontas* at Jamestown (1906), by William Ordway Partridge. The Lee statue that arose with Monument Avenue is a creation of this self-conscious American Renaissance.

The Lost Cause

The Lee Monument and other Confederate monuments reflected a cult of the Lost Cause that gained great momentum in the 1880s and persisted into the 1920s. Very specifically a white Southern response to defeat, it portrayed the Confederacy as a noble effort to preserve the South's heritage and way of life. In this white Southern interpretation of the story, the Civil War—or, as some chose to call it, the War of Northern Aggression—was not about freeing African Americans held in slavery, but about defending an agrarian culture that refused to bow to the demands of Northern mercantile and industrial interests. The North fought for a union of territory, while the South's concern was with the original intention of the Founding Fathers that the states had inalienable rights, among them the right to decide for themselves the question of slavery and the right, should they choose, to secede from the Union. The *Richmond Dispatch* in 1887 commented on the Lee cornerstone

RIGHT: *Lee Monument, New Orleans, column designed by John Ray and completed in 1877, sculpture by Alexander Doyle installed in 1884. A human Confederate flag assembled at the base of the monument for its dedication in 1884. Across the South, a variety of Confederate images were being unveiled to adoring crowds in the late nineteenth century, but those of Lee commanded the most respect. (Historic New Orleans Collection)*

BELOW: *Veterans near the Davis Monument at a Confederate reunion, sometime after 1907. Writings, speeches, and gatherings sponsored by memorial organizations drastically changed memories and interpretations of the Civil War. White Southerners portrayed the Confederacy as a noble cause motivated by a desire to protect states' rights and aroused by the North's aggression. (Valentine Museum)*

dedication by asking rhetorically of the Confederate army: "Was there ever on this planet a nobler class of men?"[12] In many ways the Lost Cause took on the trappings of a civic religion, and religious imagery often pervaded its oratory and writings.[13]

In the retelling of the Confederate story, the myth of the Old South was reinforced by the pens of novelists such as Thomas Nelson Page of Richmond. Page's various writings—among them, *In Ole Virginia* (1887) and *Two Little Confederates* (1888) and his nonfiction *The Old South* (1892)—helped to foster the myth that the Northern victory in the war had wiped out a proud and cultured civilization in which slavery was not an obnoxious institution. The white Southern version of the past held that the condition of blacks in slavery was actually far better than that of Northern laborers, and indeed that most African Americans were happy with their lives. Of course the rise and spread of this mythologized history corresponded almost exactly with the enactment of Jim Crow laws and the establishment of institutionalized segregation throughout the South.

Helping to spur on the Lost Cause myth were a number of organizations, such as the United Confederate Veterans, the Southern Historical Society, and the United Daughters of the Confederacy, as well as numerous local groups. They established camps, such as the Lee Camp Number One in Richmond, to house veterans. They also sponsored the various Confederate reunions and celebrations that became commonplace throughout the South in the years after 1890. And, in many cases, these groups were responsible for sponsoring and raising funds to pay for various memorials.

In this context, the monument to Robert E. Lee is part of an interpretation of the Civil War as seen through white Southern eyes. Yet, in a sense, the focus on Lee depoliticized the war, for Lee's reputation underwent a substantial postwar shift even in the North: he became not a rebel, but a great American hero, a tragic personage of noble character caught in an irreconcilable conflict between his state and his nation.[14] The complexities of the Lee myth and its relation to the Lost Cause are revealed in a bombastic statement by former Confederate general Jubal Early on a monument to Lee:

> His fame belongs to the world and to history, and is beyond the reach of malignity; but a sacred duty devolves upon those whom, in defense of a cause he believed to be just, and to whom he remained true to the latest moment of his life, he led so often to battle. . . . We owe it to our fallen comrades, to ourselves, and to posterity, by some suitable and lasting memorial to manifest to the world for all time to come, that we were not unworthy to be led by our own immortal chief, and that we are not now ashamed of the principles for which Lee fought and Jackson died.[15]

The Site

The two rival Richmond-based groups formed to promote construction of a Lee monument—one male and filled with ex-Confederates, the other the Ladies' Lee Monument Association—were united in March 1886 by an act of the General Assembly. The leader of the united groups, now called the Lee Monument Association, was Virginia's newly elected governor, Fitzhugh Lee, a former Confederate general and also a nephew of Robert E. Lee, who was determined to get a monument built in Richmond. Already there had been

Camp Gordon, north side of Broad Street, May 30, 1907. Huge encampments were organized to accommodate the large numbers of veterans who came to Richmond for Confederate reunions. Streetcar tracks provided access to festivities downtown, and the mess hall offered refreshments for the aging comrades. (Virginia Historical Society)

Festive occasions, like this gathering at the Lee statue, accompanying the unveiling of the Stuart Monument in June of 1907, attracted large audiences to nostalgic shows that gradually made partisan posturing a mainstream activity. (Valentine Museum)

several competitions, which brought forth a number of proposals for a site. Initially, the Ladies' Association preferred Hollywood Cemetery, but its members eventually came to the conclusion that the isolated location would diminish a monument's didactic impact. Over the years other sites were discussed, including Capitol Square near Crawford and Rogers's *Washington* and various of the city's other squares, such as Monroe. A letter to the Richmond paper *The State* suggested a tall column (similar to the one in New Orleans) with Lee's face toward the rising sun and his arm extended to the south, "indicating that the sun of the New South has arisen."[16] Another favored site, Gamble's Hill, a plateau of several acres overlooking the James River, would, according to its proponents, make a monument put there "a landmark for miles and miles."[17] The site receiving the strongest support, Libby Hill, lay in the east end of the city, on a bluff overlooking the James River. C. P. E. Burgwyn, the consulting architect for the Lee Monument Association, reported that monuments look best when viewed from below.[18]

Hence it came somewhat as a surprise when, in mid-1886, it was reported that a site west of downtown was under consideration.[19] On June 18, 1887, the Lee Monument Association announced its choice of the site just outside the western city limits, or West End, of Richmond. One of the advocates for this western site was Dr. J. William Jones, the secretary of the Southern Historical Society and former chaplain of Lee's Army of Northern Virginia. Jones had followed Lee to Washington College in Lexington and from this position appeared to speak for Lee. Jones argued that the tide of Richmond's population was moving westward, and he reasoned: "On the whole, there occurs to me no more desirable site than at the point Franklin Street strikes Lombardy Street and is stopped by the Allen property. . . . Let a circle be secured there, let Franklin Street be opened through to the Boulevard." He further explained: "And I confess that I should be glad to have it there because it would be in full view of the Soldiers' Home, and the veterans of Lee would be able to gaze on the figure of their great chief."[20] Jones's reference was to the recently established Lee Camp Number One, a home for destitute Confederate veterans. Founded in 1883, the organization purchased thirty-six acres the next year on what became Reservoir Road, and later the Boulevard. The camp lay about one mile southwest of the proposed Lee Monument site. Cottages were erected around a common that doubled as a parade ground; the veterans wore uniforms and stood guard duty. In 1887 a Confederate memorial chapel, designed by Marion J. Dimmock, was erected on the site.[21] But also, as the *Richmond Dispatch* reported, "Some time in the not-remote future Franklin Street will be extended through this property, and those who favor this site propose that it shall be widened so as to make a grand boulevard, with room for rows of trees down the middle"; additionally, the paper stated, "The city is growing rapidly in this direction, and property is steadily advancing in price in all that section."[22]

Although flat and bare, this West End site possessed several possible advantages. One Richmond newspaper described it as a broad, open space on one of the "greatest elevations of the city . . . several feet above the Capitol site." The newspaper went on to explain, "A too close proximity of buildings has ruined some of the finest monuments in Europe."[23] This opinion reflected perhaps the sentiments of C. P. E. Burgwyn, the architect for the Lee Monument Association, who had traveled in Europe observing monuments in situ. Exactly what he saw remains unclear, but he could have seen the broad, open expanse of the equestrian statue of Anne de Montmorency, Constable of France, at Chantilly. On a wide grassy circle at the intersection of two avenues stands the Chantilly statue, presenting a silhouette against a skyline.

The site of the Lee Monument lay within a tract of fifty-eight acres just beyond the western edge of the city. The acreage closest to the city limits had been used most recently, from 1883 to 1885, as a baseball field.[24] The entire tract was owned by the heirs of William C.

Fitzhugh Lee, a former Confederate general and Robert E. Lee's nephew, took control of the Lee Monument Association soon after his election as governor of Virginia. (Virginia Historical Society)

TOP: *Lee Camp Number One, a home for destitute Confederate veterans, began developing a complex of buildings on Reservoir Road in 1884. Robinson House and the chapel remain today, on the campus of the Virginia Museum of Fine Arts. (Virginia Historical Society)*

BOTTOM: *One of the attractions of the Allen site as a location for the Lee statue was the opportunity to shape the surrounding streetscape. The Lee Monument stood alone for over a decade after its dedication, offering a convenient parade ground for veterans' maneuvers. (The Library of Virginia)*

ORIGINS

Allen, who had died in 1874. Allen had been a very successful builder who had accumulated a good deal of property. His son, Colonel Otway S. Allen, was a socially prominent Richmond businessman, a friend of Governor Lee and later a member of Richmond's board of aldermen. Allen offered to donate a site to the Lee Monument Association and to build two broad intersecting boulevards around the monument to be given to the City of Richmond. Arguing for the selection of his property at the western end of Franklin Street as the site, Allen said: "There is a prospect of the street being opened, and a place similar to Monument place in Baltimore being laid out. Should this be done, where is a situation to compare with it?"[25]

Also important were land economics; Richmond was expanding to the west, and Governor Lee noted the tax advantages that could accrue to the city. In a "plain business statement" to the city council, Governor Lee argued that if Richmond annexed the property, it would receive nearly $4,000 a year in additional tax revenues.[26] This point, though attractive to Richmonders, irritated some of the groups across the South who had contributed funds to the monument scheme. Why, they asked, should their money be used to further develop real estate in Richmond? In 1892 the state legislature passed a law allowing the Allen tract, the Lee Monument and another 292 acres in the area, to be annexed by the City of Richmond.[27] As Monument Avenue was extended in the following decades, it also passed through land owned by John P. Branch and his heirs, and the Sheppard family.

Although it took many years for Monument Avenue to be built, the concept of a grand boulevard stretching to the west was intended from the very beginning. A newspaper account of the debate surrounding the Lee Monument site stated that the supporters of the Allen tract declared that they proposed to widen Franklin Street and "make a grand boulevard, with room for trees down the middle &c., and to intersect Reservoir avenue [the Boulevard] in the neighborhood of the Soldiers' Home."[28]

For the planning of Monument Avenue, Otway S. Allen, who gave eleven acres to the city for its construction, engaged the consulting architect to the Lee Monument Association, Collinson Pierrepont Edwards Burgwyn. Born on a North Carolina plantation, Burgwyn graduated from Harvard in 1874, received an engineering degree two years later, and worked in Cambridge until 1877, when he returned to Richmond, where he had lived as a child. In Richmond Burgwyn supervised improvements to the James River channel and assisted city engineer Wilfred Emory Cutshaw in the construction of the new city hall, among other projects. He also wrote a play and a novel that extolled the virtues of the South. Burgwyn's scheme indicated knowledge of American and European boulevards. He laid out cross-axial boulevards with a 50-foot-wide median and a circle of 200 feet in diameter, at the center of which would be placed the Lee Monument. The property was subdivided into standard Richmond-sized lots, with a 30-foot frontage and a depth of 150 feet. Lots facing the circle had more eccentric shapes. Burgwyn wrote in the deed that "no tree or other object of sufficient size to interfere with the view of the monument shall ever be planted or located or allowed to be upon or above the centerline" of either avenue.[29]

Located at the west end of an extension of prestigious Franklin Street, Monument Avenue aligned to the east with Capitol Square. Inside the Capitol stood Houdon's Washington, outside to the west was Crawford and Rogers's Washington Monument, and the rough axis would conclude with a statue to Lee. Now a monument was needed to realize

Otway Slaughter Allen, the original developer of Monument Avenue. (The Library of Virginia)

Collinson Pierrepont Edwards Burgwyn, who served as the consulting architect to the Lee Monument Association and laid out the plat for the initial development around the monument. (The Library of Virginia)

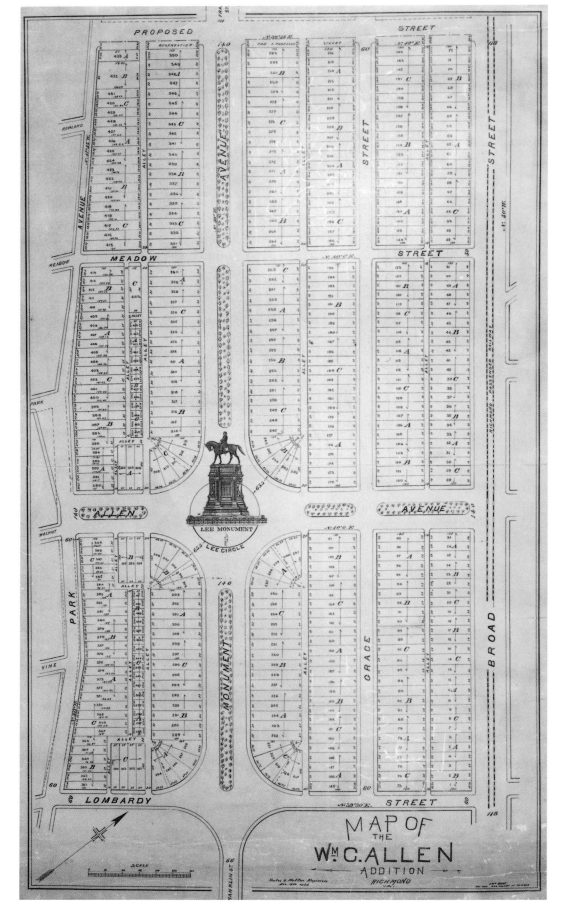

"Map of the Wm. C. Allen Addition, Richmond, Va.," design attributed to C. P. E. Burgwyn, drafted by Bates and Bolton, engineers, 1888. This plat, embellished with a silhouette of the proposed monument and showing landscaping details in the median, delineates the initial proposal for the development of the Allen property. The Allen heirs probably worked out the details with Burgwyn, whose 1887 drawing of the plan accompanied the deed between the Allens and the Lee Monument Association. (Valentine Museum)

ORIGINS

this vision. By late June 1887, the newly combined Lee Monument Association had selected a sculptor. Even though several more years would be needed to model, cast, transport, and erect a statue, the group wanted to push ahead and secure the spot for it. Hence, on October 27, 1887, a dismally wet day, a parade filled with former Confederates headed west from downtown to conduct a cornerstone dedicatory ceremony at the intended site. Governor Lee made the introductory remarks; the minister of Second Presbyterian Church, Dr. Moses D. Hoge, who had spoken at a reburial of Confederate dead in Hollywood Cemetery in 1872 and the dedication of the Jackson statue in Capitol Square, offered a prayer; and Colonel Charles Marshall, Lee's military secretary, gave the oration.[30] Many still complained about the site, but the deed was done—even though nearly three years would elapse before, on May 29, 1890, with the unveiling of the Lee Monument, the avenue became a reality.[31]

THE STATUES

Monument Avenue derives its name, and its distinction, from the six statues unveiled along its route between 1890 and 1996. First, of course, was the Robert E. Lee Monument. Then followed monuments to J. E. B. Stuart and Jefferson Davis; next, the Thomas Jonathan "Stonewall" Jackson and Matthew Fontaine Maury Monuments; and finally, a statue honoring Arthur Ashe. Their subjects forever caught in poses of action or contemplation, the statues memorialize the varied accomplishments of these six very different individuals. Placement of the statues on the avenue meant more than honoring the memory of an individual; it also involved political and cultural symbolism. The stories the statues tell as artistic and cultural creations vary: the sculptures can be read as monuments to martial exploits, as symbols of the Lost Cause, as a parade of Virginia's heroes, or as triumph over adversity. There is more to these monuments than just the image seen today; meanings change over time. Behind their creation and the decision to locate them on Monument Avenue lie tales that frequently reveal divergent interests and acrimonious discord.

Common to the erection of all the statues on Monument Avenue—and indeed to most monumental statuary groups—was a complex, and frequently lengthy, process of discussion, decision-making, and construction. The time frame varied from a few years to several decades. All began with the idea of a monument, the formation of a committee, the attempt to raise funds, the seeking and securing of a site, the commissioning of a design and a sculptor (frequently several times), the production of the monument, and finally the dedication. Conceiving of a monument was the easy task; more complex was creating a committee and finding leaders who would remain committed to the project over the years. Fund-raising always proved to be a problem; and while appeals to former comrades, friends, or interest groups were always made, in the end, either openly or covertly, the city or state government helped to supply a portion of the funds. Seldom would governmental support be openly acknowledged since the statue would always be described as coming from "the people."

Site selection for the projected monument could be agonizing and contentious. Monument Avenue was not necessarily the first—or second—choice for the placement of the

*The Lee Monument,
Monument Avenue at
Allen Avenue, 1890,
Marius-Jean-Antonin
Mercié, sculptor.*

statues eventually located there. Agreeing on a design and a sculptor could also be painful. Competitions normally were held, and public scrutiny along with the uninformed advice of the judges could create havoc. Even without a competition, the public's belief in their right to express their taste could threaten to derail any project. But finally, after years, the monument would be done, and then an elaborate ceremony would attempt to heal the wounds and give the monument meaning—often only to create another arena for discord.

The Lee Monument

Identified with the simple yet grand inscription, LEE, the statue that inaugurated Monument Avenue presents the quintessential representation of the commanding general of the

The Lee Monument.

Army of Northern Virginia. Lee sits bareheaded, stoic and impassive, gazing into the distance on his horse Traveller, who moves forward, heading south. Created by the internationally known French sculptor Marius-Jean-Antonin Mercié, the simplicity of the image masks the tremendous, and frequently bitter, twenty-year campaign to get a monument to Lee constructed in Richmond.

Immediately after Lee's death in 1870, two rival groups interested in memorializing him were founded. One was controlled by former officers of the Army of Northern Virginia and led by Confederate general Jubal Early; the other was a group of patrician Richmond women led by Sarah Nicholas Randolph.[1]

The men's group floundered under Early, a general with an undistinguished record. He gloried in his "irreconcilable" status and wanted only former Confederate soldiers to do-

LEFT: *Sarah Nicholas Randolph spearheaded efforts to erect a monument to Lee. Randolph hoped that the portrait would simultaneously meet the exacting recollections of Confederate veterans and be a great work of art. She felt that an accurate likeness placed on an awkward sculpture would not honor Lee's memory appropriately, maintaining, "'Art is long' though 'time is fleeting.'" (Maryland Historical Society)*

RIGHT: *Jubal Early, a former general of the Army of Northern Virginia renowned for his irreconcilable attitude in matters of the Lost Cause and his irascibility, complicated the early drive for a monument to Lee by refusing donations from anyone but Confederate veterans. Later, he insisted that the statue must be the most exacting portrait possible, and even threatened to blow up the finished monument if the committee accepted the proposal of Charles Henry Niehaus, which he found particularly irritating. (Virginia Historical Society)*

nate funds for the monument. Early's disorganization finally prompted members of the group, in 1875, to turn its meager funds over to a newly created male group chartered by the General Assembly and led by the recently elected governor and ex-Confederate, James Kemper. Intending to widen its base of support, Kemper's group extended its fund-raising efforts to take in school groups and even approached blacks for support. In October 1877, this male Lee Monument Association announced a competition for a statue. The Ladies' Lee Monument Association initially cooperated in the competition but pulled out when the results proved disappointing.

The competition failed since it had no prize money, no pledge of erection, no announced winner, and an inexperienced jury. The jury, composed of about two dozen Southerners, had no artistic background and tended to view the entries as final works of art rather than a means of selecting a sculptor. Hence, they judged the entries by how well they captured Lee and his horse, Traveller. The model of Edward Valentine, the Richmond sculptor, already a favorite because of his Recumbent Lee, proved to be the most popular. Valentine had even modeled Lee from life. Criticisms of Valentine's entry frequently focused on the horse, especially its neck and bridle. Another entry by a former Richmonder, Moses Ezekiel, at the time living in Rome, portrayed Lee's horse in a partially crouching position. This pose, claimed one of the competition's judges, would only be possible if Lee was lassoing a wild animal.[2] A. E. Harnish, another American living in Rome, portrayed Lee being led into Valhalla by Fame. The jury selected Vinnie Ream, a self-taught female sculptor, but, perhaps because of her gender, she was never announced as the winner. The *Richmond State* characterized the various models on exhibit in the State Library as "Trash in the Library." Calling it a "deadhead exhibition of monstrosities," the *State*'s reporter described the statues as "horses on their tails, soldiers on stuffed bags, ramping beasts of no special genus, and dancing girls representing prophetesses."[3] Undaunted, the men's group tried another competition the next year, but with only four entries—including one from Valentine—it generated little enthusiasm.

The campaign for a Lee monument in Richmond languished until 1884, when the women's group announced a competition and, after several extensions, set the due date for submissions as February 1, 1886. Quite unlike what the male group had done, the ladies held an exhibition in Washington, D.C., at the Corcoran Art Gallery, offered cash prizes, and gathered an impressive jury consisting of Augustus Saint-Gaudens and John Quincy Adams Ward, two of the most eminent sculptors in America, and Edward Clark, the architect of the United States Capitol. The other major difference between the men's and women's approaches was summed up by Sarah Nicholas Randolph, who argued, "'Art is long' though 'time is fleeting,'" and "the work whose execution we are directing will stand long after our generation is lost in oblivion."[4] She held that the monument should be art rather than fact. By now, Edward Valentine, who had been through two competitions, declined to participate. Moses Ezekiel entered again with a composition similar to his earlier proposal of Lee on a rearing horse and received second prize. The jury selected as the winner Charles Henry Niehaus, a young sculptor from Cincinnati, Ohio, who portrayed a bareheaded Lee mounted on a spirited, prancing horse. Both Niehaus and the jury obviously knew little of Confederate and Virginia gentlemen's horses, since the winning entry showed Traveller with a bobtail. When the statues were put on display in Richmond, fervent criticism broke forth, with one newspaper claiming the gaffe in regard to Traveller's tail was tantamount to Lee having "his hair banged" and quoting with great relish Jubal Early's threat to "blow up the thing with dynamite" if it was erected.[5]

Marius-Jean-Antonin Mercié's entry in the 1886 competition showed Lee "upon a galloping or rearing horse trampling upon, and supported by, the bodies of wounded or dead soldiers."[6] Not particularly popular with the public—indeed, as one critic proclaimed, "a relic of . . . antiquity"—the dying soldiers, Mercié later claimed, were Lee's own men, "stretching for a last affectionate glance of their leader."[7] But Mercié possessed several major advantages that help to explain why the commission was ultimately awarded to him, including an international reputation and a friendship with the American sculptor Augustus Saint-Gaudens, who had been a classmate in Paris. A writer noted: "It is alleged that Mercié owes his good fortune in no small degree to the good offices of one of the members of the jury who, if he did not urge his appointment, yet give it be understood that in

CHARLES A. NIEHAUS.

his opinion the best result could be obtained only through placing the work in the hands of a sculptor of Mercié's known ability."[8]

A Parisian academic sculptor, Mercié studied at the École des Beaux-Arts in the atelier of François Jouffroy, where he met Saint-Gaudens, and then in the atelier of Jean-Alexandre-Joseph Falguière. He won the *Prix de Rome*, the highest honor of the French Academy, in 1868 and spent the next several years studying in Rome. Extremely popular in France as a sculptor of public monuments, Mercié had won the Grand Cross of the Legion of Honor in 1872 for his *David with the Head of Goliath* and the highest award at the 1878 Paris Exposition for his statue *Renommée* (Fame), which stood in front of the Palais du Trocadero. His fame was ensured with his immensely popular memorial to the fallen French from the Franco-Prussian War of 1870–71 entitled *Gloria Victis* (1872–75), in which a winged figure symbolizing victory holds a wounded soldier. The statue was said to be so beloved that it assisted the French in accepting their defeat. In 1889, while at work on *Lee*, Mercié received the highest award of the Paris Universal Exposition held that year and was elected to the Institut de France. Mercié stood at the forefront of French academic sculpture.[9]

The exact circumstances surrounding Mercié's commission remain unclear. Certainly Saint-Gaudens pulled strings, and perhaps Governor Fitzhugh Lee acceded to the ladies' demand that they pick the sculptor while he chose the site, the Allen property.[10] But, equally important, Lee's memory required the imprimatur of an artist of international

Marius-Jean-Antonin Mercié, probably the most revered French sculptor of his time, seated in his studio with the model of the Lee statue in 1890, the year of its completion. (Bibliothèque Nationale, Paris)

stature. The women's committee saw very well that engaging a respected French sculptor would move Lee from being a merely local hero to having the status of great military leader, in the company of Alexander the Great, Caesar, and Napoleon. Allowing a French sculptor to provide a statue for Richmond would propel the city into the cultural big leagues, on a par with Boston or New York.

Others agreed that for a Lee monument to transcend the specifics of the war, a special type of statue was needed. The *Richmond Times* observed: "In a statue to represent him, we should be careful that the artist comprehends his theme in order to make a work that will set forth a hero of all humanity, a soldier, but at the same time a man whose example was so great and good that it rises above the locality, and teaches all the world how duty may win love and admiration, though it may fail."[11]

Mercié received directions to resubmit a model of Lee with all four of Traveller's feet on the ground. His second submission found great favor; he received a contract and went about creating the bronze image. Still another model would be sent and displayed in the State Capitol in August 1888.[12] Extensive debate arose over such details as portraying Lee with a bare head, his hat in his right hand, and with his coat collar turned up on one side. Mercié insisted on both. Reports on details were elaborately scrutinized by Governor Fitzhugh Lee and the Lee Monument Association. The association sent Mercié Lee's death mask so that the subject's face could be more accurate. The general's daughter Mary Custis Lee, along with the former head of the Ladies' Association, Sarah Nicholas Randolph, visited Mercié in Paris several times, bringing Lee's spurs, one of his hats, and the boots he had worn at Gettysburg.[13] Lee's sword presented problems: Mercié originally had it hang in the French style but learned that the Americans wear it differently, so he corrected it.

THE STATUES

OPPOSITE, TOP LEFT: *The pedestal for the Lee Monument, designed by French architect Paul Pujol, was sculpted in the United States. Figural groups originally planned for the base proved too expensive, and the ornately designed shields at the front and back replaced them. (The Library of Virginia)*

OPPOSITE, TOP RIGHT: *The model, or maquette, of the Lee Monument proved to be a more serene version than Mercié's original concept, and more in keeping with the evolving image of Lee. In order to achieve the most realistic portrait possible, the committee supplied Mercié with a variety of relics to study, including Lee's spurs, a hat, boots, and even his death mask. (Valentine Museum)*

OPPOSITE, BOTTOM: *Lee's horse, Traveller, shown here, was judged by Mercié to be too small for Lee's proportions, so a slightly larger horse was used as a model for the monument. (Valentine Museum)*

Reports estimated that between 10,000 and 20,000 Richmonders took turns hauling the Lee Monument to its site, in much the same way that the Washington Monument had been hauled to Capitol Square. Over the heads of the crowd in this photograph taken on May 7, 1890, on Broad Street near Belvidere can be seen two of the four crates in which the statue was shipped from Europe. (The Library of Virginia)

The ropes that were used to pull the Lee Monument were cut into pieces, tied with ribbons, and handed out as souvenirs. Families saved scraps and passed them on for generations. (The Library of Virginia)

The first crate containing part of the Lee statue beginning its ascent, with the shroud in the foreground behind two armed guards. (Valentine Museum)

It took two days to bolt the nine pieces of the Lee sculpture back together. Then it was covered in a protective shroud, and the trestlework built up underneath it was lifted by jacks, alternating on either end, until it was level with the top of the pedestal. Workmen then dragged the statue onto the granite base and readied it for the unveiling. (Valentine Museum)

THE STATUES

Mercié modeled the saddle from one lent by the Duc de Chartres, who had served with the Union army during the war. Mercié explained that, on seeing the Lee statue, the Duc observed: "'Ah! I see you wish to make the South fighting victorious.' 'No,' I replied. 'The war is over.'"[14] Avidly followed in the Richmond press, Mercié's work met with some criticism, since many of the locals saw his selection as a slight to Valentine. Always comparisons were made with the earlier Washington statues, and one reporter claimed that "next to Houdon's Washington it is the greatest work of art which has ever been intrusted to a European artist for execution by Americans."[15] But Mercié's work drew positive comments too: from Paris came a report that one Confederate veteran viewed the statue and experienced "all the old-time emotions, and his heart told him, 'That's Marse Robert.'"[16]

Mercié's statue, as completed, depicts Lee facing stoically forward, with Traveller's reins held loosely in his gloved hands. Traveller's feet are all on the ground, widely placed at the four corners of the plinth; his head is slightly bowed, and a full tail streams out behind. Mercié based his portrayal of Lee and Traveller on photographs taken prior to Lee's death. Traveller, a small horse, would have appeared curiously overwhelmed by his rider if their sizes had been enlarged evenly. Hence Mercié slightly increased the horse's size, making him more like a French thoroughbred.

As Mercié's modeling process went forward, another problem was created by, as one

The Lee Monument's legend began long before the unveiling. This unidentified group posed even before the scaffolding was removed. Note the workman within the structure, almost at the center, and the group on top. (Valentine Museum)

critic noted tongue-in-cheek, "the archaeological citizens of Richmond."[17] The original proposal for a statue of "heroic proportions" specified an image of about thirteen feet in height standing on a base of approximately thirty-five feet. But as some Richmonders pointed out, the Washington Monument on Capitol Square by Crawford and Rogers stood sixty feet, three inches, more than ten feet taller than the projected Lee monument. Accordingly, a change was ordered, and Mercié, who at first hesitated but then acquiesced, enlarged the statue to twenty-one feet and the pedestal to forty. Lee would stand taller than Washington.

The increase in size increased the cost of the bronze statue from $12,000 to $18,000. For the pedestal, the French architect Paul Pujol supplied the design, which originally contained allegorical groups of figures projecting from the front and rear. Pujol and Mercié intended to place a group of Southern women offering laurels to Lee at the front, while at the rear they envisioned the angel of peace taking weapons from the goddess of war. Sarah Nicholas Randolph requested that the front group be modified to a figure of Liberty, taken from the state's coat of arms, holding laurel over the head of a seated Confederate soldier. But the cost of the figural groups proved to be too high, and they were never installed. Instead, the high pedestal has shields with lions' heads surrounded by laurel on the front and rear, and two columns on each side. The actual carving was carried out in the United States, with some of the sculpted features done by Casper Buberl. Altogether, the pedestal cost $41,500.[18]

In February 1890 the Lee Monument Association sent C. P. E. Burgwyn, who had laid out Lee Circle and Monument Avenue, to Paris to inspect and approve the statue. In March the statue went on display in Paris, and Burgwyn reported that "thousands of people" viewed the statue and "the general judgment is that there is nothing in Paris superior to it."[19] Burgwyn cabled back frequently, recounting his visits to "nearly all the leading cities of Europe to look at the celebrated works of art." He reported that the equestrian statue of Frederick the Great in Berlin was "a magnificent work of art, but is only about two thirds as high as the Lee monument." Burgwyn went on to suggest, "with true American pride," as the *Richmond Dispatch* reported, "that in spite of the wonderful works of art and erudition, Europe was not keeping apace with America. He could not but observe that though in the arts and sciences they are far ahead of us, yet they are behind us in that push and vigor which constitutes the American idea of 'hustling.'"[20]

Thubout Brothers in Paris cast the statue in nine large pieces, each weighing several thousand pounds. The press avidly followed the progress of the statue across the ocean to New York, and then by rail to Richmond. The bronze statue arrived in Richmond on May 4, 1890.[21]

When Crawford's equestrian Washington had proved too heavy for the mules that were to pull it to the site, Richmond's citizens pitched in and assisted in lugging the statue up the hill from the James River to Capitol Square. Recalling what had become a Richmond legend, the Lee statue was similarly transported on May 7, 1890.[22] This time, though, the event included an organized parade. Dispensing with mules, citizens grabbed the ropes of the wagons and pulled them across town. The crowd, estimated at between 10,000 and 20,000, took as souvenirs pieces of the ropes, which became the equivalents of holy relics. Newspapers reported that citizens pinned the rope pieces to their gowns or buttonholes.[23]

The actual erection took the next several weeks, as the statue was hoisted up onto the pedestal and the pieces bolted together. Fastened to the sides of the pedestal by bolts covered with stars was the imposing plaque reading LEE. Then the statue received a shroud, awaiting the unveiling. A poignant photograph at the conclusion of construction illustrates the bareness of the site and shows two nattily attired businessmen with ties and hats posed on the pedestal, a youth sitting on Traveller's hoof, and a less formally attired man, who may have been a worker, standing beside one of Traveller's hind legs. Off to the left and also to the right, not on the pedestal, stand four black workers, one gesturing to the camera.

The irony of the photograph is unmistakable; *Lee* may have been depoliticized, but the fact remained that one of the issues of the war was the question of freedom for the Southern black population, which was still in a subservient position. Richmond's city council had several black members, and they refused to vote funds for either the 1887 cornerstone ceremony or to support a city appropriation for the 1890 dedication of the monument. One of the black council members, John Mitchell, the editor of the *Richmond Planet*, observed: "The men who talk most about the valor of LEE, and the blood of the brave Confederate dead are those who never smelt powder or engaged in a battle. Most of them were at a table, either on top or under it when the war was going on."[24] "The capital of the late Confederacy has been decorated with emblems of the 'Lost Cause,'" he editorialized, and the placement of the Lee statue handed down a "legacy of treason and blood" to future

Various people, their roles hinted at by their positioning and clothing, pose at Traveller's feet and on the scaffolding in this photograph. The grandstand erected for the unveiling is visible in the bottom right corner; slightly above it, a baseball game is in progress. Richmond College is to the left, at the tip of Traveller's tail. (Valentine Museum)

This photograph records the completion of the work and the last chance to get a photograph before the Lee statue scaffolding was removed. Its composition betrays the complexities inherent in public sculpture and commemoration, which can rarely please its entire audience, or even all those involved in its creation. (Virginia Historical Society)

THE STATUES

*The shroud removed
and the scaffolding dis-
assembled, the Lee statue
stood exposed until the
ceremonial veil was draped
over it. The blocky towers
of the state fairgrounds,
near the future site of
Broad Street Station,
are visible on the right.
(Valentine Museum)*

THE STATUES

These decorated bicycles led the parade that took place before the Lee Monument unveiling ceremony. (Virginia Historical Society)

Flags, banners, and bunting hung from every immobile object the day of the Lee Monument dedication. Looking west down Franklin Street, the monument can just be seen on the horizon between the trees in the distance. (Virginia Historical Society)

ABOVE: *The banners and waving flags, the varied hats and striped umbrellas, and the boys and men crowding right up onto Lee's pedestal convey the excitement of the festivities of Monument Avenue's first unveiling ceremony on May 29, 1890. (Valentine Museum)*

LEFT: *This image caught the veil falling from the Lee statue and the crowd jostling each other, craning to catch the first glimpse. (Valentine Museum)*

generations.[25] In another editorial Mitchell noted, "He [the African American] put up the Lee Monument, and should the time come, will be there to take it down."[26]

In this latter editorial Mitchell reported on the reaction of one black man to the statue: "'The Southern white folks is on top—the Southern white folks is on top!'" But then, "a smile lit up his countenance. . . . 'But we've got the government! We've got the government!'"[27] This was wishful thinking, however, as historian Kirk Savage has pointed out, for in the next two decades Mitchell and other blacks would be disenfranchised.[28] It took a while, but the annexation of white suburbs diluted the black vote, there was white fraud at the polls, and then in 1902 the Virginia Constitution imposed a poll tax and other restrictions on voting. In 1903 Richmond's city council abolished the black voting block of Jackson Ward, eliminating the possibility of black councilmen.[29]

The dedication of the Lee statue took place on May 29, 1890, in a celebration witnessed by an audience estimated at between 100,000 and 150,000. A parade of over four miles in length wound through Richmond, passing Lee's former home. At its head as chief marshal rode former governor and general Fitzhugh Lee. More than forty other generals either marched or rode in the parade, along with governors from former Confederate states and 15,000 veterans. Accorded special honor were the widows of Stonewall Jackson and George Pickett. At the monument, the prayer was followed by the playing of "Dixie," after which Jubal Early introduced Colonel Archer Anderson, a prominent businessman with the Tredegar Iron Works, and a member of the Lee Monument Association. Anderson's long address covered a number of themes. He began with the standard "a people carves its own image in the monuments of its great men" and went on to place Lee in the company of Virgil, Sir Isaac Newton, Frederick the Great, Napoleon, and Washington. Virginia, he claimed, had "produced two such stainless captains," and "the monument of George Washington has found its only fitting complement and comparison in a monument to Robert Lee." Essentially, Anderson attempted to depoliticize Lee once again with rhetoric, claiming that the general's character represented "the perfect union of Christian virtues and old Roman manhood." Anderson recounted Lee's war record, but, in conclusion, he dedicated the Lee Monument not as a memory to the Confederacy, but as a testament to "personal honor," "patriotic hope and cheer," and an "ideal leader."[30]

Then former Confederate general Joseph E. Johnston approached the statue; after a dramatic pause, he pulled the chord and the canvas slid off. The *Richmond Dispatch*, declaring that Lee's name was "woof and web" of his country's history, recorded the scene: "The men went wild. Veterans shouted and cried and hugged each other. . . . The women and children waved handkerchiefs, parasols, [and] fans. . . . The artillery thundered; the musketry followed, volley upon volley." Richmond had its Lee Monument.[31]

From the North came a few expressions of outrage that a statue of Lee could be erected: a Philadelphia newspaper compared Lee to Benedict Arnold, while the *New York Mail and Express* proposed a congressional law that would ban monuments to Confederates as well as display of the "stars and bars."[32] But Northern sentiment was divided, and not everyone saw the erection of the monument as a rebellious act. Lee was brave and honorable, as the *New York Times* editorialized; "his memory is, therefore, a possession of the American people."[33]

The Lee Monument became a site of pilgrimage and a tourist destination. Richmond began to promote itself as the "City of Monuments," and glowing newspaper stories told

The Lee Monument,
just after the unveiling.
(Valentine Museum)

of the Lee Monument and others, including the monument to Washington.[34] As a result of the severe economic depression that gripped the entire country during the 1890s, however, building in Richmond ground to a halt, and for the next decade nothing was constructed to accompany the Lee statue on nascent Monument Avenue. Henry James, visiting Richmond in 1905 as part of his "pilgrim's return," viewed the statue and described it as a "stranded, bereft image." Of its site, he wrote, "The place is the mere vague center of two or three crossways, without form and void, with a circle half sketched by three or four groups of small, new, mean houses."[35] Nonetheless, the statue of Lee had begun a narrative, and soon other chapters would be added to it.

The J. E. B. Stuart Monument

The unveiling of the General J. E. B. Stuart Monument on May 30, 1907—and the dedication of the Jefferson Davis Monument four days later—helped shift the focus of the narra-

This famous photograph records a tobacco crop in front of the Lee Monument, not because the statue was erected in the middle of a working farm, but because empty lots all over the country were planted with useful crops during World War I. (Valentine Museum)

tive of Monument Avenue to a more explicit celebration of the Lost Cause. Whatever ambiguity there may have been in the Lee statue disappeared in the overt homage to the military exploits of Stuart, a Confederate cavalry general. Located one block to Lee's east and, in a military sense, protecting his left flank, Stuart's statue marked the entrance to Monument Avenue from West Franklin Street.

A graduate of West Point, where Fitzhugh Lee had been a classmate, Stuart gained international renown for his audacious cavalry tactics as Lee's eyes and ears. He fought at nearly every major battle in which the Army of Northern Virginia was engaged. His most famous exploit involved the "Ride around McClellan," in which his cavalry brigade completely encircled the Union army, capturing 170 prisoners and more than 300 horses and mules, while losing only one man. Stuart was dashing and dressed the part, with gold lace, large gauntlets that reached his elbows, plumes, and yellow sashes. He suffered a mortal wound in May 1864 at Yellow Tavern, just north of Richmond, and was brought to a house on West Grace Street, where he died. The house was only a few blocks from where the Stuart statue would be erected; and his funeral service took place at St. James's Episcopal Church at Fifth and Marshall Streets, its location before the congregation moved to West Franklin Street. He was buried in Hollywood Cemetery.[36]

Sentiment in favor of erecting a monument to Stuart began to be expressed almost immediately after his death, but nothing happened until 1875, when the unveiling of the English sculptor John Henry Foley's statue of Stonewall Jackson in Capitol Square sparked the Richmond City Council to pass a resolution calling for the city to erect an equestrian statue of Stuart. There matters stood until 1891, when, flush with the success of the Lee

ABOVE: *The General
J. E. B. Stuart Monu-
ment, Monument
Avenue at Stuart Circle,
unveiled 1907, Frederick
Moynihan, sculptor.*

LEFT: *The Stuart
Monument, seen in
the foreground in this
photograph from the
1930s, erected one block
east of the Lee statue,
marks the entrance to
Monument Avenue.
(Dementi-Foster Studios)*

In 1892 Captain M. J. Dimmock sketched this suggestion for a Stuart Monument. He brought it up for discussion at an 1896 Confederate reunion, but it was not until 1903 that a competition was announced. The sketch's remarkable resemblance to the finished statue is probably no coincidence. It is likely that even before he did the sketch, Dimmock had discussed the statue with Moynihan, the sculptor who won the commission. (The Library of Virginia)

Monument, Fitzhugh Lee helped organize the Veteran Cavalry Association of the Army of Northern Virginia with the express goal of erecting a monument to Stuart. Lee created the Stuart Monument Association and a committee to oversee its efforts that included the artists John A. Elder, William Sheppard, and perennial Richmond favorite Edward Virginius Valentine. Elder was a painter who lived in Richmond and gained fame after the war by painting Confederate scenes and portraits. Sheppard would provide the Howitzer Monument (1892) on Grove Avenue and the Soldiers and Sailors Monument (1894) on Libby Hill, which earlier had been a suggested site for the proposed Lee monument.

In 1896, during a reunion of Confederate veterans, Captain Marion J. Dimmock, a former cavalryman and the architect of the Confederate Chapel at the Lee Camp, submitted to the Stuart Monument Association committee a sketch for a statue of Stuart riding a rearing horse and brandishing a sword.[37] The source for Dimmock's sketch was John Henry Foley's statue of the English general Sir James Outram, which had been unveiled in 1874 and stood in Calcutta, India. The Stuart memorial group met again in 1902, but funds still eluded them.[38] By 1903 approximately $10,000 had been raised, and the group announced a competition for a statue of Stuart to be held the following year. The winning entry by Frederick Moynihan of New York followed in many details the Dimmock suggestion of seven years earlier.

Moynihan not only knew Dimmock's entry, he had probably ghosted it for him—though, in October 1896, he told Edward Valentine, "I don't think Captain Dimmock did much good with his model for Stuart."[39] Moynihan had spent considerable time in Rich-

mond working as a modeler for Valentine, and he also had been Foley's assistant in England. Moynihan had worked on Foley's *Jackson* in 1874, the year Foley died. And, although no direct evidence of the fact exists, given that the Outram sculpture was also unveiled in 1874, Moynihan may well have worked on it; he certainly knew it very well.[40] Foley, a leading, prolific English sculptor, specialized in extravagant images of British might and power, such as the snorting horse and magisterial *General Outram*.

Frederick Moynihan was born on the Isle of Guernsey, won several medals while attending the Royal Academy, worked for the English court sculptor Baron Marochetti, and then worked for other academicians, including Foley. Moynihan arrived in New York about 1883, hoping to snare some of the large sculptural commissions that were beginning to be awarded in America thanks to the nation's post–Civil War prosperity. Initially though, Moynihan earned a living through teaching and also modeling for sculptors, including Daniel Chester French, Augustus Saint-Gaudens, Hiram Powers, and Launt Thompson. Modeling entailed taking a sculptor's small maquette and enlarging it so that it could be cast in bronze or carved in stone. Few, if any, turn-of-the-century sculptors actually worked on the final sculpture that the public would see.

Moynihan came to Edward Valentine's attention in 1887 and subsequently came to Richmond to model Valentine's statues of Thomas Jefferson, for the Jefferson Hotel, and Williams C. Wickham, a Confederate general honored in Monroe Park. Independent works by Moynihan included the Georgia state monument, *Confederate Infantryman*, at the Chickamauga battlefield and the Griffin A. Stedman Monument in Hartford, Connecticut. The

General Sir James Outram, *Calcutta, India, 1874, John Foley, sculptor. Moynihan had worked with Foley in England and would have known of Foley's statue of Outram. Some parties insisted that Moynihan's work amounted to plagiarism, but the scandal soon died down, and the monument's drama appealed to Stuart's admirers. (Barbara Groseclose)*

The model for the Stuart Monument dwarfed sculptor Frederick Moynihan, pictured here in his studio. (Virginia Historical Society)

large-scale success Moynihan sought eluded him. One of the reasons might have been alcohol, of which, in a letter to Valentine, Moynihan writes: "I know you will be glad to learn that I have successfully over come my bad habits. I have kept away from it since I have returned to this City, and would not return to it to save my life."[41] In other letters to Valentine dating from 1895, Moynihan refers to a large equestrian statue,[42] which supports the conclusion that Dimmock's 1896 sketch for a Stuart statue was based on Moynihan's concepts.

Moynihan's winning design of 1904 caused immediate controversy because of its clear resemblance to Foley's Outram statue. The day after the Stuart Monument Association made its announcement, the *News-Leader* published photographs of the three finalists' entries: Eugene Morahan's and Louis Gudebrod's, along with Moynihan's, and also a photograph of Foley's *Outram*.[43] The next day, a dissenting member of the Stuart Monument Association's executive committee, Jeffrey Montague, published a letter criticizing the choice as "almost an exact replica," and a "second-hand design."[44] A commotion ensued in the press, with letters and editorials flying back and forth.[45] Dimmock found it "peculiar" that the dissenting member, a "young man who had never seen Stuart should set up and contend for his view over that of veteran soldiers on the committee," who had known Stuart.[46] In spite of the newspapers' attempt to inflame the battle, it died down within a month. However, over the years, controversy over Moynihan's source reappears, only to die again.[47]

Moynihan made changes the committee asked for, and on December 5, 1904, the Stuart Monument Association accepted his final model. A *Times-Dispatch* reporter who visited Moynihan while he was at work on the model for the statue described him as "very bohemian in a white working apron with plaster simply besprinkling him from head to heels." Moynihan noted that Fitzhugh Lee "spent a whole day here with me [and] is satisfied that the likeness cannot be improved upon. He suggested certain changes, notably of forehead and cheeks which I have made." A question regarding the depiction of Stuart's horse came up, but Moynihan reported, "General Lee said to me, 'That horse is hard to beat.'" Lee's opinion of the statue was much valued, as Moynihan explained, for "General Lee was with General Stuart two years at West Point in his student days, and there is no man living that is so well able to recall Stuart as is General Lee." Moynihan also reported that Stuart's widow approved of the model and the great pains he had taken to copy Stuart's uniform from photographs and to render accurately his sword, which hung in the Commonwealth Club.[48]

Originally, the Stuart Monument Association hoped to place the statue in Capitol Square, but the city's board of aldermen appropriated $20,000 on the condition that the statue be placed somewhere else in Richmond.[49] Since the association had raised only $10,000 of the projected cost of more than $30,000, acquiescing to another location became imperative. In September 1904 they selected a site at the beginning of Monument Avenue at Lombardy Street.[50] In addition to being adjacent to the Lee statue, the site further recommended itself by being close to the site of Stuart's death and the church from which he was buried.

The Stuart Monument differs significantly from the Lee. Instead of showing a calm field general passing into eternity, the statue provides an active display of martial glory. The pedestal, a large piece of granite sitting on a stepped platform, contains Stuart's name, dates, and military rank, as well as quotes from Lee and Jackson regarding his military prowess. Encircling the base is an iron fence of upturned cannons, spears, and crossed cavalry swords.

The statue depicts Stuart twisting in his saddle, brandishing a sword as he looks down Franklin Street toward the State Capitol. His bearded face appears defiant, surveying the field of action. His horse seems to be diminutive, or conversely, Stuart appears too large. Portrayed in action, the horse moves with one leg lifted and its tail straight out behind. Moynihan claimed the horse was "Kentucky-bred" and was perhaps true to the nature of horses used during the war by the cavalry. Instead of the stately thoroughbred Mercié made of Lee's Traveller, Stuart's mount is a quarter horse, a breed known for its quick turns and maneuverability.[51]

The dedication of the Stuart Monument took place on Memorial Day, May 30, 1907, at the beginning of a Confederate reunion that would last for five days. A large parade brim-

RIGHT: *The bronze equestrian statue of Stuart was hoisted to the pedestal by a system of steam engines and winches. (Virginia Historical Society)*

BELOW: *On May 30, 1907, as the Stuart Monument sat in the distance waiting to be unveiled, soldiers and bands paraded up Monument Avenue and crowds milled around on the median and the curbs. The shiny new dome of Temple Beth Ahabah can be seen near the monument, with the Cathedral of the Sacred Heart and the City Market further to the right. (Valentine Museum)*

THE STATUES

ming with Confederate veterans marched through town, and Stuart's granddaughter, Virginia Stuart Waller, unveiled the statue. After many speeches, Mayor Carlton McCarthy accepted the statue for the city. Following the ceremony, the crowd proceeded to Hollywood Cemetery for the Memorial Day commemoration.

The Jefferson Davis Monument

Four days after the dedication of the Stuart Monument, on June 3, 1907, the ninety-ninth anniversary of the birth of Jefferson Davis, a monument to the former Confederate president was unveiled before a crowd variously estimated at between 80,000 and 200,000. Located four blocks west of Lee, Davis stands in front of a giant, sixty-foot-high Doric column capped by "Vindicatrix," while behind him a screen of columns represents the Confederacy and those states that sent delegates to the Secession Convention. Symbolic politically, the Davis Monument quite clearly shifted the meaning of Monument Avenue even further toward representing a vindication of the Confederacy.[52]

Jefferson Davis died on December 11, 1889, in New Orleans, and on December 21, 1889, a Jefferson Davis Monument Association was formed in Richmond. It had two goals, to erect a monument and to transfer Davis's body to Richmond. In 1893 his widow, Varina, agreed to the reinterment of his body next to that of his son in Hollywood Cemetery. The realization of the monument would take much longer and become a project of the newly formed United Confederate Veterans and ultimately of the United Daughters of the Confederacy.

The reputation of Davis underwent a substantial rehabilitation in the 1880s and 1890s from its nadir after the war. A graduate of West Point, and a hero of the Mexican-American War, Davis had served in the U.S. Congress and as secretary of war before accepting the call to become the president of the Confederate States of America. Initially, Davis was viewed by many in the South as the person most responsible for the Confederacy's defeat. Caught fleeing and reputedly disguised in women's clothes (which offended Southern male sensibilities), Davis became a point of much ribaldry in both the North and the South. He never became an absolute hero, as Lee or Jackson did. Imprisoned by the federal government immediately after the war but then released without prosecution, Davis existed in limbo, only rarely giving speeches, until 1886, when he accepted a series of speaking engagements throughout the South. Thereafter, Davis increasingly became a symbol of the righteousness of the white South's cause, a glorification of the Confederacy.[53]

With Varina Davis's approval, in 1892 the City of Richmond granted a site in Monroe Park to serve as the location of a memorial to Davis. Led by Richmond businessman Norman V. Randolph, a drive was launched throughout the South to raise $250,000 for a monument. The promotional literature stated: "The men and women who fought for the Confederacy and their descendants must quarry this monument out of their heart's blood if need be."[54]

The competition for a memorial to Davis on the Monroe Park site was announced in March 1896. The specified cost was to be between $100,000 and $200,000, and a statement of price, including construction, had to accompany all designs. The *News-Leader* warned the selection committee that "slick designs" would not be acceptable.[55] Twenty-five

The Jefferson Davis
Monument, Monument
and Davis Avenues, 1907,
Edward V. Valentine,
sculptor, William
Churchill Noland,
architectural designer.

entries were received, including designs from the sculptor Charles Niehaus, architects Carrère and Hastings of New York, and Marion J. Dimmock of Richmond. In late June the
Davis Monument Association, by now joined with the newly formed United Daughters of
the Confederacy, announced the winners. William C. Noland of Richmond received third
prize with a screen of massive Doric columns sheltering a statue of Davis, with lower wings
in a more simplified Doric order. Second prize also went to a Richmond architect, Edgerton Rogers, son of the sculptor Randolph Rogers, fresh from his triumph with the Virginia State Building at the World's Columbian Exposition in Chicago. Rogers submitted a
complex baldacchino—an ornamental canopy—with a multiplicity of statuary accompani-
ments. First prize went to New York architect Percy Griffin, who entered a massive domed
temple with four equal facades that owed a debt to Richard Morris Hunt's Administration
Building at the World's Columbian Exposition, as well as Palladio's Villa Rotonda.[56] An
elaborate cornerstone ceremony for the proposed monument took place, as part of the
annual Confederate reunion, in Monroe Park on June 25, 1896, with Mrs. Davis, two of
her daughters, a number of Confederate generals and veterans, and various dignitaries
present.[57] Griffin's winning entry would cost an estimated $210,000. The Davis Monu-
ment Association attempted to raise the funds but found after three years that they had little to show for their efforts. In 1899 they turned the entire enterprise over to the capable
hands of the United Daughters of the Confederacy (UDC) and Norman V. Randolph's
wife, Janet.

The UDC gave up the Monroe Park site and put forth a new proposal: a memorial arch

on Broad Street at Twelfth, adjacent to both the Virginia State Capitol and Davis's former residence at the White House of the Confederacy. The UDC increased the money available to more than $40,000, and again held a competition in 1902. The winning entry was by Louis Gudebrod, a New York sculptor who had also entered the Stuart competition. Gudebrod adopted one of the most venerable of ancient monuments, the Arch of Titus in Rome. His arch measured sixty-five feet high; the archway was forty feet tall, seventy feet wide, and twenty-four feet in depth. Embellishing the arch would be inscriptions honoring Davis, the Great Seal of the Confederacy, and state seals. The UDC suggested removing an eagle Gudebrod projected, and he complied. Gudebrod's arch proposal did not find great favor with Varina Davis, however; and though she eventually went along, fundraising again proved a problem.[58] An extravagant fund-raiser in the spring of 1903 failed, and Gudebrod quit.

Daunted but not defeated, the UDC changed its tactics and in June 1903 went directly to William C. Noland and Edward Virginius Valentine for a design within its budget. The announcement of the design came in late 1903, but the site of the monument still remained in question. The *Richmond Times-Dispatch* commented on the state of things, noting, "The choosing of the site will be important and has not been done yet," and adding that "the design suggests its placement at the end of a vista."[59] Following the lead of the Stuart Monument Association, which had obtained a location on Monument Avenue in September 1904, the UDC approached the city council. The council complied with their request, granting the UDC a site four blocks west of the Lee statue at Cedar Avenue (later renamed Davis Avenue) and also appropriating $1,000 toward the construction of the monument's foundation.[60] But Noland and Valentine's Davis Monument demanded more room, and again the city complied by cutting off corners of adjacent property to create the needed space, compensating the property owners for the diminished value of their lots.[61] The location contained symbolic value beyond its proximity to the Lee Monument. On the site had stood a fort, a piece of the Confederate inner defense line surrounding Richmond. (Subsequent to the erection of the Davis Monument, in 1915, the Confederate Memorial Literary Society and the City of Richmond installed a cannon just east of the monument to commemorate the defenses.)

The UDC's choice of Valentine and Noland for the proposed Davis monument reflected frustration with the competition process and the hope that these two professionals would work within the available budget. Edward Virginius Valentine, well known for his various portraits of Lee and other work, was Richmond's and Virginia's aesthetic conscience in the late nineteenth century. He was the only artist with any national stature that the state could claim. Born in 1838 into an old Richmond family, Valentine studied briefly in Paris with the painter Thomas Couture and the sculptor François Jouffroy before moving to Berlin, where he sat out the Civil War studying under August Kiss. Exposed to the art treasures of Europe during his extensive travels, he returned to Richmond and opened a studio on Leigh Street during Reconstruction. He flourished, sculpting portraits of Confederate heroes, local notables, and the occasional grand piece. He met Jefferson Davis in July 1870, and in August 1873 he recorded in his diary, "I got some measurements of Mr. Davis' face." He was Richmond's major connection to the grand art traditions of Europe, the major local representative of the American Renaissance.[62]

William Churchill Noland, the architectural half of the team, personified a younger generation of the American Renaissance. Born in 1865 in Hanover County, Virginia, Noland learned architecture through apprenticeships with architectural firms in New York, Richmond, and Philadelphia. He worked for the well-known Philadelphia firm Cope and Stewardson. He then traveled and studied for two years in Europe prior to returning to Richmond in 1893 and setting up a firm with the engineer Henry Baskervill in 1897. Noland acted as the main designer of the firm and brought to Virginia the new imperial swagger and fidelity to original historical details common to New York firms such as McKim, Mead, and White and Carrère and Hastings. Among his major projects from the turn of the century was the extension of Jefferson's State Capitol (1902–6). He was regarded as the state's leading architect.[63]

The monument that Noland and Valentine designed received its dedication at a massive

Louis Gudebrod, a New York sculptor, designed this triumphal arch, the winning entry in the second Davis Monument competition. This project, which was intended to stand on Broad Street at Twelfth, turned out, like the first proposed monument, to be too ambitious. (Valentine Museum)

TOP RIGHT: *For those attached to the Lost Cause, even the remnants of fortifications were considered hallowed ground by the turn of the century. In 1915 the Confederate Memorial Literary Society and the City of Richmond installed a cannon on the median just east of the Davis Monument to commemorate the fort that had stood there, strengthening the line of defense around Richmond. (Valentine Museum)*

BOTTOM LEFT: *Edward Virginius Valentine, who designed the sculptural components of the Jefferson Davis Monument, poses in his studio. After two earlier competitions had come to naught, the United Daughters of the Confederacy finally approached two Richmonders—Valentine and William C. Noland, both entrants in the previous competitions— about designing a more modest Davis monument. (Valentine Museum)*

BOTTOM RIGHT: *William Churchill Noland, a young architect, collaborated with Edward Valentine on a scheme for the Davis Monument. (Virginia Historical Society)*

THE STATUES

ABOVE: *When the Davis Monument arrived, schoolchildren pulled it to the site where it was to be erected. On April 18, 1907, 3,000 children, accompanied by revelers of all ages, hauled the statue—still crated and draped with bunting and flags—down Franklin Street. (Valentine Museum)*

LEFT: *Many curious bystanders turned out to supervise as Vindicatrix, an allegorical figure personifying memory and the spirit of the South, was raised to her perch on a sixty-foot-tall Doric column in the center of the Davis Monument. (Valentine Museum)*

The Davis Monument was unveiled four days after the Stuart Monument, on June 3, 1907, Davis's ninety-ninth birthday, at the largest Confederate reunion ever held. The parade, in which over 1,000 veterans and their sons marched, lasted over two hours in front of crowds estimated to be as large as 200,000. The speaker is sheltered under the awning at left. Although historians dissect the text of speeches offered at public events like the one pictured here, few of the attendees actually could hear them in the days before public address systems. (Valentine Museum)

ceremony on June 3, 1907, eighteen years after the project was first broached. By this time, the transportation of a statue to its site had become a Richmond tradition, and 3,000 area schoolchildren pulled the bronze statue of Davis, cast by the Gorham Company of Providence, Rhode Island, through the city on April 18, 1907. All of the children were requested to "bring a small Confederate battle flag." They were followed by veterans from the Lee Camp.[64] On May 30, the *Times-Dispatch* printed its front page partially in color, with portraits of Lee and Davis and the monument.[65] The parade for the dedication lasted for two hours and featured an estimated 1,200 veterans and their sons. The widows of Generals J. E. B. Stuart, Stonewall Jackson, A. P. Hill, and William Mahone attended. Varina Davis had died the year before, but the ex-president's only surviving child, Margaret Howell Hayes, and her two sons participated in the unveiling. Orations came from General Clement A. Evans of Georgia, and Governor Claude Swanson of Virginia, who presented the monument to the city, and Mayor Carlton McCarthy. All of the speakers expounded on the greatness of Davis and his trials and tribulations, but also they explained the rightness of the Confederate cause. As the *Times-Dispatch* noted, the occasion was "a noble tribute to the memory of the 'Lost Cause.'"[66] The governor proclaimed: "In this war the South contended for the sovereignty of States against Federal Aggression and power. She fought for the great principle of home rule against outside, illegal interference."[67]

"Dixie" was played, Confederate flags flew, and fireworks flared at the dedication. One newspaper quoted an aged, hobbling veteran who sighed after the event, "I was a boy again while the march lasted, but now that it's over, I'm an old broken man, ready to die."[68]

THE STATUES

Later that evening, the Stonewall Brigade Band of Staunton, Virginia, which participated extensively in the event, serenaded Mrs. Jackson, who was staying at the Jefferson Hotel. In addition to the familiar Southern tunes, the band concluded its concert with "America" and the "Star-Spangled Banner."

The theme of reconciliation present in the musical selections indicates some of the changes that were taking place in relations between the North and South. During the Spanish-American War former governor and Confederate general Fitzhugh Lee wore the blue uniform of the U.S. Army, as did many other white Southerners. Former Confederate soldiers were accepted as American heroes, and Davis now would join that pantheon. But the reconciliation took place on white Southern terms, as the Davis Monument explicitly indicated. The design of the monument drew upon several prototypes, perhaps most obviously Trajan's Column in Rome, but was recast with new meanings. The central feature, the sixty-foot-tall Doric column, was topped by a provocatively named, classical female statue, "Vindicatrix," intended to personify memory and the spirit of the South. Locally she became known as "Miss Confederacy." Her base contains the inscription DEO VINDICE (by God the protector), a phrase that had appeared on the Confederate seal, indicating her identity as "Vindicatrix." Two bands on the column contain the words PRO JURE CIVITATUM (for the rights of states) and PRO ARIS ET FOCIS (for hearth and home). Toward the bottom, a third band contains the seal of the Confederacy and the inscription JEFFERSON DAVIS PRESIDENT OF THE CONFEDERATE STATES OF AMERICA 1861–1865. Valentine's eight-foot-tall bronze statue of Davis stands in front, facing down the avenue toward Lee, the Washington Monument in Capitol Square, and the State Capitol, which had served as the capitol of the Confederacy. A reporter for the *News-Leader* explained Davis's gestures, "His right arm is outstretched as if he were expounding the Southern Doctrine, and was on the point of pleading with his countrymen to stand by the things for which so many had laid down their lives."[69] His left hand rests upon an open book, which has been interpreted as either a bible or a book on constitutional law. More books are stacked behind him. Supporting the open book is a fluted Doric column that emerges from a rough-hewn boulder. The boulder is inscribed with the date 1776, and near the bottom, the words JAMESTOWN 1607. The pedestal on which Davis stands also contains inscriptions, and the one in front reads, JEFFERSON DAVIS / EXPONENT OF / CONSTITUTIONAL PRINCIPLES / DEFENDER OF / THE RIGHTS OF STATES / CRESCIT OCCULTO VELUT / ARBOR AEVO FAMA. The Latin inscription is a quote from Horace: "The fame from a remote age grows like a tree." Quite clearly, the argument Davis is orating derives from the principles of American history and independence.

Embracing these central motifs is a curved screen, an exedra, of thirteen columns and two end piers, eighteen feet high. Seating was initially provided around the exedra, but subsequently the city closed it off by erecting a decorative iron fence. The thirteen columns represent the eleven states of the Confederacy and the two states (Kentucky and Missouri) that sent delegates to the Confederate Congress but did not secede. In the frieze above the columns are fourteen state seals, adding one more state, Maryland, as an honorary Confederate state. Inscribed in the entablature is an excerpt from Davis's speech to the United States Senate when he resigned to join his native Mississippi in secession, including the phrase: "the high and solemn motive of defending and protecting the rights we inherited."

TOP LEFT: *Floral tributes littered the base of the Davis Monument on the day of its unveiling.* (*Valentine Museum*)

TOP RIGHT: *In his monument, Jefferson Davis, who had been known for his oratory, was depicted speaking, and the words he offered as his resignation from the U.S. Senate were quoted along the frieze of the screen of columns behind him.* (*Valentine Museum*)

BOTTOM: *The Jefferson Davis Monument.*

OPPOSITE: *Vindicatrix rises dramatically over the statue of Jefferson Davis in this photograph of the monument at sunset.*

THE STATUES

THE STATUES 73

The terminating piers at either end are dedicated to the Confederate army and navy and carry bronze plaques, while on top stand funerary urns bedecked with the "Stars and Bars" of the Confederacy.

The Davis Monument—in image, architecture, and inscription—shifted the meaning of Monument Avenue in a substantial way. No longer a celebration primarily of character, loyalty, and martial exploits, it now unabashedly proclaimed the rightness and glory of the Lost Cause. It represented a reassertion of the political and constitutional views held by Davis in 1861 and by many white Southerners in 1907.

The Thomas Jonathan "Stonewall" Jackson Monument

The monument to Thomas Jonathan Jackson, unveiled October 11, 1919, at the corner of Monument Avenue and the Boulevard, combines the visual serenity and nobility of the Lee Monument with the martial sentiment of the Stuart Monument. The latter was certainly fitting, given Jackson's legacy: his uncanny understanding of military strategy made him Lee's star subordinate, but, impressive as his accomplishments were in life, his legend grew even larger after his early death.

As a professor of military tactics and the commander of the cadet corps at Virginia Military Institute before the Civil War, Jackson had a reputation as an odd, intensely religious man. Once the war started, his fervor and brilliance on the battlefield made him a legend and Lee's most trusted general. In the Valley Campaign, Jackson's strategy enabled him to use his 17,000 men to flummox more than 125,000 Union troops by darting ahead of and around them for over a month. His clever maneuvering, hard-driving leadership, and relentless pursuit of fleeing Union troops won several improbable victories. On May 2, 1863, returning at dusk from a reconnaissance ride during the battle of Chancellorsville, he was accidentally shot by his own men. His shattered left arm was amputated the next day. Lee's prophetic comment was, "He may have lost his left arm, but I have lost my right." Jackson contracted pneumonia and died May 10. His body lay in state at the Virginia State Capitol and in the Governor's Mansion, where thousands paid their respects, mourning his passing and what it might mean to their cause.

The growth of Jackson's postwar reputation can be attributed to a number of factors, including his military brilliance, a melancholy sense of unfulfilled promise that came from his death before the South's defeat, and the appeal of his rigid puritanical streak to the preachers and churchgoing citizens of the South. As the myths surrounding the leaders of the Confederacy grew, Jackson rose to the top along with Lee and Davis. Jackson was the first individual Confederate soldier commemorated, with the Foley monument in Capitol Square. Several other monuments honored Jackson in the years following the war, including a memorial placed on the spot where he fell in 1888, a statue by Edward V. Valentine erected over Jackson's grave in Lexington, Virginia, in 1891, and a statue by Moses Ezekiel commissioned for the West Virginia state capitol, a copy of which was made for Jackson's alma mater, Virginia Military Institute, and dedicated in 1912. Still, none of these was an equestrian monument, and the prevailing sentiment among surviving Confederates was that Jackson would not be appropriately honored without one.

After a reenactment of Jackson's famous ride through the Valley of Virginia, the Rich-

The Thomas Jonathan "Stonewall" Jackson Monument, Monument Avenue at Boulevard, 1919, F. William Sievers, sculptor.

mond Howitzers called for a meeting to discuss a monument. On November 29, 1911, the Jackson Monument Corporation was founded at the Lee Camp Hall. The Reverend James Powers Smith, the sole survivor of Jackson's staff, was elected president. On April 29, 1914, the corporation held a rally at City Auditorium with Mary Anna Jackson, widow of the general, as honored guest. Two days later, on May 1, a "flag day" filled the streets of Richmond with members of the United Daughters of the Confederacy selling Confederate flags, raising $5,000 for the statue.[70]

The cornerstone was laid in a penetrating rain at the end of a Confederate reunion on June 3, 1915. A grand parade progressed from Capitol Square to Monument Avenue, but only about 150 spectators stayed to see the ceremony. The speech given that day by Major William A. Anderson, a member of the Stonewall Brigade, again praised both Jackson's devotion to God and his military superiority. He was hallowed along with Lee, "kindred as they were in the unselfishness of their ambition, the nobility of their ideals, the righteousness of their conduct, the purity of their motives, and the greatness of their souls . . . we, their followers can make no comparison of their goodness and greatness."[71]

The sculpture itself was not commissioned until 1916. By this time, a reconciliation between North and South had been constructed that combined both forgiveness and a careful manipulation of history by those who believed in the South's righteousness and honor. The South's enthusiastic response to the call for troops during the Spanish-American War had ameliorated much of the rancor that remained. Talk of patriotism and reunification filled newspapers and veterans' meetings. Previous monuments had established a pattern, exemplified by the Lee Monument, stressing honor, nobility, and righteousness. Time had passed, and fading memories had mellowed most Americans' view of the Civil War. Now, more than a generation away from the war, a tentative reconciliation had been reached, one that was to a large extent influenced by the white Southern view of the war, often communicated through monuments.

A competition had been announced in April 1915. After two rounds of altered models, the selection committee, composed of veterans and Richmonders, but with no artistic representation, had narrowed the field from thirty-one entrants to four finalists by March 1916. These four sculptors—Frederick William Sievers, Charles Keck, Edward Clark Potter, and Pompeo Coppini—were asked to submit another round of models.[72] Sievers had gained several small commissions in Virginia before he won the commission for the Virginia Memorial at Gettysburg in 1910, when he moved to Richmond. Keck, a New Yorker and member of the National Sculpture Society, would later receive several commissions in Virginia, including, interestingly, a statue of Stonewall Jackson for Jackson Park in Charlottesville in 1921.[73] Potter, a New England sculptor famous for his skill with equestrian subjects, often collaborated with Daniel Chester French. Coppini, a prolific sculptor who hailed from San Antonio, had numerous Confederate commissions in Texas.[74]

On May 25 the committee announced the selection of Sievers, and on June 10 a contract was signed. Keck and Potter, both better known nationally than Sievers, evidently lost because of Sievers's dogged pursuit of an accurate portrait. The debate over giving preference to accuracy or to artistic expression had begun with the Lee Monument and was generally decided, for each statue, by the makeup of the committee designated to choose the artist. Sievers had gone to great lengths in his Gettysburg memorial to capture Lee. He had also passed out a questionnaire, quizzing veterans on arcane details about uniforms and arms to better represent the soldiers at the base of the sculpture. The committee knew that Sievers would be sympathetic to their desire for an exacting likeness. Reporting on the selection of Sievers, one newspaper suggested that the sculptor would be asked to alter his model because Jackson was in "complete repose" but some members of the committee were known to "be of the opinion that the horse should show more action." However, the paper commented, "The likeness of Jackson is excellent and the whole pose of the statue is said to be characteristic of the great soldier."[75]

Sievers was born in 1872 in Fort Wayne, Indiana. He was raised there and in Atlanta, where he began sculpting at eighteen. He came to Richmond at twenty-one and found work as a carver of frames and furniture. He studied from 1893 to 1898 at the Mechanic's Institute under Frederick Moynihan, the sculptor of the J. E. B. Stuart Monument, before becoming an instructor himself. By 1898 he had saved enough money to go to Europe.

He enrolled at the Royal Institute of Art in Rome; he may also have attended the Academy Julian in Paris at some point, but he maintained a studio in Rome until 1901. In 1902 he settled in New York, helping to model work for the 1904 Louisiana Purchase Exposition in St. Louis and coming into contact with the finest American sculptors of the period, including Daniel Chester French, Henry Kirke Bush-Brown, Solon Borglum, and possibly Edward Clark Potter. He received minor commissions in the South, and then in

1910 he won the Gettysburg competition. In that year, Sievers and his wife moved to Richmond.

The City of Richmond donated $10,000 to the Jackson Monument Corporation, and the General Assembly of Virginia did the same. Together with the money raised earlier, the total available for the monument reached more than $40,000, and it was in hand when the contract with Sievers was signed. Sievers completed the model in the spring of 1919 and sent it to the Gorham Foundry in Providence, Rhode Island, for casting in bronze.

The unveiling came on October 11, 1919, the first on Monument Avenue not to be held during a Confederate reunion, though the sentiments surrounding it were thoroughly Confederate. The unveiling was preceded by a ceremony at the Museum of the Confederacy in which Jackson's granddaughter, Mrs. E. Randolph Preston, presented Jackson's sword as a gift from the family. The requisite military parade began with the cadets from Virginia Military Institute and included 2,000 soldiers in all. By this time, relations between the North and South had been further eased by their shared experiences in World War I. The Jackson Monument, which had been commissioned before America's entry into World War I, still reflected the martial sentiments more frequently asserted in earlier Confederate monuments. Speeches praised both Jackson's devotion to God and his fervid commitment to the Confederacy. Colonel Robert Edward Lee, a grandson of Jackson's commanding officer, said, "In every quality that goes to make a perfect fighting machine, Jackson and his foot cavalry were unsurpassed, not only in the War Between the States, but no war since has seen their superior."[76] Anna Jackson Preston, a great-granddaughter of the general, aided by William Daniel Sievers, the sculptor's son, tugged on the veil; but the wind had tangled the cords, and a workman had to climb the statue to cut them and release the veil.

The bronze statue rests on a twenty-two-foot-high, capsule-shaped pedestal of granite from Mount Airy, North Carolina. It depicts a firm, composed Jackson facing north on an attentive horse with all four feet firmly planted on the ground. The pedestal's inscriptions read STONEWALL JACKSON on both sides, and on the north face, BORN 1824 / DIED CHAN-CELLORSVILLE / 1863. There is no significant difference between the finished sculpture and the model described earlier, indicating that the Jackson committee either did not suggest changes, or was persuaded by Sievers that this sculpture was preferable. Sievers achieved a realistic likeness of Jackson, partially by using the death mask modeled by the sculptor Adalbert Johann Volck, owned by the Valentine Museum. Little Sorrel, Jackson's favorite horse, was not used as a model; instead Sievers modeled Jackson's mount after a thoroughbred named Superior, chosen for its proportions.

Legends about Civil War statues abound with elaborate theories of orientation and composition. Do they face north because their subjects were killed in battle, or is that why their horses rear up on their hind legs? When do they doff their caps, and what does it mean when they face east or west? Although we know that sculptors did not necessarily consider these factors, which were, after all, never codified, there is some evidence that the public, and hence the committees that commissioned these artworks, may have made iconographical assumptions. In the case of the Stuart statue, the orientation of most viewers has shifted. When the statue was unveiled, Stuart's figure, turned in the saddle, faced the traffic entering Monument Avenue from Franklin Street on the east. But since 1946 West Frank-

lin Street has been one-way heading east, and most vehicular traffic now views Stuart's back and his horse's side as they approach. The Jackson committee and Sievers struggled with Jackson's orientation. Sievers preferred to have the general face south, the direction from which most traffic would approach. Major Anderson and the soldiers at the Lee Camp disagreed, claiming that it would be inappropriate for Jackson to, in effect, turn his back on the North. The old soldiers won.[77]

Although Jackson was celebrated for his military genius, his piety likewise endeared him to generations of white Southerners. Sievers seemed to draw on Jackson's intense spirituality in the sculpture, in which he seems completely at ease, even serene. Jackson's last words, "Let us cross over the river, and rest under the shade of the trees," are often quoted as indicative of his composure and faith. Although his fame originated with his ferocity in battle, his legend emphasizes his spirituality, and so does the statue in which he is immortalized on Monument Avenue.

The Matthew Fontaine Maury Monument

The erection of the Matthew Fontaine Maury Monument signaled change for Monument Avenue. Unveiled in 1929, the Maury Monument depicts the only hero on the street who, for many, needs an introduction. Maury, known as the "Pathfinder of the Seas" for his achievements in charting the winds and currents of the world's oceans, was honored primarily for his scientific achievements, though he was a Confederate and the statue was supported financially by the United Daughters of the Confederacy. As the South cemented a reconciliation with the North, a legacy of military prowess, as expressed in the Stuart and Jackson Monuments, was deemphasized. In Maury, Virginia had a hero who had achieved prominence through peacetime endeavors. He had literally transformed our understanding of the world, and this reflected glory back to his home state. His statue also represents

THE STATUES

ABOVE: *To the sculptor's displeasure, at the insistence of Confederate veterans Sievers sited Jackson facing north. He would have preferred to have the general face south, the direction from which most of the intersection's traffic approached, but the old soldiers would not hear of Jackson turning his back on the North. (Valentine Museum)*

LEFT: *Monument Avenue's standing as a gathering place and public arena sometimes attracted crowds and parades, sometimes just a weekday group of small children and their nannies. (Valentine Museum)*

OPPOSITE: *The Stonewall Jackson Monument.*

The Matthew Fontaine Maury Monument, Monument Avenue at North Belmont Street, 1929, F. William Sievers, sculptor.

an attempt by Frederick William Sievers, the sculptor of the Stonewall Jackson Monument, to break away from his traditional sculptural style, to express something more abstract than military valor and might.

In 1906 Gaston Lichtenstein, a Richmonder visiting Germany, was struck by the reverence shown for Maury at a naval museum in Hamburg. Lichtenstein came home and ruminated on the fact that Maury was practically unknown in his own country. Six years later, Lichtenstein wrote a letter to a Richmond newspaper suggesting that there should be a monument to Maury in the city. Katherine Stiles of the Museum of the Confederacy then published a biographical booklet by Maury's son, Richard L. Maury, as a means to raise money for a memorial. In 1915 Lichtenstein wrote another letter, and a few days later, an as-

THE STATUES

sociation formed. It was reorganized a year later, at which time Elvira Moffitt was named president.[78] Moffitt, an activist who had moved from North Carolina to Richmond in 1909, came to the project with great spirit and a long list of previous accomplishments. Her volunteer work for groups in her home state had included varied projects for historical societies, patriotic organizations, groups advocating peace and school reform, and women's clubs.[79]

Matthew Fontaine Maury was born near Fredericksburg, Virginia, in 1806. He was raised on a farm in Tennessee and joined the United States Navy in 1825. He rose quickly from midshipman to lieutenant, and sailed around the world. After his return, he wrote a new treatise on navigation, which was thereafter used by the navy. He was unable to sail again after he suffered a disabling knee injury in a stagecoach accident in 1839. In 1842 he was appointed the first head of the U.S. Naval Observatory, where he took on the task of mapping both the stars and the oceans, describing sea lanes that still aid navigation today. The maps he constructed of seabeds helped in laying the first transatlantic cable. Maury also studied land forms and their effects on storms and hurricanes to aid Southern agriculture and shipping. He is considered the father of oceanography, and his work laid the foundation for the U.S. Weather Bureau. He also served in the Confederate navy as a technical expert. In the basement of a house on Clay Street, he conducted experiments that led to his invention of an electric torpedo, a device that protected Confederate harbors. Later, he went abroad as an agent of the Confederate government. Out of the country when the war ended, he remained away for several years. Eventually he was persuaded to return, and he took a teaching post at the Virginia Military Institute, where he died in 1873.[80]

World War I interrupted the Maury Association's work, but in 1920 the group pushed a bill through the state legislature to appropriate $10,000 toward the monument. With a little-known hero and the passage of almost sixty years since the Civil War, the Maury Monument Association struggled to find the rest of the money that would be needed. Maury's birthday was set aside as a day for schoolchildren to observe, and they were urged to donate money to the cause. The United Daughters of the Confederacy donated $5,000, and its members threw themselves into fund-raising, too. Then, the City of Richmond offered the land at the intersection of Belmont Street and Monument Avenue.

The cornerstone was laid June 22, 1922, during a Confederate reunion, and the ceremony was attended by Governor E. Lee Trinkle, the commander-in-chief of the Confederate veterans, Mrs. Moffitt, the leaders of the UDC, and Gaston Lichtenstein. In their remarks on the occasion, both the governor and Dr. A. B. Chandler, president of the State Normal College for Women, chastised Americans for recognizing Maury's greatness so late.[81]

Earlier that spring, F. William Sievers, the sculptor of the Jackson Monument, had approached Moffitt with a proposal for the Maury Monument. He claimed Maury as one of his heroes. A line in Stiles's pamphlet—"The voice of the wind and the voice of the waters were music to his ears"—inspired him, and he presented a portrait of Maury seated in front of a large globe around which swirled a figural group being battered by storms. This interpretation synthesized the committee's aims, putting Richmond in a world context both figuratively and literally.

The association was immediately taken with the model and Sievers's idea. They resolved

TOP LEFT: *A full-size model of the storm group and the globe for the Maury Monument almost filled Sievers's studio. A small maquette, or model, of the entire monument sits on a platform to the right. Sievers placed the globe behind Maury because he felt only a globe could sufficiently represent the size and importance of the scientist's ideas. Those ideas, rendered looming over the figure of Maury, were to Sievers literally bigger than the man himself. (The Library of Virginia)*

TOP RIGHT: *The Gorham Foundry cast the portrait and the globe separately, and the statue of Maury was delivered and installed months before the globe was completed. (The Library of Virginia)*

BOTTOM: *In a mishap like that at the unveiling of the Jackson Monument, the veil caught on the Maury Monument as two of his great-grandchildren tried to uncover it at the Armistice Day ceremony on November 11, 1929. A naval officer climbed up and disentangled the veil while the crowd waited. (The Library of Virginia)*

LEFT: *The figural group at the base of the globe above the Maury statue embodies mankind's struggles with nature, in keeping with Maury's scientific studies aimed at helping us understand weather systems, particularly dangerous ones. Sievers illustrated Maury's work by sculpting struggles with a storm at sea, on the left, and on a farm, at the right.*

BELOW: *After his explorations in Antarctica, Richard Evelyn Byrd, brother of former Virginia governor Harry F. Byrd, traveled to Richmond and placed a wreath at the Maury Monument in recognition of Maury's pioneering efforts at mapping the oceans. (The Library of Virginia)*

that there would be no competition; Sievers would sculpt the monument. However, they would not be able to sign a contract with Sievers until they had raised the $60,000 necessary. With the fund stalled at $37,000, a group of Richmond businessmen came to the aid of the organization, persuading the city to donate $10,000 and raising the rest by subscription. The association signed a contract with Sievers on May 10, 1926.[82]

The statue of Maury was cast by the Gorham Foundry and put in place months before the model for the globe and the figural group were completed. A fence had to be erected around the site to protect the portrait. After some trouble with the casting of the globe, Sievers telegraphed from New York on October 16, 1929, "Bronze OK May Proceed with Unveiling Program."[83]

Significantly, the unveiling took place on Armistice Day, November 11, 1929. The South's restored place in the unified nation was reinforced by the choice of a national holiday that celebrated the country's armed forces and the end of World War I. In earlier years, officials probably would have scheduled the unveiling of a monument to a Confederate hero for another day. By 1929, though, Richmonders clearly felt that there was no reason to do so.

An American Legion memorial service began the day downtown. A military parade formed at the Lee Monument at two o'clock and marched out to Belmont Street, where Governor Harry Flood Byrd gave the address at the unveiling. Two of Maury's great-grandchildren, Matthew Fontaine Maury Osborne of Norfolk and Mary Maury Fitzgerald of Richmond, pulled the cords to reveal the completed monument. The simple inscription reads, MATTHEW FONTAINE MAURY / PATHFINDER OF THE SEAS. The parade turned back down to the Boulevard and marched to the newly constructed City Stadium, also slated for an Armistice Day dedication, which took place that afternoon with fireworks and speeches as the grand finale to the day's activities. Before marching in the parade, the band from the Norfolk Naval Base had serenaded Elvira Moffitt as she lay ill at Johnston-Willis Hospital near the new monument. She died about six months later, at the age of ninety-two, having accomplished her last goal.

Sievers had explained to the Maury Association committee that the portrait of Maury would have to communicate the power of his mind as well as represent him physically. He placed a seated Maury in front of a globe. The globe, much larger than Maury and placed higher than him on a drum-shaped pedestal, represented the focus and breadth of Maury's ideas to Sievers. He said, "It occurred to me that certainly a man's creative mind and his concepts are bigger than the physical man himself, so it would be logical to make the allegory, which symbolizes that mind and its work, bigger than the actual figure of the subject." Sievers pointed out in a description of the sculpture that the classical approach would have shown Maury holding a model of the earth in his hand. He felt his composition was more meaningful.[84]

The detailed, realistic portrait of Maury contrasts with the idealized and sometimes vague figures behind him. These figures represent humanity and its struggles with storms and the sea. Maury's intention in studying patterns in the weather was to aid mariners and farmers, so Sievers stressed the human side of Maury's scientific achievements. An ox and a capsized lifeboat add to the chaos and help tie the composition to the everyday applications that motivated Maury. The sea lanes and weather patterns he mapped appear accurately depicted on the globe. The sculptor imprinted fresh- and saltwater fishes, swallows, bats, and other creatures on the base and pedestal of the monument. These animals symbolize parts of Maury's investigations; for instance, the electric ray suggests deep sea exploration, as well as the electric torpedo. Sievers intended the elaborate iconography to help identify Maury and to clarify his design concept.

The departure of the Maury statue from the overt celebration of the Lost Cause and martial glory of the previous four monuments on the avenue reflects the changed intellectual and cultural climate in Richmond during the 1920s. Some Northern critics belittled culture in the South, which H. L. Mencken referred to as the "Sahara of the Bozart," and Richmonders felt the need to refute this reputation. Not that sympathy for the Confederate version of the war disappeared, but another sensibility also ruled. Many white civic leaders in Richmond saw themselves as part of the new sophisticated cosmopolitanism of big business, and they needed to persuade outsiders that this was the case. Foreign travel increased, and instead of glorying in the provincialism of being Southern, Richmonders actively sought to broaden their cultural horizons, in the process seeking the approbation of Northerners, as with the extraordinary patronage they afforded to the New York architect William Lawrence Bottomley. Hence, while Maury certainly was a Confederate, he is shown as a "man of the world," an exemplar of Virginia's contribution to world knowledge and culture. Science and technology were the darlings of commerce, and recognition of a Virginian's scientific genius could only enhance Richmond's reputation as a modern city.

The Arthur Ashe Monument

The Arthur Ashe Jr. Monument, dedicated July 10, 1996, sixty-seven years after the Maury Monument, challenged and changed the narrative of Monument Avenue. It suggested a reconciliation of the Old South personified in the various Confederate statues with the achievements of African Americans in the late twentieth century. Although the campaign for the Ashe Monument required only three years from concept to completion, much less time than the decades needed for some of the earlier monuments, the battle over its location proved to be perhaps the fieriest yet. Unlike the case of the earlier monuments, the leader and instigator of this battle was the sculptor of the statue, Paul DiPasquale.

Between 1929 and 1996 Richmond both grew and shrank as it experienced the same vicissitudes as most major American cities during this complex time of prosperity, depression, and postwar boom. Geographically, Richmond expanded, annexing many areas and growing from nearly 23 square miles in 1914 to 62.5 in 1970. The city reached its population peak in the 1950s, with approximately 230,000 residents, and then lost as the significant growth shifted to the suburbs. By 1990 the city's population stood at 202,000, while the surrounding metropolitan-suburban area stood at over 700,000. What happened in Richmond occurred elsewhere: the central city declined as vast interstate highways pushed through neighborhoods, the large department stores closed, and a significant portion of the population, largely white, departed for the suburbs.

Richmond had always been a city of two races, with the whites dominant. As noted earlier, around 1900 Jim Crow laws substantially disenfranchised the African American population and solidified a racially segregated society. The U.S. Supreme Court's *Brown v. Board*

The Arthur Ashe Monument, Monument Avenue at Roseneath Road, 1996, Paul DiPasquale, sculptor.

of Education decision of 1954 outlawing school segregation brought about "massive resistance" in the city, championed by the editor of the *Richmond News Leader*. Although Richmond never closed its public schools to resist, as did many other Virginia localities, school integration proceeded very slowly. Massive resistance collapsed in the 1960s under pressure from the civil rights movement, business leaders, and other activists, but the concept of racial equality remained a goal beyond reach. The Voting Rights Act of 1965 and amendments to the Virginia Constitution helped restore the right to vote to the city's black population, increasing its majority population as "white flight" to the suburbs continued at a pace that was not offset by the annexation of some white residential areas. A few parts of the city remained predominantly white, however, despite overall trends. Monument Avenue was one of these, remaining throughout the post–World War II years a staunchly white enclave. In 1977 the black majority on the city council elected Henry Marsh as Richmond's first black mayor. In 1990, L. Douglas Wilder, whose grandparents, former slaves, had moved to Richmond in the 1880s, took the oath of office as the first black governor of the Commonwealth of Virginia. Into this mixture of a newly enfranchised black majority and a white minority, Paul DiPasquale, a white sculptor, introduced the idea of a statue to Arthur Ashe.

Arthur Ashe, an African American, achieved fame as an international tennis star, helping to break the color barrier in that sport. Born in 1943 in Richmond, he learned to play tennis in the city on strictly segregated courts. Ashe attended the University of California at Los Angeles and then embarked on a tennis career, becoming the first black to represent the United States on a Davis Cup team, winning the U.S. Open in 1968, and defeating Jimmy Conners for the Wimbledon Championship in 1975. Ashe devoted much of his later life to supporting black youth and their education. An humble man not given to boasting, Ashe wrote in his autobiography, *Days of Grace*, about his youth in Richmond. He remembered "the huge, white First Baptist Church. That church confirmed its domination and its strict racial identity by its presence on Richmond's Monument Avenue, the avenue of Confederate heroes."[85] Although Ashe lived with his wife and child in New York, he reconciled himself with Richmond, where many of his family still lived, and devoted significant time and funds to benefit its black youth. During an operation in 1983, Ashe received a tainted blood transfusion. He subsequently contracted the AIDS virus and died of pneumonia on February 6, 1993. He was buried in Richmond in a historically black cemetery.

Shortly before his death, Ashe and a few colleagues advanced the concept of a hall of fame for African American athletes to be located in Richmond.[86] Ashe had become very interested in black athletes and had written a book on the subject.[87] He had also founded a philanthropic organization to mentor public school students, Virginia Heroes, Inc. Ashe met the sculptor Paul DiPasquale during a 1992 visit to conduct a tennis clinic in Richmond. DiPasquale, impressed with Ashe's accomplishments and his commitment to youth, wrote him with the idea of sculpting his likeness and creating an "authorized and approved public sculpture." Ashe agreed and in subsequent communication told DiPasquale that the sculpture should be as "straightforward as possible." He suggested an informal pose, with books and perhaps a tennis racket.[88] After his death, an Arthur Ashe Monument Committee was formed under the umbrella of the Virginia Heroes organization to further DiPasquale's project. Jeanne Moutoussamy-Ashe, Arthur Ashe's wife, worked with DiPasquale.[89] Fund-raisers for the project included state senator Benjamin Lambert and the chief executive officer of Dominion Energy, Inc., Thomas N. Chewning, who ironically—given Ashe's printed comments—worshiped at the First Baptist Church on Monument Avenue.[90]

Born in New Jersey, Paul DiPasquale graduated from the University of Virginia in 1973. He was accepted by the law school there, but decided instead to study architecture in

RIGHT: *The mold created for the casting of the Arthur Ashe portrait, in DiPasquale's studio. (Paul DiPasquale)*

BELOW: *Paul DiPasquale working on the clay model for the Ashe statue in his studio. (Jay Paul)*

THE STATUES

LEFT: *A detail of the plaster proof of the Arthur Ashe Monument. (Lynn S. Harkins)*

BELOW: *The entire nation watched Richmond's agonizing debate about locating the Ashe Monument. Finally the base was set in place at the intersection of Roseneath Road and Monument Avenue. (Douglas J. Harnsberger)*

Boston and then sculpture back in Richmond, where he received a Master of Fine Arts from Virginia Commonwealth University in 1977. He lived and taught in the northern Virginia area for several years prior to returning to Richmond in 1983 to pursue a career as a public sculptor. He created the enormous Indian head, *Connecticut*, installed at The Diamond, Richmond's baseball stadium (home of the Richmond Braves); the bronze *Headman* on Brown's Island, which depicts a bateauman navigating the nearby James River and Kanawha Canal; a bust of Governor Mills Godwin for the Capitol; and a bust of Oliver Hill, Richmond's distinguished civil rights lawyer, for the city's Black History Museum. The necessity of earning a living from his sculpture provided DiPasquale with the patience and fortitude to promote his Ashe monument through some venom-filled discussions.

By February 1994, DiPasquale had completed a twelve-foot model and shown it to Ashe's family members, including his widow, Jeanne, and brother, Johnnie. They approved the basic design and the figure's likeness. The Ashe Monument Committee, through Virginia Heroes, then approached the City of Richmond concerning placement of the statue on city property. At an early showing, former governor Wilder suggested Monument Avenue, but as DiPasquale recalled: "Nobody agreed with him. . . . Everybody thought it would just be too much of a fight."[91] Richmond's black mayor, Leonidas B. Young, appointed several city council members to a site selection committee, which also included DiPasquale, Chewning, and Randy Ashe, a cousin. The committee identified five locations, including one on Monument Avenue near Roseneath Road, which, until the avenue was extended in 1915, had been its terminus. Criteria for the location included visibility, safety, fund-raising potential, and approval by the Ashe family. The Monument Avenue site best met the criteria in the view of a majority of the committee. Jeanne Moutoussamy-Ashe, who traveled to Richmond privately and viewed the possible sites, agreed.[92]

The Ashe Monument Committee began the laborious process of winning approval by various city agencies and boards, attending, for example, a meeting of the Public Art Commission, a meeting of the Urban Design Committee, several meetings of the City Planning Commission, and four meetings each of the Architectural Review Committee and the city council.[93] Opposition developed in several quarters and took a variety of forms, including denigration of the artistic merits of DiPasquale's work and criticism of the site. Among complaints concerning the statue were the comments that it was "too informal," "too casual," "awkward," "uninspired," and created to be viewed from only one side. DiPasquale continued to modify the statue, adding weight and muscularity while maintaining the facial features and eyeglasses of Ashe from shortly before his death. The head of the statue, which started the process with a downward gaze, was tilted up in response to criticism, and then shifted back down again when that was criticized. Some felt that when the statue was viewed from behind, Ashe looked "as if [he] were being arrested or held up," and consequently DiPasquale adjusted the position of the arms.[94] Objections toward the sculpture were raised for months, and a group of artists and patrons even raised pledges to conduct a competition but were later told that the city had already accepted DiPasquale's sculpture.

Placement on the avenue also remained a major issue, with arguments ranging from those that complained that the site at Roseneath would defame Ashe, to those that reverted to the claim that Monument Avenue's program was to memorialize the Lost Cause. Although many Richmonders had moved beyond that position, not all had. At a city council hearing, Richmonders who embraced the notion of the Lost Cause came out in sizable numbers to protest, prompting the *Times-Dispatch* to note that these white citizens "almost unfailingly said Monument Avenue would be reserved for Confederate figures."[95] Other Richmonders, both black and white, offered thoughtful contributions, wondering what people elsewhere would think if Richmond excluded Ashe from the street, exulting over the thought of a hero to whom they could relate on what had seemed a forbidding street, and urging a symbolic break with the past.[96] Outsiders offering their opinions included the president of the Danville, Virginia, chapter of the Heritage Preservation Association, who declared, "I don't think the man was significant enough in the history of Virginia or the country to be included along with these monuments that are along that avenue." He continued: "These men [the generals] contributed more to the founding and the values of this country than a tennis player."[97] All the other sites were revisited countless times during a yearlong battle, as the site selection moved through the bureaucratic and political fog. Dissension crossed all party and racial boundaries, with many complex issues at stake. Some African Americans felt that Ashe did not belong on Monument Avenue with Confederates and that he would not have wanted to be there. Some whites liked the idea of siting the monument on the avenue but wanted a different sculpture. And other individuals argued that it was time for the whole city to be represented on Monument Avenue.

Finally, early in the morning of July 18, 1995, after a seven-hour public hearing, the city council voted seven to zero to place the Ashe statue on Monument Avenue at Roseneath Road.[98] Prior to the meeting, Mayor Young suggested placing the statue in a local park, next to the tennis courts where Ashe had learned to play, an idea that former governor Wilder quickly characterized as "moronic." Young changed his mind. Local commentators noted that the "eyes of the nation were truly on Richmond," but a "national embarrassment of disastrous proportions . . . was avoided until another day."[99]

Although the city council revisited the matter of the statue and its site several more times, the decision stood, and on August 15, 1995, a ground-breaking ceremony took place.[100] Fund-raising continued, under the leadership of Chewning, for the estimated $500,000 needed to finance the statue. The dedication took place on July 10, 1996, the fifty-third anniversary of Arthur Ashe's birth.[101]

The site of the Ashe statue at Roseneath Road, three blocks west of the Maury Monument, had earlier been selected by the City of Richmond as a location for a future monument, and in 1925 the city rounded off the corners of the blocks and set aside a circle forty-four feet in diameter.[102] In 1996, for the Ashe Monument, the city installed traffic barriers and widened the site. Barry Starke of Earth Design Associates designed the base, while Doug Harnsberger of D. J. Harnsberger and Associates produced the working drawings of the base.

The bronze statue created by Paul DiPasquale and cast by the Bronze Craft Foundry in Waynesboro, Virginia, depicts Ashe standing in a warm-up suit, his arms upraised in a victory salute, but carrying in his left hand a tennis racket and in his right several books. He rises above four upward-looking children, modeled from the waist up; each one also raises an arm. The contrast between the subject—Ashe—and the supporting context is an inversion of the Maury statue's composition. Also related to the Maury Monument are DiPasquale's modeling techniques, with an emphasis on texture that recalls Sievers's treat-

ment of bronze. The bronze base of the statue contains Ashe's name in capital letters. The granite pedestal doubles the twelve-foot height of the statue and is inscribed on the front with a quote Ashe chose for his autobiography from Hebrews 12:1, "Since we are surrounded by so great a cloud of witnesses, let us lay aside every weight, and the sin which so easily ensnares us, and let us run with endurance the race that is set before us." The rear of the pedestal carries Ashe's name and dates, and a brief statement that the purpose of the monument is "to inspire children and people of all nationalities."

*The Arthur Ashe
Monument
(Paul DiPasquale)*

The Ashe statue faces west, which proved to be controversial, though the orientation received approval by the City Planning Commission. DiPasquale argued that the lighting from the south and west would be best, and that the high trees to the east would frame the frontal view without shading the figures' faces.[103] The monument's dedication did not stop the arguments and criticism, or the praise.[104] In any event, the statue has proved to be tremendously popular, drawing a substantial number of visitors in the years since its dedication.

As a work of public sculpture and a memorial, the Arthur Ashe Monument proved to be effective. Its most apparent weakness is the massiveness of the columnar pedestal, the plainness of which cries out for more relief. Ashe leans slightly forward toward the children, his arms with books and racket outstretched in a gesture of victory—not one of excessive hubris and ego, but rather an imploring statement. The children, two girls and two boys, emerge from the base. Fittingly, they are black, white, and Asian. As a sign of the times, one of the boys has his baseball cap on backward. The message the statue conveys is immediately apparent to the observer. Here is an individual who excelled in a sport, had a passion for learning, and was committed to children. The physical likeness to Ashe is very strong: it is clearly the face of a person with some age and wear. That his back is toward the other statues on Monument Avenue and toward downtown Richmond does convey a message—that Ashe turns his back on the past. Facing west is also symbolic, since embedded in American culture is the myth of the West as the future, as hope and freedom.

The Arthur Ashe statue completed the statuary program of Monument Avenue for the twentieth century. Certainly, in the future other monuments will be proposed, and perhaps some will be placed on the avenue—but that is a question for the new century. The Ashe statue does not mark the end of the avenue's story, but rather opens the narrative to new interpretations. History still resonates, and the addition of the Ashe statue to the others illuminates possible themes of reconciliation. It also explains why Monument Avenue has captured the imaginations of several generations, demonstrating that public sculpture helps shape and impose a collective memory that is constantly evolving. The Monument Avenue sculptures are both artifacts and a portrait of America.

THE STATUES

Chapter 3

BUILDING A NEIGHBORHOOD

Real Estate

The creation of Monument Avenue involved many people with a variety of motives. Ostensibly, Monument Avenue began as the site for a monumental statue of Robert E. Lee, but behind that project and the later statues lay another agenda, one fundamental to American culture: financial return, in this case, real estate speculation and building. Ellen Glasgow, one of Richmond's preeminent novelists and a chronicler of the city's life, caught the spirit in a novel of 1916 in which the new "metropolis" is described. One of the characters says excitedly: "Just watch as we go up Franklin Street to Monument Avenue . . . just wait until you see Monument Avenue. It's the handsomest boulevard south of Washington. It's all new, every brick of it. There's not a house the whole way up that isn't as fresh as paint, and the avenue is just as straight as if you'd drawn it with a ruler."[1]

Many individuals saw Monument Avenue as a commercial enterprise that could provide significant returns to the original property owners and to those who chose to speculate or build. The impressive layout of wide medians, double rows of trees, and grand vistas provided a spectacular setting for the Lee Monument and also established the beginnings of an elegant neighborhood with generous lots in the western end of Richmond, at the end of the city's most prestigious address, West Franklin Street. The sculptures and their symbolism provided a background against which real estate owners, speculators, builders, architects, and patrons could play the great American game of proving you have arrived by building a large house at a prestigious address. As time passed, Monument Avenue became more than just a series of large houses, evolving into a neighborhood that contained churches and some of Richmond's most impressive apartment houses as well.

Richmond, like all American cities in the nineteenth and early twentieth centuries, was a city built upon real estate speculation. As noted in Chapter 1, Richmond began to expand west in the late eighteenth century, and that pattern continued well into the twentieth. The various neighborhoods of Richmond, such as the Fan District and Oregon Hill, and the odd jogs of Main and Cary Streets at Belvidere and Harrison Streets were produced by different real estate developments, which, in many cases, took years to build out.[2]

Monument Avenue's fresh new architecture and landscaping reach from the Lee Monument to the Davis Monument in the distance in this photograph taken from the upstairs porch at 1637 Monument in 1925. (Valentine Museum)

At the beginning of the street's development, the houses, like these in the 1600 block, looked much like those being built in the neighboring Fan District.

By the late nineteenth century, several real estate developments had surrounded parts of the area that today contains the historic core of Monument Avenue—Stuart Circle west to Roseneath Road. To the south lay a large neighborhood known as Sydney, which had begun as early as 1817, when three developers—Jaquelin Harvie, Benjamin Harris and George Winston—formed a partnership to develop the property. They laid out a grid of streets but shifted their alignment from that of the streets in central Richmond. Sydney continued the dominant Richmond pattern of wider east-west streets serving as main transportation arteries, while north-south streets were narrower. The complex geometry of triangular blocks at the intersections of the grids became a distinctive feature of the area that is today known as the Fan. Because of economic depressions, Sydney took years to develop; it was built primarily as a residential area, though it also included a racetrack and some commercial enterprises. To the north of what would become Monument Avenue lay Broad Street, originally developed as the Deep Run Turnpike in 1804. A major east-west highway, Broad Street became intensely commercial, with factories clustered along it and railroad lines running down the center of the street. To the south of Sydney, the City of Richmond built a reservoir and began to develop what became known as Byrd Park. Between the reservoir and Broad Street ran a road that was renamed the Boulevard in 1883. Along it in 1884 was established the Robert E. Lee Camp, a home for Confederate veterans. The gap between the Sydney and Broad Street neighborhoods became the site of Monument Avenue. Period photographs reveal the future site of Monument Avenue to be a vacant, desolate area lying ripe for development at the end of prestigious Franklin Street.[3]

The Original Landowners

Three families originally owned most of the property that would become Monument Avenue: the Allen family owned the area from Lombardy to Allison Streets; the Branches owned most of the property from Allison Street to the Boulevard; and the Sheppards owned the area west of the Boulevard to Roseneath Road. In addition to these families, the real estate partnership of James W. Allison and Edmund B. Addison owned a short stretch of property at Allison Street. The avenue developed from east to west, with most blocks being built up as the block to the east was completed. The primary landowners had different goals for their property, and consequently the avenue's character changed as development moved westward.[4]

The original owner of the Allen tract was William C. Allen, a sensible, hardworking builder who started out as a brickmason. He came to Richmond about 1810 and became a building contractor and small developer, quietly amassing a considerable fortune. Allen built many attractive, simple, and well-constructed houses throughout the first two-thirds of the nineteenth century. He bought property in the western end of Richmond as a long-term investment but did not seem to have any particular plans for development.

William C. Allen's son, Otway, used his father's fortune to become a gentleman. Social, a member of many prestigious clubs, and with a modest political career, Otway Allen utilized his connections to make his property the site of the Lee Monument. Otway and his three sisters—Mary C. Sheppard, Bettie F. Gregory, and Martha A. Wise—were the developers of the site that contained the Lee Monument. City engineer C. P. E. Burgwyn, who

was also a consultant to the Lee Monument Association, drew the earliest plat of the property, dated June 1887. As noted earlier, Burgwyn created a circular feature to be the site of
the monument, and Franklin Street, now renamed Monument Avenue, was increased in
width to four lanes with a central median. It also included a cross-axis named Allen Avenue. Allen Avenue was an extension of Sydney's Walnut Street. The first sketch did not
show the irregularities in the property, nor did it show the extension of Grace Street.

By 1888 Burgwyn had refined the scheme and clearly platted the lots. The lots were 30
feet by 150 feet, wider and longer than those on neighboring streets. Burgwyn projected
double rows of trees separated by a row of shrubbery down the median. The plan showed
pie-shaped lots facing Lee Circle at the intersection of Monument Avenue and Allen Avenue. Burgwyn proposed the same treatment for the lots at the intersection with Lombardy
Street, curving the lots on the east side of the intersection. Franklin Street reverted to its
original width at the western edge of the Allen's property.

Burgwyn's scheme, as noted in Chapter 1, owes a great debt to Boston's Commonwealth
Avenue and also to other American real estate prototypes. Apparently, Otway Allen admired Mount Vernon Place in Baltimore with its cross-axial alignment and the central
monument, Robert Mills's giant column dedicated to Washington. Allen even called the
Lee statue site "Lee Place" on the original 1887 plat. But in contrast to the layout in Baltimore, Burgwyn created a plan capable of infinite expansion to the west, a possible development centered on not one monument, but many.

After the dedication of the Lee Monument in May of 1890, Allen sold lots, but the Panic
of 1893 stalled the economy of Richmond for almost a decade and few improvements were
made. The city signed a contract to grade Monument and Allen Avenues in 1893, though
the work was not accomplished until 1901. By 1894 only one house had been constructed.
Located at 1601 Monument and built by Otway Warwick, a partner in the tobacco supplies
firm of Warwick Brothers, the Queen Anne–style townhouse that had been the avenue's
first building was torn down in 1978. In 1901 the street was curbed and guttered as far as

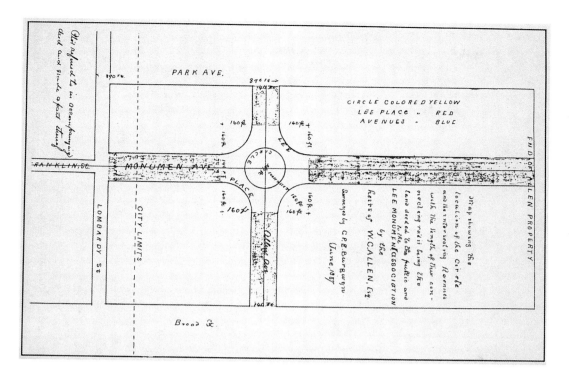

Burgwyn's first plan for the Allen property merely indicated Monument Avenue and a cross-axis to be named Allen Avenue beyond the city limits between Broad Street and Park Avenue. In the intersection of the two streets was a circle set aside for the monument. (Richmond Deed Book 133A:222)

Meadow, and the city installed utilities along both the street and adjoining alleys. Of the 134 original building lots, the Allens had sold 84. Scarlet and sugar maples were planted in 1904, a double row on the median and a row along newly built sidewalks.

Otway Allen never actually lived on Monument Avenue. He died at the age of sixty in February 1911, while his house at number 1631 was still under construction. At least 60 houses were already built or under construction by that time, and why he waited so long is unclear. In any event, his wife, Mary McDonald Allen, moved into the elegant Colonial Revival house designed by Claude K. Howell. Next door, his sister-in-law and her husband, Jennie McDonald and B. Randolph Wellford, built an equally impressive Colonial Revival house. Around the corner on Allen Avenue lived Otway's sister Mary C. Sheppard. His other sister, Martha Allen Wise, and her husband built a house designed by Isaac T. Skinner at 1808 Monument Avenue, just west of the Lee statue, in 1926. The Allen family's building pattern illuminates how the avenue became a neighborhood, with families moving into close proximity to each other.

The second major landholding family on Monument Avenue, the Branches, owned most of the section from Strawberry Street to the Boulevard. A venerable Virginia family, the Branches' lineage went back to the early days of Virginia, but their fortune had been acquired more recently. Prior to the Civil War the Branches had been involved in a number of commercial enterprises. After the war, John Patteson Branch and his brother James Read Branch, in partnership with their father, Thomas Branch, formed Thomas Branch and Company, which proved enormously profitable. Along with a brother-in-law, they founded the Merchants National Bank in 1870 and then other enterprises, becoming one of Richmond's wealthiest families. John Patteson Branch acquired most of his property on what would be Monument Avenue in the 1880s and transferred portions of it in 1912 to the Kingsland Land Company, run by his son, John Kerr Branch, and nephew, Robert G. Cabell. He

ABOVE LEFT: *The first house built on Monument Avenue, number 1601, was erected in 1894 for Mr. and Mrs. Otway Warwick. It actually faced Lombardy Street at Stuart Circle. It was demolished in 1978 to make way for a parking garage. (Valentine Museum)*

ABOVE RIGHT: *This photograph (ca. 1907) shows a remnant of Civil War earthworks beside new civic improvements. (Valentine Museum)*

RIGHT: *The Otway S. Allen house, 1631 Monument Avenue, 1911, Scarborough and Howell, architects. Allen's house was still under construction when he died in 1911, so he never lived on the street he created. (The Library of Virginia)*

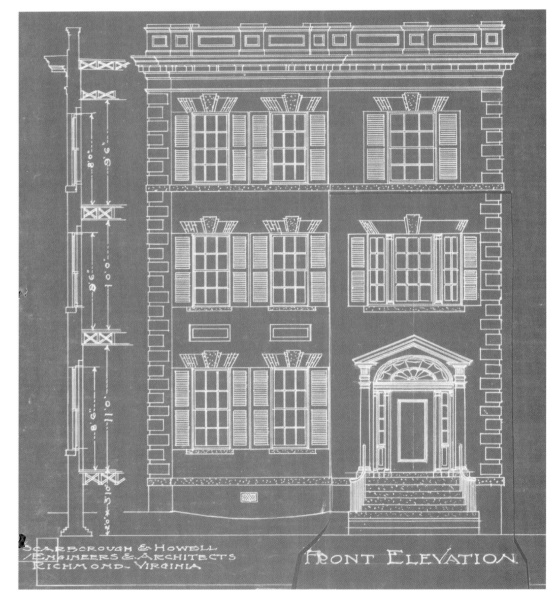

*1808 Monument Avenue,
1926, Isaac T. Skinner,
architect. Martha Allen
Wise was the last member
of the Allen family to
build on Monument. The
house fills one of the lots at
the northwest corner of
Lee Circle.*

never moved onto the avenue, perhaps feeling that it was too extravagant, since he was known to counsel against overspending.

Spurring the development of the Branch property (and the north side of the 2300 block, which was owned by business partners Allison and Addison along with C. W. Taylor) was the 1904 decision to locate the Jefferson Davis Monument there. Although the placement of the monument facing east would imply that this was conceived of as the end of the avenue, it was not, and the Branches began selling land to the west almost immediately after the Davis dedication ceremonies of 1907.

The contrast of the Branches with the Allens is apparent in the house that John Kerr Branch and his wife Beulah built at 2501 Monument Avenue between 1917 and 1919. They built the largest, most expensive, and most notable house on the street, after designs by John Russell Pope. John Patteson Branch kept his business interests within the family, involving his sons' and son-in-law's landholding company and stockbrokerage. In addition to John Kerr Branch, Robert Gamble Cabell, a great-nephew, built on Monument Avenue,

ABOVE: *John Kerr Branch and his wife, Beulah, built the largest house on Monument Avenue. (Virginia Historical Society)*

TOP: *The Branch house, 2501 Monument Avenue, 1917–19, John Russell Pope, architect.*

The Cabell house, 2601 Monument Avenue, 1926, William Lawrence Bottomley, architect. Robert G. Cabell's house is currently the home of philanthropist and art collector Frances Lewis. She and her husband, Sydney, donated much of the art and furniture that they lived with in this house to the Virginia Museum of Fine Arts.

ABOVE: *The parlor at 3201 Monument Avenue, 1911, Carneal and Johnston, architects. The Virginia author James Branch Cabell and his wife entertained many famous guests here. (Valentine Museum)*

LEFT: *The Taylor house, 2325 Monument Avenue, 1924, W. Duncan Lee, architect; the Blair house, 2327 Monument Avenue, 1913, Walter D. Blair, architect. The irregular lot sizes in the Branch section allowed for grander houses. (Valentine Museum)*

BUILDING A NEIGHBORHOOD

The streets of the Sheppard section, laid out in accordance with earlier plans, aligned with Monument Avenue at varying angles, creating several odd intersections, such as the one that is the site of the Maury Monument.

The density of apartment buildings between the Jackson and Maury Monuments alters the character of the street as one moves west.

an elegant house at 2601, after designs by William Lawrence Bottomley. Melville C. Branch, another nephew, lived at 2200 Monument Avenue between 1916 and 1921. Finally, another great-nephew, James Branch Cabell, lived at 3201 Monument Avenue in a house more modest by Branch standards but still quite substantial. The house's façade, which seems irregular, might be seen as reflective of the artistic nature of James Branch Cabell, a successful novelist, known for his fantasy tales, who never joined the family business. In reality,

BUILDING A NEIGHBORHOOD

however, the house was originally built in 1911 and not purchased by Cabell and his wife Priscilla Bradley until 1925, by which time he was well established as a novelist. Richmond never cared much for Cabell's novels. But, along with Ellen Glasgow, he represented the city's claim to an intellectual life, and visitors to his house included H. L. Mencken and other literary lights. In addition to his novels, Cabell authored *Branchiana* (1907), in which he traced—at times with tongue in cheek—the genealogy of his family. Reacting to then-current peccadilloes within the Branch family, Cabell reported of their Virginia origin in 1619: "the authentic forebearer of this family was merely an honest and God-fearing yeoman whose reputation is not attestedly enhanced by even the tiniest infraction of the Decalogue."[5]

In contrast to the Allens, who followed the orderly plot plan created by C. P. E. Burgwyn, the Branches subdivided their property irregularly, mixing large and small lots. They sold some larger properties to friends of the family. The Branch house stayed in the family until 1953, when it was given to the United Way by Zayde B. Rennolds. Subsequently, the house became the offices of an insurance company. Two doors to the east at 2325 Monument stands the second-largest surviving house on the avenue, the Jaquelin P. Taylor house, on an oversized lot purchased from the Branches. Throughout the Branch portion of the street, the larger lot sizes provided for a greater variety of house plans, and fewer homes related to the traditional Richmond townhouse design. The large lots with free-standing houses give a more suburban and spacious look to the area. The large and irregularly sized lots also permitted the construction of large apartment houses. The Westover, built in 1914, and the impressive Stratford Court and Kenilworth Apartments of 1917–18 were erected at the beginning of a torrent of apartment building that would dominate the street in the 1920s. These apartment houses face the Branch House, and it is notable that the Branch family seemed to have had no objection to sharing the block with apartments.

Modern zoning regulations that separate land uses into distinct districts were not part of Monument Avenue's concept, although the deeds for property prohibited apartment houses. Apparently the property owners chose not to enforce this stipulation, because apartment dwellings were introduced very early. Large numbers of apartments for persons of comparatively modest income were introduced to the street in the second decade of the twentieth century. These made a Monument Avenue address accessible to the prosperous middle class.

The third major landholding family on Monument Avenue, the Sheppards, owned most of the property from the Boulevard and the Jackson Monument west to Roseneath Road. The Sheppard family came from Buckingham County, Virginia. The patriarch, John F. Sheppard, was originally a doctor, but he passed the Civil War years as an investor in New York. Even though John Sheppard never lived in Richmond, he participated in real estate speculation there both with his brother Nicholas, a doctor who lived nearby in Henrico County, and with James Dooley, the railroad magnate who would later donate "Maymont," his estate, to the City of Richmond. In the 1870s Sheppard purchased as speculation the land that would become part of Monument Avenue. The Sheppards were neither socially prominent nor much engaged in local business or politics. No Sheppard lived on Monument Avenue. Instead, two of Nicholas's offspring lived in their farmhouse, now demolished, near the present-day intersection of Roseneath and Grace.

The original plan of the Sheppard family properties shows them in 1883 as an extension of the Sydney development, before there was any thought of Monument Avenue. When the city decided to extend Monument westward in 1907, it was necessary to adjust the plat, creating several difficult-to-build-on triangular lots. The Sheppard family's only interest in Monument Avenue was to sell the property; hence the character of the street changed once again when the land they owned was developed. While the Allens saw in the avenue a grand civic gesture and a wealthy development, and the Branches concurred at least in the development, the Sheppards do not seem to have had a distinctive vision for their part of Monument. The number of large apartment houses increased dramatically. Although large houses did appear, there was also an increase in the number of smaller residences. The Sheppards may have played a role in this, but suburban growth probably helped as well, as by the 1920s many larger houses were being developed in new suburban areas, such as Windsor Farms and Westmoreland Place. The area near the Stonewall Jackson Monument also marks the last development in Richmond before the introduction of modern zoning in 1926. The density of the stretch between the Jackson and Maury Monuments is remarkable. Three-story walk-up apartments fill every inch of their sites. The north side of the 2700 block is notable in that respect. Most apartment houses were built on the north side of the avenue, receiving southern sunlight. Deep porches shade the living rooms in summer but allow light to enter during the winter months. The light also created dramatic shadows that emphasize the architectural trim of these buildings.

Today the Sheppard section is distinctive in its vegetation, since its trees create a true canopy over the street. Further east, in the Allen and Branch sections, the original trees have been replaced, but the trees in the Sheppard section, which are oaks rather than maples, are more mature. The last two monuments on the avenue are also located in the Sheppard section: the Maury Monument, unveiled in 1929, and the Ashe Monument, dedicated in 1996. And perhaps typical of the lower profile of monuments built since the 1920s, they fit more gracefully into the context of the median strip. The Sheppard section does not repeat the monumental cross-axes used earlier on the avenue.

Builders of the Avenue

Each of the statues and each of the landholding families helped to give Monument Avenue a special character; but also important were real estate speculators and builders. By the time development of the avenue got under way, Richmond had not just recovered from the defeat and destruction of the Civil War—it had expanded, grown, and thrived. Richmond desired a place as the centerpiece of the New South, and the business community wanted to show the world that it was a major city again. Architecture provided the physical symbol of new prosperity. Chamber of commerce publications of this period often show the homes of illustrious citizens. Impressive homes were a measure of civic pride; they were tangible indications of prosperity and wealth. The business community of the time did not need a modern advertising executive to explain the importance of image.

Most prominent among the earliest residents of Monument Avenue were not the landed gentry or Confederate veterans, but individuals involved in the building trades—contractors, building materials suppliers, and real estate developers. In one of the earliest blocks,

the 1800 block, names associated with building and real estate include H. H. George, a building contractor; civil engineers Frederick Phillips and Edward Hoadley; lumber merchants Bayard Ellington, Charles Guy, and Thomas T. Adams; real estate agents O. H. Funsten, James B. Elam, and Garrett Wall; building materials supplier William Whitehurst; and Bertha Binswanger, the widow of a glass supplier. It is notable that both partners of two important firms—Ellington and Guy, lumber retailers, and Elam and Funsten, a real estate firm—lived in the same block at 1815, 1817, 1825, and 1834 Monument Avenue.[6]

Richmond's building trades clearly recognized that Monument Avenue was a place to display their skills and products. Nowhere is this better represented than in the Binswanger houses. The Binswanger Glass Company was a major glass supplier for the Richmond region. Bertha Binswanger's house at 1840 Monument Avenue was one of four houses the glass family built on the street. Harry S. Binswanger built two houses, 2220 and 2222, on the same block as Moses I. Binswanger's house at 2230. All four houses boast high-quality architectural glasswork, and clearly the houses were showplaces for the firm's products.

Monument Avenue was, of course, a great opportunity for the construction business and trades in the city. Richmond, in common with many American cities, had a great fear of fire; and hence materials were restricted in certain areas to brick or stone for the exterior walls. On Monument Avenue this became the rule. Iron, steel, and concrete for floor slabs were generally absent, except in churches and some of the larger apartment houses. Although a builder, or later a contractor, can be identified for many of the houses, focusing

1825 Monument Avenue, 1907, architect unknown. Businessmen associated with real estate and the building industries were among the first attracted to the new street. This house was built for real estate man James B. Elam, whose partner O. H. Funsten built on the same block. (Valentine Museum)

ABOVE: *1817 Monument Avenue, 1905 (left); 1834 Monument Avenue, 1908 (right). Business partners in a lumber supply house Bayard Ellington and Charles Guy lived across the street from each other in these two houses in the 1800 block.*

RIGHT: *1840 Monument Avenue, 1905. Bertha Binswanger, the widow of a glass supplier, lived in this Romanesque-style house. It was the first of the Binswanger family's homes on the street.*

2220 Monument Avenue, 1908, Claude K. Howell, architect. Harry S. Binswanger built this house and another (2222) on the same block.

The beautiful glass used in the Binswanger house at 2220 Monument Avenue advertised Harry Binswanger's glass supply business in particular and Richmond's prosperity in general.

2024 Monument Avenue, 1910, D. Wiley Anderson, architect. R. J. Gallespie, a small contractor, constructed this house from plans by Anderson for James F. Walsh, an executive with the Chesapeake & Ohio Railroad.

upon one builder or firm denies the complications of any project. In most cases the builder had a crew that would be responsible for the basic construction in keeping with the plans of the architect. A few of the larger builders and contractors, such as Davis Brothers or J. T. Wilson, employed in-house designers who produced plans. And Davis Brothers probably had a full line of employees who could dig the foundations, pour the cement, lay the brick or stone, cut the timber, and plaster the walls. A smaller builder—such as R. J. Gallespie, who constructed a house for James F. Walsh, general superintendent of motive power (locomotives) for the Chesapeake & Ohio Railroad, at 2024 Monument Avenue in

Developer William J. Payne speculated on the north side of the 1600 block of Monument with these four townhouses that followed stylistic patterns set in the Fan District. (Valentine Museum)

1909–10—probably hired independent craftspeople to come in and do specialized work. In the case of the Walsh house, Gallespie was following plans provided by D. Wiley Anderson and constructed the house for $10,000.[7] He undoubtedly hired day laborers, probably black, to dig the foundation, built the basic house with his crew, and hired plasterers for interior work. Many of the trim details, both interior and exterior, came from lumber yards and building suppliers. Although this system continues, the rise of large, full-service construction firms such as Davis Brothers or Claiborne and Taylor—who built many of the houses that Bottomley designed—meant more consolidation of work as a single company was responsible for a complete project.

An example of real estate speculation at work on Monument Avenue is the 1903 group of houses at 1616, 1620, 1626, and 1634, all put up by the developer William J. Payne and among the earliest built on the avenue. This group consisted of four townhouses in two designs. Payne bought the lots and developed the site utilizing brick construction in the Romanesque style.[8] The two central houses were of one design, and the two houses flanking them were of another, but all relied on typical Romanesque materials and ornament. These townhouses followed the pattern that had already been established on West Franklin Street and elsewhere in Richmond, particularly the Fan District. Also typical on this block is the fact that the north side was built first. It provided the most sun for the public rooms and front porches. The houses that were built later to fill the other lots on the 1600 block followed Payne's lead in size and shape but more frequently employ Colonial Revival detailing.

The first residents of William Payne's recently completed development in the 1600 block were the Putney, Cohen, Strause, and Coleman families. These families embodied many of the characteristics found in the early residents of Monument Avenue. Langhorne Putney was the first vice-president of the Stephen Putney Shoe Company, whose factory, one of the most impressive industrial buildings in the city and now the headquarters of the Virginia Department of Taxation, was on nearby Broad Street. Charles Cohen and Jacob Coleman were partners in M. Cohen Son and Company, a wholesale dry goods firm. Leon L.

TOP: *3123, 3125, and 3127 Monument Avenue, 1928, Carl Lindner, architect. C. Custer Robinson, an architect himself and the son and colleague of architect Charles M. Robinson, who designed many houses in Richmond, lived in 3125, the center house in this photograph.*

BOTTOM: *Richmond's streetcar line crossed Monument Avenue at Sheppard Street, providing transportation to many residents of the neighborhood. (Virginia Historical Society)*

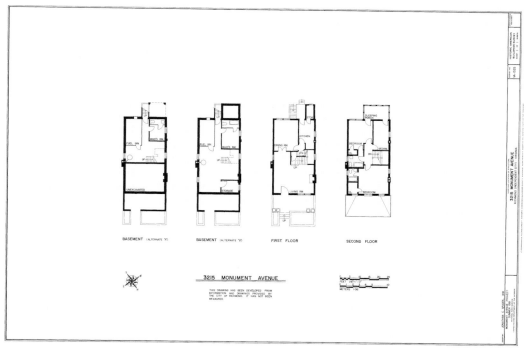

BASEMENT (ALTERNATE "X")   BASEMENT (ALTERNATE "Y")   FIRST FLOOR   SECOND FLOOR

3215 MONUMENT AVENUE

THIS DRAWING HAS BEEN DEVELOPED FROM
INFORMATION AND DRAWINGS PROVIDED BY
THE CITY OF RICHMOND. IT HAS NOT BEEN
MEASURED.

Floor plan, 3215 Monument Avenue, 1920, Davis Brothers, builders (left); and facades, 3219 and 3221 Monument Avenue, 1920, Davis Brothers, builders (above). The Davis Brothers constructed houses for middle-class families all over the city. This plan was chosen for six houses in the 3200 block of Monument. (left, Historic American Buildings Survey; above, John O. Peters)

Strause traded in leaf tobacco and served as president of the Chelf Chemical Company. His brother, Isadore, rented a house a few doors down, and after Isadore's death, his widow, Ada, commissioned a house on the same block. These early residents were excited about Richmond's prospects as exemplified in this beautiful new avenue, and they wanted to live on it.

The south side of the 1600 block remained in the Allen family's control and is where Otway Allen began building his house, though, as noted, he died prior to its completion. Built later, the houses on the south side of 1600 are more consistently Colonial Revival in detailing. By 1910 the First English Lutheran Church had purchased property at 1603 Monument Avenue, indicating that the avenue was becoming a neighborhood.

Further west in the Branch section the same involvement of real estate developers and builders occurred. Among residents of this section of the street, Robert Cabell was associated with the Arvonia-Buckingham Slate Company, J. Scott Parrish with Economy Concrete Company, and Lee Paschall with the Wise Granite Company. In addition, Paschall and fellow residents Jonathan Bryan, James Pollard, and Henry Wallerstein were major real estate developers.

Across the Boulevard in the Sheppard section of Monument Avenue, the pattern of builders and real estate entrepreneurs continued, with subtle differences. In addition to real estate agents Merrill E. Raab, Manley Hubbard, Charles H. Phillips, and Samuel G. Meredith, architects Max Ruehrmund, Carl Ruehrmund, and C. Custer Robinson made their homes in this section. Building in the Sheppard section was dominated by developers more than elsewhere on the avenue. As noted above, parts of the Allen section were built by speculative developers and then sold, but the overall pattern for the Allen and Branch sections (with the exception of apartment houses) was for an individual to commission an architect to design a house. In the Sheppard section, however, lots were sold to developers who built houses and apartments as speculative investments. Two groups dominated construction on the Sheppard property: the Davis Brothers and the Ruehrmund-Lindner group.

Davis Brothers was a large contracting and development firm that worked throughout the western suburbs of Richmond between 1905 and 1932. Their work is easily identified in the blocks immediately west of the Jackson Monument. The firm was indeed run by brothers, augmented by cousins and other relatives, an extended family connection that provided a stability lacking in many business partnerships. Beginning as carpenters, Charles W. and Oswald J. Davis opened C. W. Davis and Bro. in 1905, changing the name to Davis Brothers, General Contractors, about 1908. With another brother, J. Lee Davis, they set up Davis Bros., Inc., and Davis Land Company, which engaged in property development. Also active in the firm were L. Otis Spiers, E. Leslie Davis, and George K. Davis.[9]

On Monument Avenue, Davis Brothers built as speculation the group of houses at 3215, 3217, 3219, 3221, 3223, and 3225 within the years 1919–23, and the apartment houses at 2810, 2812, 2820, 2822, 2824, and 3029 within the years 1919–26. The houses at 3215–25 were constructed as pairs of single-family dwellings, and the plans and construction tectonics are the same for all. The facades differ, with alternating gables, columns, and facade materials. The heavy brackets and imaginative porch details provide a sense that each of these identically planned houses is individual. The architectural effect is bold rather than refined. The

The Frankmont Apartments, 3029 Monument Avenue, 1926, Davis Brothers, builders. The Davis Brothers designed houses and apartments in the Sheppard section of Monument Avenue, offering more modest residences than those further east.

land on which they sit had passed through numerous hands over the years prior to their construction. For instance, the lot at 3217 had fifteen different owners between its sale by the Sheppard heirs in 1909 and its purchase in 1920 by Walter R. Taylor, the first owner of the house there.[10]

The Greenwood and Seminole apartment houses at 2810–12 Monument Avenue (1919) illustrate the Davis Brothers' style, with multitiered porches that have deep, overhanging roofs, creating a dramatic play of light and shadow. The multitiered porch was especially in evidence in the Davis Brothers' less expensive apartments, for example those at 2820–24 Monument Avenue, erected in 1924. Their plan is similar to that of the Greenwood, but

Sulgrave Manor Apartments, 2902 Monument Avenue, 1921, Davis Brothers, builders.

The Greenwood and Seminole Apartments, 2810 and 2812 Monument Avenue, 1919, Davis Brothers, builders. The Arts and Crafts style was applied to these apartments with the repeating pattern of three-tiered porches.

the architectural style is distinctive, with overtones of the Arts and Crafts and Craftsman styles, sometimes accented by California Mission. The architecture is both simple and imposing, relying on broad effect rather than architectural detail. Davis Brothers' architectural work integrates Monument Avenue with the neighboring areas in a way that the mansions designed by Bottomley or Duncan Lee do not.

The Ruehrmund-Lindner group was an informal association of architects and real estate developers who were part of the same extended family. They also left an imprint on the

The Lord Fairfax Apartments, 3101–15 Monument Avenue, 1923, Lindner and Phillips, architects. Carl Lindner made his mark on the Sheppard section of Monument Avenue, especially with these stylish apartments. (Valentine Museum)

Sheppard section. Architect Carl Lindner, for instance, designed nine houses in 1926 for the 3100 block (between 3117 and 3133) that cost $11,111 apiece for Jeanette A. Mayo, who built them.

With the stock market crash of 1929 and the Great Depression of the 1930s that followed, construction stopped on Monument Avenue. When house construction resumed in the years following World War II, the taste for building elaborately had passed. Ranch houses replaced the two- and three-story houses of the older sections of the street. Richmonders built some fine houses in the areas along the avenue to the west of the Sheppards' properties, but they do not have the same cohesive effect. The combination of impressive mansions and 1950s-era ranch houses breaks the earlier consistency.

The builders, real estate speculators, and architects—along with the suppliers of concrete, slate, and lumber—who shaped, and often lived on, Monument Avenue represented one of the major sources of wealth in Richmond. As in many other American cites, in Richmond real estate and building activity have been at the heart of commercial success and economic expansion.

Apartment Houses

Apartment houses, which appeared on Monument Avenue as early as 1909, were rare in the Allen section, more prominent in the Branch section, and a dominant building type in parts of the Sheppard development. This shift is largely attributable to an increasing acceptance by Americans, and Richmonders, of the apartment as a suitable habitation. Although apartments were introduced in New York during the 1860s and 1870s by the École-des-Beaux-Arts-trained architect, Richard Morris Hunt, many Americans viewed them with skepticism. The reason lay in the supposedly Parisian origin of the building type, though London apartment buildings were in fact an equally important model. The Parisian influence was suspect for many Americans because they considered French morals lax, a view reflected in Edith Wharton's description in *The Age of Innocence* of a bedroom arrangement "which recalled scenes in French fiction, and architectural incentives to immorality such as the simple American had never dreamed of." Wharton explains: "That was how women with lovers lived in the wicked old societies, in apartments with rooms on one floor, and all the indecent propinquities."[11] But by the early twentieth century, with the new cosmopolitanism exemplified in the American Renaissance, apartment houses and buildings began to be more accepted and indeed became a mark of modernity and progressive attitudes. New York's apartment houses were too big for the scale of Richmond, which required a lower and generally more compact building type. Hence, Washington, D.C., became the touchstone for apartment design in Richmond.[12]

Richmond's earliest apartments were high-rise structures built on or near Franklin Street and Monument Avenue. Given their size and complexity, either architects or large building contractors were always involved in the design. Stylish architects Noland and Baskervill designed the city's first apartment building, the Chesterfield, in 1902. It sits on Franklin Street, facing the extravagant mansion of Lewis Ginter, a tobacco magnate. In 1904, German-born architect Carl Ruehrmund designed the Shenandoah on Allen Avenue next to the Lee Monument, and in 1909, Carneal and Johnston designed the Gresham Court, near Temple Beth Ahabah, also on Franklin Street. The Shenandoah apartment house has protruding bay windows reminiscent of progressive Midwest modernism from Chicago, but its heavy cornices and other details recall historical styles.

In 1909 Carneal and Johnston designed the earliest apartment house on Monument Avenue, the Stafford (at 2007), a distinguished classical design in red brick with stone trim. The Stafford introduced the three-level porch to Monument Avenue. This arrangement gave each of the front apartments a porch or deck providing an outdoor living area, an important amenity before the advent of air-conditioning. The multilevel veranda became the most popular architectural element for apartments in the Fan District and the defining element of the building type in Richmond.

The high-quality architectural detail of the Stafford clearly established that this apartment building offered stylish accommodations for well-off residents, not just rooms for those who could not afford a house. This set a distinguished precedent for later apartment buildings on Monument. Carneal and Johnston's next luxurious apartment building, the Brooke Apartments, was built in 1912 at 2215 Monument. This spectacular Beaux Arts–style building did not, however, follow up on the stacked porches scheme of the Stafford.

Albert Huntt designed one of the most impressive architectural ensembles on the street, the matching Stratford Court and Kenilworth Apartments at 2510 and 2512 Monument Avenue built in 1917 and 1918. These buildings made graceful use of the giant order, a column more than one story in height. The Westover, built in 1914, and the Lawrence Apartments of 1915, at 2616 and 2018 Monument Avenue respectively, first used the giant order on the street, but Huntt refined it two years later in the Stratford Court and Kenilworth, which rival the largest public buildings in their display of classical elements. Four identical triple-tiered porches are supported by no fewer than twenty-four, two-story Corinthian columns. With classical balustrades, Palladian windows, and a grand entrance feature as well, the

The Stafford Apartments, 2007 Monument Avenue, 1909, Carneal and Johnston, architects. Carneal's design for this apartment house makes it looks like a private residence, setting a high standard for apartments on the avenue. The three-tiered porch would become a characteristic of apartment houses in Richmond.

apartments are a true tour de force. The extravagance of these buildings, built during World War I, reflects the prosperity of the period. Still, impressive as they are, each building cost $35,000, a sum dwarfed by the $160,000 cost of the Branch mansion across the street.

The golden age of apartments was from the eve of World War I to the stock market crash in 1929, precisely the period when the Sheppard section was being built up. The Rosemary Apartments (1913) at 2828 Monument set a high standard as the first apartment building erected west of the Boulevard. It is particularly elegant, with an elliptical porch, French doors opening onto the porch roof deck, and small elliptical balconies serving the third-floor units.

Real estate developer and general contractor Samuel G. Meredith built the Meredith in

The Brooke Apartments, 2215 Monument Avenue, 1912, Carneal and Johnston, architects. Carneal followed the Stafford with this beautiful, Beaux Arts–inspired design, ignoring his own precedent of stacked porches at the Stafford.

the side yard of his large house at 2910 Monument in 1914. The building, following the lead of the Stafford, had single-story columns supporting each of the three tiers of porches. D. Wiley Anderson designed both Meredith's house and the apartment building.

The architects of some apartments attempted unusual arrangements. Upscale apartments were popular, but many developers hedged their bets by developing split apartment houses. The Rixey Court, for example, built in 1924–25 at 2235 Monument Avenue, contained three luxury apartments facing Monument, backed up by six more modest units entered from Allison Street (now known as Strawberry Street). The front apartments occupy the entire frontage, with living and dining rooms at either end of a curved entrance hall. They have three bedrooms, each with a bath, and a kitchen, breakfast nook, maid's room, and maid's bath. Their size is that of a standard modern house, occupying 2,300 square feet. The rear apartments are smaller, two-bedroom units with only 900 square feet. The apartments of the early twentieth century were smaller and more efficient than the large houses that had been built on the avenue, but they were by no means austere or simple. Bascom Rowlett, who had worked for Albert Huntt, was the architect of Rixey Court. The front is imaginative and unusual, and it is tempting to see Huntt's influence there.

The apartment buildings erected between the end of World War II and 1960 are utilitarian in the worst sense. They combine small, tight, inconvenient plans with low ceilings and small windows. The prewar apartment houses constructed on Monument Avenue were Richmond's last efforts to treat apartments as a major, architecturally distinctive building type.

ABOVE: *The Kenilworth (right) and Stratford Court (left) Apartments, 2510–12 Monument Avenue, 1918 and 1917, Albert Huntt, architect. The clustered columns of the Kenilworth and Stratford Court Apartments form one of the most impressive architectural statements on Monument Avenue.*

LEFT: *The entrance of the Stratford Court Apartments.*

RIGHT: *2830 Monument Avenue, 1928, W. Duncan Lee, architect; 2828 Monument Avenue, 1913, The Rosemary Apartments, Carneal & Johnston, architects. The Rosemary Apartments, the first apartment building erected west of the Boulevard, resembled a single-family residence, much like the Stafford.*

BELOW: *2910 Monument Avenue, 1913, D. Wiley Anderson, architect; the Meredith Apartments, 2906 Monument Avenue, 1914, D. Wiley Anderson, architect. Contractor Samuel Meredith built the Meredith Apartments in the side yard of his house.*

Residents

Although Monument Avenue was planned to be an impressive street, its character would depend on those who chose to live there. The residents commissioned and purchased houses and also brought churches to the street. The avenue provided an opportunity for Richmond families to display their wealth and taste. The original residents were prosperous men of business and their families. Their fortunes came from commerce and finance. Initially, few members of the landed gentry and few families that had any direct connection to the Confederacy built on the street. Lewis H. Blair appears to have been the only Confederate veteran to build on the street—at 2327 Monument Avenue, in 1913—in front of the Davis Monument. After Otway Warwick's first and lonely foray in 1894 at 1601 Monument Avenue, the next houses appeared in 1902, when John Harwood, a wholesale oil merchant, built at 2000 Monument Avenue and George Guvernator, an ice merchant and brewer, put up a home at 1842 Monument Avenue. Mr. Harwood and his brother R. Henry Harwood also had extensive real estate interests on Monument Avenue. They were followed quickly by other merchants who built on the avenue.

A subtle shift both in occupations and in the size of houses began after 1910. The opening of the Branch section may have been a contributing cause, since larger houses were now possible; but also it was after 1910 that building activity really accelerated. The United States, and Virginia in particular, experienced sustained prosperity up to and after World War I. Although an initial economic downturn occurred immediately after 1918, the big recovery of the 1920s led to the construction of many of the houses by which Monument Avenue is best known, the stunning Colonial Revival homes designed by William Lawrence Bottomley, W. Duncan Lee, and other architects. It is noteworthy that during the 1920s many of the more difficult sites around Lee and Stuart Circles were filled in. As already indicated above, it was not unusual to find some families that built several houses on the street, usually clustered together. Parents and children, as well as cousins and in-laws, are found on the street. The Allens clustered near Lee Circle; the Branches near the Davis Monument.

Although Monument Avenue gained and maintained a reputation as the avenue of Richmond's elite, it was always the home of many middle-class families as well. They lived in the more modest houses and apartments in all three sections of the street. Whether upper- or middle-class, however, the residents of Monument Avenue always remained white. Covenants prohibiting black ownership were standard in all land titles. Religiously, the avenue's residents were more diverse, as is evidenced in the different houses of worship clustered along its route and nearby on West Franklin Street and the Boulevard.

Richmond's Jewish community was well represented on Monument Avenue. For a time, Edward N. Calisch, the distinguished rabbi of the Temple Beth Ahabah, located nearby on Franklin Street, lived on Lee Circle. Rabbi Calisch had three homes on Monument in the first three decades of the century. In the 1600 block, besides Calisch, Jewish residents included the families of Charles Cohen, Jacob Coleman, Isadore Strause, Ada Strause, Leon Strause, Isaac Hutzler, Isaac Lichtenstein, and Emanuel Raab. Their presence on the avenue was not accidental. Calisch emphasized ecumenism and the need to integrate Judaism with American culture.[13] His congregation, the sixth oldest in the nation, was largely German in ancestry and had been playing an important role in Richmond for

2319 Monument Avenue, 1926, Merrill C. Lee and Clifton Lee, architects. This Mediterranean design includes a window cut through the chimney. Building styles and sizes began to vary more in the 1920s in the Branch section.

1842 Monument Avenue (left) and 2000 Monument Avenue (right), architects unknown, were the first houses to appear on Monument Avenue in the twentieth century, being built in 1902.

2702 Monument Avenue, 1910, Charles K. Bryant, architect (top left); 1643 Monument Avenue, 1910, Scarborough and Howell, architects (top right); 3104 Monument Avenue, 1928, Davis Brothers, builders (left). Rabbi Edward Calisch, the revered leader of Temple Beth Ahabah, lived in these three houses on Monument Avenue. He built 2702, a transitional house in a mixture of Jacobean and Colonial Revival styles, for himself in 1910. Five years later he moved to 1643, a symmetrical Colonial Revival house, which had been built at the same time as his first house. Later he lived at 3104, a Mediterranean design built for his son Harold by Davis Brothers.

generations. He wanted Jews to share the cultural, business, and social activities of their Christian neighbors, and residing on Monument could help fulfill these goals. Still, that the Jewish residents clustered together is also telling. As the son of one of the families who built on the street explained, the integration of the Jewish and gentile communities had led to many interfaith marriages. Some Jewish families hoped that by clustering together, they could interact with their Christian friends and neighbors while still offering their children proximity to a circle of friends from whom they could choose spouses, helping to maintain the faith.[14] In the Branch section, the Straus, Levy, Hofheimer, Schwarzschild, and Gunst families attest to the continued German and Jewish presence on the street. Edward Calisch built the first of his three residences on Monument Avenue in 1910 at 2702 on property purchased from the Branches. In 1915 he moved to 1643 Monument Avenue, a house built five years earlier for John G. Farland, president of the Sydnor Pump and Well Company. In the Sheppard section, the rabbi had his final Monument Avenue residence at 3104 (built in 1928), where he lived with his son Harold. The Straus, Raab, and Schwarzschild families also built houses in this area. Members of the Greentree family lived at 2902, 3102, 3208, and 3302 Monument.

Houses of Worship

Religious structures provide a point of identification and a bond for most American communities. Churches and synagogues frequently dominate the neighborhoods where they are found and act not just as places of worship but as social centers too. In the first years of the twentieth century, Richmonders created a clustering of religious buildings on Monument Avenue and Franklin Street that have been important in the creation of the neighborhood and lent it architectural distinction. Although they are among the largest and most monumental buildings on the street, the churches play a somewhat secondary role since the central axis of Monument Avenue contains the statues. Thus, for example, while Grace Covenant Presbyterian Church (1922) and First Baptist Church (1926–27) are among the largest churches ever built in Richmond, they sit to the side, not occupying the central position frequently expected of neighborhood churches. The churches on and near Monument Avenue display a variety of forms and styles befitting their various religious denominations.[15]

There are five churches in the historic area of Monument Avenue, but several other nearby religious structures contribute to the street. The steeple of St. James's Episcopal Church (1911–13) by Noland and Baskervill, at 1205 West Franklin Street, is visible for many blocks from the eastbound lane of Monument. For their design, the architects drew on St. Martin-in-the-Fields in London by James Gibbs, while the tower recalls the churches of Sir Christopher Wren. One more block to the east, at the corner of Ryland Street, sits the dominant Doric portico and low-rising dome of Temple Beth Ahabah (1903–4), also by Noland and Baskervill. Chronologically, Temple Beth Ahabah was one of the first religious structures in the immediate area of Monument Avenue, and it provided a focus for the Jewish population that settled there. Since 1922, yet another Noland and Baskervill structure, St. Mark's Episcopal Church, with its prominent steeple, has been an important focal point on the Boulevard.

All these houses of worship and the others on the avenue moved from older parts of the city. Two trends encouraged churches to move to the new western residential districts. At the turn of the twentieth century the commercial and retail core of Richmond was expanding. Because of the topography of downtown Richmond, the only potential for expansion was into the older residential areas between Capitol Square and Belvidere Street. At the same time, the African American community was prospering and growing, as were the German and Jewish communities. The African American and German communities shared the area known as Jackson Ward, the residential district to the north of Broad Street. Monument Avenue and other new neighborhoods solved the squeeze for space in central Richmond. The white population left the older residential districts and moved west, leaving room for the black population to fully occupy Jackson Ward. Business uses took over the area south of Broad Street, creating modern Richmond's larger downtown. The western migration of churches illustrates the source of the new Monument Avenue neighborhood's population. German congregations founded First English Lutheran, St. John's United Church of Christ, and Beth Ahabah. St. James's and St. Mark's had served Jackson Ward, and First Baptist and Grace Street Presbyterian had served the former downtown residential areas.

The cluster of religious buildings near Stuart Circle is one of the architectural high points of the avenue. It occurs at the intersection where the four lanes of Monument contract to the two lanes of Franklin Street. The solid granite mass of First English Lutheran Church (1910) and the much more delicate limestone of St. John's United Church of Christ (1921, 1926–28) face each other diagonally across the circle. With the dynamic statue of Stuart on his rearing horse surrounded by a fence composed of cannons and swords, the ensemble is memorable.

First English Lutheran Church, at 1603 Monument Avenue, has a particularly successful siting. The name of the church relates to the language of its service (the German language remained popular at some other churches in Richmond until World War I), not the ancestry of its members, who were, by and large, of German descent.[16] The church is a cross-shaped sanctuary set between curved wings. In the center of the facade, two stone towers flank a large central window. Charles Robinson, the architect of First English Lutheran and of Stuart Circle Hospital (1913, with later additions) across the street, was a gifted architect, who unfortunately did not design any houses on Monument Avenue. At the church, Robinson's Gothic design relates to the heavier style of the 1880s and the preference for massive building associated with H. H. Richardson. The building is low, broad, and convex. The well-preserved interior is dominated by three large windows filled with green art glass. The contrast between the massive character of the building and the large window area is visually effective. The construction of this building stretched the congregation's financial resources to the limit, and to this day, church members recall the building as a leap of faith by a small congregation in a new part of town.

Architect Bascom Rowlett collaborated with Carl Lindner Sr. in the design of St. John's United Church of Christ at 503–7 Stuart Circle.[17] This is a sophisticated Neo-Gothic building derived from Continental sources. Originally located downtown, St. John's congregation purchased this land from Richmond College in 1913 because so many of its members were moving farther west. The church was built in two phases, with the parish house

St. James's Episcopal Church, 1205 West Franklin Street, 1911–13, Noland and Baskervill, architects. The eastern-most church within the Monument Avenue His-toric District, St. James's is actually on West Franklin Street, but its steeple holds an important spot on the skyline for those traveling east on Monument Avenue.

ABOVE: *Interior,*
St. James's Episcopal
Church.

LEFT: *Temple Beth*
Ahabah, 1111 West
Franklin Street, 1903–4,
Noland and Baskervill,
architects. Beth Ahabah
drew many residents and
played a very important
role in the development
of a neighborhood on
Monument Avenue.
(Valentine Museum)

ABOVE: *First English Lutheran Church, 1603 Monument Avenue, 1910, Charles M. Robinson, architect. Imaginative site planning fit the church onto its difficultly shaped lot.*

RIGHT: *Stuart Circle Hospital, 1913, Charles M. Robinson, architect. Robinson's only work on the street besides First English Lutheran Church is the hospital that faces it. (Valentine Museum)*

BUILDING A NEIGHBORHOOD

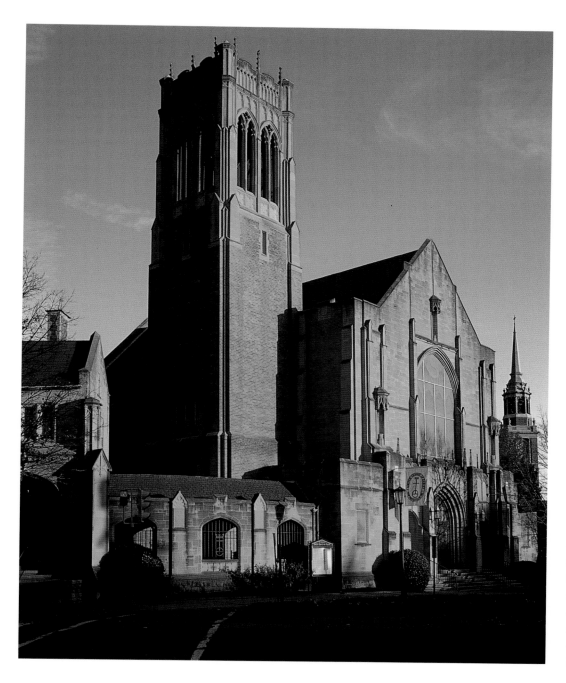

St. John's United Church of Christ, 503–7 Stuart Circle, 1921 and 1926–28, Lindner and Rowlett, architects. St. John's forms an impressive part of the cluster of buildings at Stuart Circle.

St. John's United Church of Christ, 503–7 Stuart Circle, 1921, Lindner and Rowlett, architects. The parish house, on the left, was completed several years before the sanctuary. (Virginia Historical Society)

Grace Covenant Presbyterian Church, 1627 Monument Avenue, 1919–22, John Kevan Peebles, architect. The congregations of Grace Street Presbyterian and the Church of the Covenant merged and abandoned their earlier structures when this church was completed. (Dementi-Foster Studios)

Grace Covenant Presbyterian Church, 1627 Monument Avenue, 1919–22, John Kevan Peebles, architect (left). The slender tracery of the front of Grace Covenant, as seen in its impressive stained glass window (right), contrasts with the building's massive corner pylons.

LEFT: *The Collegiate School for Girls, 1617 Monument Avenue, 1922, H. Carl Messerschmidt, architect. This school, the only one on Monument, filled the gap between First English Lutheran and Grace Covenant Presbyterian Churches.*

BELOW: *First Church of Christ Scientist, 2201 Monument Avenue, 1931, Marcellus Wright, architect.*

BUILDING A NEIGHBORHOOD

*First Baptist Church,
2709–15 Monument Ave-
nue, sanctuary begun
1927 and completed 1929,
Herbert Cain and Joseph
P. Hudnut, architects;
various subsequent
additions and architects.
The congregation of
First Baptist Church
originated in downtown
Richmond, and the
design for this sanctuary
was based on that of their
second church, designed
by Thomas U. Walter
in 1841.*

finished in 1921 and the main sanctuary in 1928. An elaborate, arched stained glass window outlined by limestone tracery dominates the facade. St. John's is the only church located on the north side of Monument Avenue, facing southwest, and the architects carefully considered the interplay of light and shadow. The church's architecture appears distinctly scholarly when compared to that of First English Lutheran across the street but not as bold as that of Grace Covenant a half block away.

Sharing the same block as First English Lutheran is Grace Covenant Presbyterian Church, at 1627 Monument Avenue. The church's congregation was formed by the merger in 1915 of Grace Street Presbyterian Church and the Church of the Covenant. Grace Street Presbyterian served an older congregation located in downtown Richmond in an area fast losing its residential character. The new Church of the Covenant had just completed a large building several blocks away on Harrison Street in 1913. Both buildings were abandoned, and the merged congregation moved to Monument Avenue.

The congregation of Grace Covenant Presbyterian Church occupied the sanctuary in 1922, three years after completing the building's Sunday School wing. The church sits on a mid-block site and has no tower; the front is dominated by a huge stained glass window. The late Gothic, English Perpendicular style inspired architect John Kevan Peebles's design for the sanctuary, one of the largest in the city at the time. The repetitive pattern of tracery and the soft grays of the Celtic interlace stained glass define the sanctuary. The rich Gothic architectural tradition sometimes coexists uneasily with the austerity associated with the

Protestant architectural tradition. Peebles's solution for this church is particularly appropriate. The geometrical flat patterns of late English Gothic provide richness without demanding statuary.

Between Grace Covenant and First English Lutheran Churches, at numbers 1617 and 1619, once stood the only school located on Monument Avenue, the Collegiate School for Girls, founded by Helen Baker in 1916. H. Carl Messerschmidt designed the building at 1617, which still stands. Constructed out of red brick, it fit in with the residential character seamlessly. The school later moved to the far western suburbs, and 1619 was destroyed in order to put in a parking lot. Medical offices occupy 1617 today.

The First Church of Christ Scientist, 2201 Monument Avenue, on the corner of Allison Street, traces its Richmond roots to 1901, though the building on Monument dates from 1931. Designed by Marcellus Wright, a member of the congregation, the church features a severe neoclassical limestone facade, articulated with giant order Doric columns.

At the Boulevard intersection with Monument Avenue, number 2715, First Baptist Church began the construction of a new building in 1927. This is the largest complex of buildings on the avenue, taking up an entire city block. Herbert Cain, a Richmond architect who specialized in Baptist churches, provided the design; he was assisted by Joseph P. Hudnut, who was head of the architecture program at the University of Virginia. Hudnut went on to become one of the major supporters of radical modernism in American architecture and, as dean of the School of Design at Harvard, brought Walter Gropius, of

First Baptist Church. Over time, the congregation of First Baptist has filled the entire south side of the 2700 block of Monument Avenue with a remarkably consistent complex of buildings.

1811–21 Monument Avenue. The first blocks of Monument Avenue were filled with townhouses that respected consistent boundaries but explored various materials and styles.

Bauhaus fame, to this country, but the conservative nature of the design of First Baptist indicates Hudnut's earlier proclivities. The lot was evidently very boggy, and no one had been tempted to use it before 1927. The land was purchased through a gift from Whitmell S. Forbes, a wealthy grocer, who owned a large house just past Roseneath Road that is now demolished. Additions to the church, which faces Monument, have transformed it into an E-shaped complex. Cain's original design has a Doric distyle portico in antis—a recessed portico supported by two columns—derived from the congregation's 1841 building designed by Thomas U. Walter in downtown Richmond on Broad Street. The style is remarkably consistent throughout the complex, though later architects' additions have lightened the severe classicism.

The houses of religion on Monument Avenue and in its environs include examples of most of the popular church building styles of the early twentieth century. The churches are grand and monumental, but they do not attempt to rival the monuments. They are good neighbors, adding architectural variety to the predominantly residential ambience of the street without ever disrupting the flow. They punctuate rather than interrupt the streetscape.

Otway Allen and C. P. E. Burgwyn did their best to establish a modern, wealthy residential district that would impress both Richmonders and visitors. Their draft of a wide, tree-lined boulevard centered by a monument definitely set the stage for what followed. The development attracted prosperous merchants and professionals, who brought along other members of their social groups, drawn from their businesses, families, and religions. The residences they built formed consistent rows of handsome townhouses, which gradually changed to freestanding mansions when lot sizes and building styles changed. But real cities are more complex than ideal ones, and the rarified atmosphere of Monument Avenue soon expanded to include a variety of building types. The eventual addition of apartment buildings, a school, and houses of worship increased the diversity of the streetscape and attracted a wider range of families, affording the avenue the vitality of a real neighborhood.

Chapter 4

HOUSES, STYLES, AND ARCHITECTS

Houses

The success of Monument Avenue involves the complex interplay of the plan of the street, the statues, and the houses and their architects. One can make grand plans and lay out broad boulevards and even dedicate a statue or two, but unless individuals commission great buildings and there exists a cadre of architects with a common vision, most grand plans come to naught.

Although Monument Avenue contains churches and apartment houses, it was most especially a scene for the construction of houses marked by what the American economist Thorstein Veblen in 1899 labeled "conspicuous consumption."[1] The great wealth accumulated by some Americans at the turn of the century found expression all across America in a variety of large building projects—libraries, museums, city halls, and especially grand houses. The so-called American Renaissance, in which the architectural styles of the European and American past were revived and employed, found its Richmond outlet on Monument Avenue.[2] Certainly not all of the propriety and restraint of older Richmond disappeared, but the new age required a different display. A hubris enveloped many architects and their patrons, and a quest for swagger and public preening became the order of the day. Ellen Glasgow, in her 1916 novel *Life and Gabriella*, caught the spirit quite well when one of her characters says to another: "Look at that house now, that's one of the finest in the city. Rushington built it—he made his money in fertilizer, and the one next with the green tiles belongs to Hanly, the tobacco trust fellow you know, and this whopper on the next square is where Albertson lives. He made his pile out of railroad stocks."[3]

This transformation occurring in Richmond had national dimensions. As two of America's most important architectural critics—Harry Desmond, the editor of *Architectural Record*, and Herbert Croly, a distinguished social commentator—observed shortly after the turn of the century in their book *Stately Homes in America*, "Our American residences . . . will not be understood unless it is frankly admitted that they are built for men whose chief title to distinction is that they are rich, and they are designed by men whose architectural ideas are profoundly modified by the riches of their clients." Desmond and Croly

claimed that American wealth differed from European wealth because American society was both more "plastic" and "fluid."[4] Monument Avenue became Richmond's "prosperity row," and again Ellen Glasgow captured this new spirit perfectly when she observed: "Here and there, one might discover an authentic antique among all the varnished reproductions scattered to the far end of Monument Avenue." As she perceived, "Imponderables might be respected, but possessions were envied."[5]

Monument Avenue is known as a unified street of grand houses, and as one proceeds up the boulevard, a consistency seems to arise through the repetition of similar elements. But a closer view reveals that the succession of columnar porches breaks up into a variety of sizes and shapes, some one story, a few two stories in height. Similarly, the initial impression of an unending stream of red brick facades breaks down into a display of ornamental detail—pediments, finials, bay windows, cornices, and gables, the grand past of world architecture pulled from the books and put up for admiring anew. And while many of the houses are large and some grand, many more modest dwellings appear, so that the overall unity begins to take on a contrapuntal rhythm. Yes, unity exists—a common basic height of two or three stories, plus attic and roof, and a common setback—but variety is an important note. Red brick in various shades was the preferred building material, but at times yellow and tan brick appears, and facades in stucco and limestone break the rhythm. Many roofs were originally covered with wood shingles, now replaced by asphalt shingles, but for the more pretentious houses, slate or green, red, or orange tile was used. Subtle shifts in the size and spacing of houses are evident, from the narrow homes, almost row houses,

1815 Monument Avenue, 1905, Claude K. Howell, architect. A desire to display wealth and prosperity infused Monument Avenue with exuberant architectural statements.

at the eastern end, to the larger houses set alone on lots with plenty of space further west. The key to Monument Avenue's importance and appeal is the unity within the diversity, a common background and the respect of one architect for another.

Initially, most of the houses on Monument Avenue were derived from the common Richmond building type of three-bay townhouses, one room and a hall wide. In contrast to Northern cities, Richmond rarely assembled houses in long rows. The detached town-

1816–26 Monument Avenue. The initial impression of an unending stream of red brick in the eastern blocks of the street breaks down into a varying display of ornamental detail upon examination.

house favored in Richmond was a row house in every other respect, but it was freestanding and offered superior air circulation for hot summer months. Typically a three-foot-wide space separated Richmond's urban houses. This space was vital for both ventilation and fire protection. Most Richmond houses shared the same plan, but few elevations matched. Often the street facade was the only elevation that received any obvious attention from the designer/builder. Varied compositions, alternating materials, and different colors and elements characterized the city's house fronts. This variation is superficial but visually effective, giving each residence an individual facade and creating the character of neighborhoods.

The three-bay townhouse became the initial building stock of Monument Avenue but was soon supplemented with the five-bay house and even larger dwellings. In the eastern, or Allen, section, many of the houses are three bays; then five-bay dwellings begin to appear with the Lee statue; and in the Branch section, grand mansions sit in semi-isolated splendor on their lots. In the far western, or Sheppard, section, which dates largely from the 1920s, smaller, three-bay houses make an appearance again. Although, in general, the avenue was built up from east to west, with the earliest houses constructed in the Allen end and the more recent houses in the Sheppard section, there are some exceptions to this pattern. For instance, at Lee Circle, 1800 Monument, the house of Robert M. Jeffress, a paper and cotton mill owner, designed by William L. Bottomley, dates from 1929–31. The Lee Circle lots, with their wedge shapes, were not initially considered very appealing. Occasionally lots stayed empty for many years. The house of David M. Mann, a physician, at 1635 Monument Avenue, designed by Peebles and Ferguson, dates from 1928, although

1634 Monument Avenue, 1903, architect unknown. At first, most of the houses on Monument were derived from common Richmond townhouse designs, one room and a hall wide.

many of the surrounding houses were built fifteen to twenty years earlier. Lots on the south side of the avenue, allowing for a house with a north entrance, were not generally as attractive as the northern lots, which permitted construction of a house with a south-facing facade. This pattern is not unique to Richmond, and can be found in many American cities.

Houses and the rooms therein have many purposes, ranging from the intimate to the very social and public. Monument Avenue's houses were built as homes in which to live and, in many cases, raise families. But they were also built as statements and as settings for

RIGHT: *Plan for 1832 Monument Avenue, 1907, Noland and Baskervill. The suite of rooms along the first-floor hall is easily accessible to visitors, with the service area in the back hall, separated by a wall. (Historic American Buildings Survey)*

BELOW LEFT: *Plan for the Allen house, 1631 Monument Avenue, 1911, Scarborough and Howell, architects. The service area is accessible only through a door in the dining room. (The Library of Virginia)*

BELOW RIGHT: *Plan for 2714 Monument Avenue, 1929, William Lawrence Bottomley, architect. Gradually, floor plans along the avenue reflected its wider lots and an interest on the part of residents for a flow among the rooms and into the gardens. Often the stair and a library or dining room displayed more complex geometric forms. (Historic American Buildings Survey)*

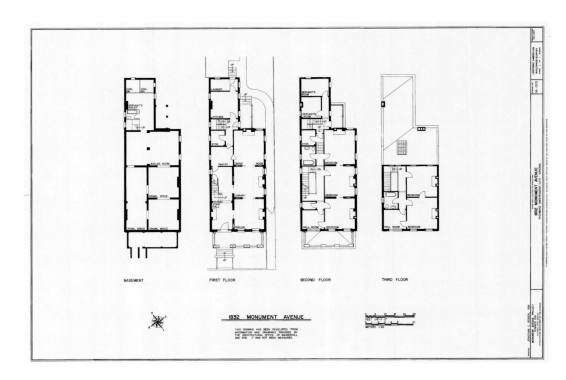

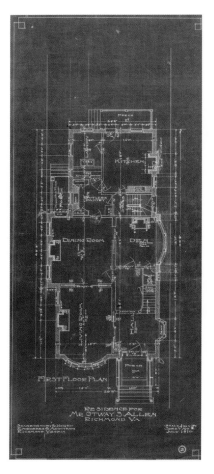

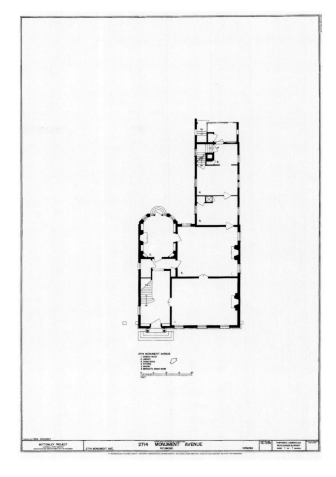

LEFT: *2714 Monument Avenue. Bottomley's houses, such as the Boykin house pictured here, reflect his knowledge of historical precedents.*

BELOW: *3216–24 Monument Avenue. A mixture of sizes and styles characterizes the area west of the Boulevard within the historic district.*

HOUSES, STYLES, AND ARCHITECTS

social success. Ellen Glasgow observed that "there was only one key to unlock modern Richmond and that key was golden. Anybody from anywhere who could afford to give a larger party became automatically, as it were, a 'social leader.'"[6] The house as a social center influenced the spatial organization of many Monument Avenue houses.

Room arrangement in Monument Avenue houses varied widely and depended on the size and cost of the dwelling, the client for whom it was built, the architect who designed it, and other factors, such as orientation. However, a few general characteristics can be noted. Most floor plans indicated the impact of Richmond's humid summer climate in the days before air-conditioning: openings were placed for cross-ventilation, and the prominent porches served as outdoor rooms for significant portions of the year. Almost all the houses were organized around a large hall and a staircase. The sequence of entry from the front door, and perhaps a porch, into a vestibule, and then a hall that might be divided into several areas, was a critical social statement. This flowing space and the staircase down which a grand entry might be made became the site for lavish embellishments on the part of the architect. Of course there were rear, or service, entrances into all the houses, and the one a person used defined his or her social class and reason for calling. Servants and tradespeople appeared at the rear, while the front door was reserved for guests and family. With few exceptions, all the major public rooms—living room, parlor, dining room, and music room—were located on the ground floor, and they usually received impressive decorative schemes. The placement of these rooms varied depending on entrance and facade orientation. Some arrangements shift the interior orientation away from the street to side or rear gardens. The second floor was the bedroom floor, though in larger houses a family sitting room might also be included. Spaces for servants, which were standard in all the houses, would be located at the rear of the second floor, or in a third floor or large attic. Rear staircases provided vertical communication for the servants. Most houses had at least one live-in servant, who was usually female and black. Many households employed more servants, either as live-ins or on a daily basis. Gardens and their placement varied; with the older row houses they were placed to the rear, but some of the larger individual residences had side gardens walled off from the street. The relation of the interior spaces to the garden also varied, with some gardens treated as extensions of the interior or outdoor rooms.

The decoration and furnishing of the major public spaces varied according to the date of a house's construction since room decoration and furnishing is always a temporal affair. Although Richmond had always followed the national trends in furniture and decoration, it had never been known as an extravagant town. Times were changing, however, a new prosperity and cosmopolitanism ruled, and, as Ellen Glasgow wittily observed in a novel whose locale is based upon Richmond: "Even in Queensborough [Richmond] where, until recent years conversation had been the favorite art, almost the only art patronized by the best circles, wealthy citizens were beginning to realize that, if books look well in a library, pictures lent even more emphatically the right note to the walls of a drawing room."[7]

The dates for the building of Monument Avenue coincide with the various editions of Edith Wharton and Ogden Codman's *The Decoration of Houses* and Elsie de Wolfe's *The House in Good Taste*.[8] Both of these books, as well as various homemaker periodicals like *Ladies' Home Journal* and *House and Garden*, while exposing different fads and trends, were decidedly anti-Victorian and rejected the overcluttered, overstuffed look that dominated

Library, 2324 Monument Avenue, 1914, Marcellus Wright, redesigned 1929, Baskervill and Lambert, architects. The houses on the avenue were built as homes in which to raise families and, often, as places to provide impressive settings for social successes.

most American interiors up to 1900. Instead they preached restraint and advised that interiors and furnishings should follow French and English models of the eighteenth century.[9] Books such as *A Chippendale Romance* or *The Lure of the Antique* asserted the superiority and nostalgic value of early American furniture.[10] Although generalizations are hazardous, most of the interiors on Monument Avenue exhibited aspects of the refined "good taste" preached by these various "authorities." Certainly, many houses contained overstuffed Vic-

OPPOSITE: *Interior, 1800 Monument Avenue, 1931, William Lawrence Bottomley, architect. Bottomley's skill with interiors was complemented by his wife's knowledge of wallpapers, moldings, and details.*

RIGHT: *Interior, 2220 Monument Avenue, 1908, Claude K. Howell, architect. Howell mixed his styles by using a Colonial Revival balustrade with some heavier Arts and Crafts details.*

BELOW: *Interior, 1817 Monument Avenue, 1905, architect unknown. Large window areas were frequently balanced by dark woodwork in the older houses on the street. (Valentine Museum)*

RIGHT: *Interior, 2614 Monument Avenue, 1912, Albert F. Huntt, architect. As the Colonial Revival style spread, more delicate woodwork, frequently painted white, appeared. (Virginia Historical Society)*

ABOVE: *Interior, 2309 Monument Avenue, 1917, William Lawrence Bottomley, architect. Bottomley's interiors vary from Georgian to Adamesque, with appropriate mantels and paneling.*

RIGHT: *Interior, 2200 Monument Avenue, 1910, architect unknown. This 1940s bedroom exemplifies the evolution to brighter and less cluttered interiors. (Virginia Historical Society)*

Living room, 2315 Monument Avenue, 1924, William Lawrence Bottomley, architect. Some interiors followed the lead of the exterior style of the house, with tapestry wall-hangings, special light fixtures, and rich oriental rugs. (Valentine Museum)

Interior, the Branch house, 2501 Monument Avenue, 1917–19, John Russell Pope, architect. The furnishings for the Branch house and others were collected on European trips and assembled to convey the owners' interests and background. (Valentine Museum)

torian furniture brought from earlier homes in the city, but for the most part Monument Avenue interiors followed the broad national trend. This meant classical paneling and/or trim for the downstairs main public rooms. The main staircase would receive special attention with balusters and newel posts. The fireplace in the drawing room—and, if the owner could afford it, the library and dining room—had an elaborate mantel. Wallpaper would have a subtle pattern, and heavy drapery was used for the windows. Rugs would be broadloom with perhaps an oriental or two. Furniture was a mixture of earlier heavy pieces and some recent reproductions of French or English eighteenth-century furniture with thinner forms, and perhaps one or two genuine antiques. Pictures would be cozy genre scenes, maybe a small landscape, but certainly nothing that might be considered "modern." Also on display would be paintings of ancestors, for, after all, this was Virginia, and family still ruled.

A few homes on Monument Avenue had special interiors with specific themes, such as the Mediterranean style of the J. Scott Parrish house (1922) at 2315 or the Tudor style of the Branch house (1916) at 2501. At least one semi–Arts and Crafts interior, in the Laura H. Johnson house at 2023 Monument Avenue, was created with abstract balusters and newel post for the stairs and a tile-covered fireplace in the matte finish popularized by the Moravian Pottery and Tile Company. Johnson's furnishings are unknown, but probably they were not as unusual. Gustav Stickley's Craftsman furniture did not have an outlet in Richmond, and indeed its thick and solid forms would have been considered primitive by most Richmonders when placed alongside American colonial or French furniture. If Stickley or other similar Arts and Crafts furniture appeared in houses on Monument Avenue, it was probably in the library, where a Morris chair for the man of the house would have been considered appropriate, or perhaps upstairs in a servant's quarters. The twelve dollar price of a Stickley side chair compared to seventy-five cents for a Sears and Roebuck chair, would, however, have made most Richmonders think twice.

Richmond's building code exerted some influence over a house's appearance and features, as did the property owner's deed. Turn-of-the-century building codes were concerned mainly with fire safety, so guidelines mandated the building material and the thickness of walls.[11] Original deeds required a setback of only twenty feet from the street, with allowances of five feet for a bay toward the street. After the introduction of sidewalks in 1904, the setback was changed to fifteen feet. Clauses required that there be a five-foot setback on at least one side of each house and that all construction be of brick or stone. Initially only private single-family residences could be built on the avenue. These clauses were mandated for twenty-five years, but apartment buildings began to appear on the avenue long before that period had passed. After a few years, restrictions were added to many deeds within the Allen section stating that blacks or "anyone of African descent" could not own or rent, although they were allowed as servants in a house.[12]

Styles

The houses of Monument Avenue represent many of the various stylistic idioms that captured the fancy of the American architects and the public in the period between 1890 and 1930. "Indiscriminate imitation," was the term one of the nation's leading architectural crit-

Interior, 2023 Monument Avenue, 1908, Claude K. Howell, architect. The Arts and Crafts interior of the Laura Johnson house extends even to the art tile fireplace surround.

ics employed to describe the reliance of American architects upon models drawn from the European and American past.[13] Competing for attention at the eastern end of Monument Avenue are the restless pyrotechnics of the earliest houses, designed in variations on the Richardsonian Romanesque and Queen Anne styles. They stand out, with their towers, rounded bays, and asymmetrical facades. After 1905 the various classical idioms would dominate. By far the most common of these was some version of the red brick Colonial Revival house.

Amid the dominant classical structures, a few stylistic heretics did appear, such as the Jacobean house built for Henry S. Wallerstein (1915) at 2312 Monument Avenue and a couple of half-timbered designs. Other alternatives included houses in the Mediterranean or the Italo-Spanish idiom, like that of J. Scott Parrish (president of a concrete company and a vice-president of the Richmond Chamber of Commerce), designed by William Lawrence Bottomley (1922), at 2315 Monument Avenue. Although the light-colored stucco facade made the house stand out against the ubiquitous darker brick of much of the avenue, stylistically the house was essentially classical. Bottomley also employed the Mediterranean idiom for the nine-story Stuart Court Apartments (1924–25), located at the eastern end of the avenue at Stuart Circle.

North side of the 1600 block of Monument Avenue. Architects and their clients examined many European and American models between 1890 and 1930, creating lively streetscapes with widely differing forms.

Another stylistic variation was the Italian Renaissance idiom, as seen in the John T. Wilson house (1911) at 2037 Monument Avenue. Wilson, a successful building contractor, made a grand statement about his arrival on the Richmond scene, since his house was not only one of the largest on the street but also, in a sense, the most institutional in design. Although classical in inspiration, the Wilson house employed an odd contrapuntal bay organization of five bays at ground level and then six window bays at the second floor,

2037 Monument Avenue, 1911, John Kevan Peebles, designer. The Wilson house, a local version of an Italian Renaissance palazzo, built by a contractor for himself, is so large that it appears institutional.

with a further division into a grouping at the attic level of eleven windows, placed in a two, two, three, two, two rhythm. John Kevan Peebles of Norfolk designed the Wilson house; he created an Americanized—and indeed Southern—version of a Italian Renaissance palazzo in red brick with limestone trim, not unlike the YWCA building on North Fifth Street downtown that would be built a few years later after designs by Noland and Baskervill.

An ornamented tympanum above the second floor windows, Wilson house.

Richmond, being an artistically conservative and relatively provincial city, tended to lag behind larger Northern cities such as Boston, and of course New York, in the acceptance of new architectural idioms. Just barely present on Monument Avenue were the new architectural idioms popularized by Frank Lloyd Wright and his followers in the first two decades of the twentieth century in the Chicago suburbs. Duncan Lee's 1913 design for the Moncure house at 1821 Monument does display some Prairie School influence, as does the design of A. G. Higginbotham, a West Virginia architect, for the 1910 Gunst house at 2208 Monument. Later, in the 1920s, more modernistic idioms appeared in the New York suburbs, but not in Richmond. The Arts and Crafts movement—in which Wright was a Midwestern player—also found a minor expression on Monument Avenue with the Laura H. Johnson house at 2023, designed by Claude K. Howell in 1908. The Arts and Crafts movement did not play a major role in the American South except for its influence on pottery and textiles, and Virginia was not particularly affected.[14] Bungalows were constructed elsewhere in Richmond, but their modest nature as inexpensive housing and their low-slung character would have been inappropriate for Monument Avenue.

Hence, the Arts and Crafts character of the Johnson house is unusual. Constructed of brick, with stucco and half-timber applied on the large front gable, the house draws upon the contemporary English Arts and Crafts work of M. H. Baillie Scott and others, which found great favor in the Philadelphia and Boston suburbs.[15] During the 1920s this "Tudorbethan" evocation would be the basis for the suburban development of Windsor Farms and for Virginia House and Agecroft Hall constructed there. However, on Monument Avenue the Johnson house stands out. Claude Howell also designed 2220 Monument Avenue for Harry S. Binswanger in 1908, and although this house has a far more conventional design, it contains notable leaded glass that resembles the glass with geometric designs developed by Frank Lloyd Wright in the Midwest. This might be expected since Binswanger

Staircase, 2230 Monument Avenue. The mix of classically inspired details with Arts and Crafts glass indicates the stylistic freedom that characterized the first two decades of the twentieth century.

was Richmond's leading glass supplier. A few doors up, Moses I. Binswanger had D. Wiley Anderson design a house in 1914. Nominally a classical design in details and facade, its green tile roof makes it stand out. Inside, Arts and Crafts glass appears next to classically inspired details, which to design purists of today seems incongruous. This glass work probably came from a stock supplier in either New York or Chicago.

These exceptions notwithstanding, overall Monument Avenue seems to present an unending line of manifestations of the Colonial Revival. As a style and as an image, the Colonial Revival is perhaps the most American creation of all the various revival styles that architects have utilized for the last century and a half. Open to many different interpretations, ranging from a statement of patriotic and progressive values to an expression of geographical identity, what is colonial depends on one's viewpoint and location. For Virginians, the red brick, two-story, symmetrical house frequently labeled "Georgian" became the dominant image of colonial domestic architecture, but in New England it might be the white weatherboarded Cape Cod cottage or perhaps a dark-shingled reproduction of a Puritan's homestead. Elsewhere, Dutch forms for the Mid-Atlantic, or two-level piazzas in New Orleans or Charleston, or Spanish missions for the Southwest and Far West indicate the variations possible within the term "Colonial Revival." But specific regional expressions disappeared very quickly, as imitation James River Neo-Georgian mansions sprang up in Newport, Rhode Island, and Boston Federal houses appeared in Richmond. What was considered colonial encompassed far more than buildings dating prior to 1776, and even included styles that came from foreign sources. Not only English Georgian architecture was considered appropriate but also, in some cases, Tudor or Stuart styles, since arguably they reflected the buildings the earliest settlers might have known. The Federal style, or the architecture of the Early Republic, became fair game, and in the South the two-story, temple-fronted portico became a specifically Southern Colonial variation. The temple-fronted portico owes its origins largely to Thomas Jefferson and his designs for Monticello, the Virginia State House, and the University of Virginia, all of which postdate the Revolution. The Lewis H. Blair house at 2327 Monument Avenue, designed by Walter Dabney Blair in 1913, demonstrates this Southern genre of the Colonial Revival, as did the Whitmell S. Forbes mansion that used to stand at 3401 Monument Avenue.[16]

The gigantic Forbes mansion of 1914, which stood just beyond Roseneath Road, was for many years one of Monument Avenue's—and Richmond's—showplaces and well illustrated the perfidies of the Colonial Revival. Forbes was a prominent business tycoon in Richmond, who owned a streetcar line and a wholesale grocery business, as well as having an interest in the Virginia Baking Company and the Richmond Guano Company. Although the identity of the designer of the Forbes house remains unknown, the mansion may well have been the work of an out-of-town firm. Constructed of yellow brick, with large wings, a tile roof, outflung balustraded terraces, and elaborate details, the house's two-story, approximately forty-foot-tall entrance portico had four elaborate Corinthian columns, and swags appeared in the entablature. The single-story porches on either side had row upon row of Ionic columns. This overdone quality set the teeth of many critics and architects on edge. Joseph Everett Chandler, a proper Boston Colonial Revivalist, restorer, and scholar, pictured a house similar to the Forbes mansion in his book *The Colonial House* (1916) and labeled it as "'Kickapoo' or 'Hoppigee' . . . or 'Virulent Colonial,'" adding, "An example of everything not to do."[17]

Although instances of the revival of colonial (or Federal) forms can be found prior to the Civil War even in Virginia, the major interest in these forms developed in New England seacoast resort areas during the 1870s.[18] By the 1890s leading architects in New York, Boston, and Philadelphia had developed the Colonial Revival idiom as an acceptable image for the homes of the wealthy, displacing the more picturesque Queen Anne and Roman-

2327 Monument Avenue, 1913, Walter Dabney Blair, architect. The giant columns are typical of the Southern version of Colonial Revival.

esque Revival styles. The Colonial Revival went hand-in-hand with the new classical orientation that overtook American architecture in the 1890s and remained dominant into the 1920s. In Virginia the adoption of the Colonial Revival lagged behind its acceptance in the North, even though Edgerton Rogers, a leading Richmond architect, had designed a copy of Mount Vernon as the Virginia Building for the World's Columbian Exposition of 1893 in Chicago. In Virginia, interest among architects in reproducing colonial forms and details first appeared in the northern part of the state when Glenn Brown measured, and published information on, some details of Alexandria houses in 1887.[19] This was one of the opening salvos in Virginia of what became an obsession of many architects: documenting in drawings and photographs colonial details and buildings to serve as sources for designs. The vast number of books and articles published on Virginia colonial architecture by architects provided the basis for much of the Colonial Revival.

There were many reasons for the popularity of the new colonial style. Like the Italianate style that had dominated Richmond's commercial and residential architecture in the middle years of the nineteenth century, Colonial Revival design could be simple and economical or complex and expensive. Colonial Revival construction used ordinary brick, and the decoration could be modest and made of wood. Just as their forerunners had been able to modernize in the 1840s by adding Italianate brackets to the box cornices of the Greek Re-

Construction of the Forbes house, 3401 Monument Avenue, 1915, architect unknown. Elaborate Colonial Revival mansions such as the Forbes house were derided by scholars and critics for being excessive. (Valentine Museum)

vival, local builders could easily make the cornices more simple and classical again. The basic townhouse form remained unchanged. Albert F. Huntt provided the first Colonial Revival house for the street, with the 1905 Henry H. George house at 1831 Monument Avenue. Huntt's design for the red brick house included tentative colonial details, such as keystones and a widow's walk. By 1909 fully realized Colonial Revival houses were under construction on the avenue, and by 1915 the style set the standard for the street.

Still, other styles and some exotic details also appeared on Monument Avenue, including fanciful Dutch gables in Charles Bryant's design for Rabbi Edward N. Calisch at 2702 Monument Avenue. The house is a visual cacophony, with a somewhat medieval bay window below the Dutch gable and then on the ground floor a wide Federal Revival window. As noted above, the half-timbered and Tudorbethan styles also appeared on Monument Avenue, though not in the profusion seen in other areas of the United States.[20] During the 1920s American residential architecture maintained the restrained classicism typified in the work of architects like Bottomley but added a new interest in the picturesque. At the western end of Monument Avenue, at numbers 3117–31, designed by Carl Lindner, this new suburban picturesque is fully visible in houses that range from Mediterranean to Gothic.

The matter of assigning significance to a stylistic choice can be difficult. Certainly, to some residents the choice had at least some meaning: a house in the colonial idiom made some sort of a hazy connection back to the origins of the country, for example, or a design could reflect a certain family heritage, as in the case of Beulah and John Kerr Branch's Tudorbethan fantasy at 2501 Monument Avenue. On another level, one should be careful not to attribute deep intellectual motives to the choice, for in most cases the styles employed on the avenue were the nationally popular idioms that appeared in cities across the country, and in books and magazines. These were the styles that architects knew; too radical a departure would not be possible and could upset the harmony of the street.

1831 Monument Avenue, 1905, Albert Huntt, architect. Huntt produced the first Colonial Revival house on Monument when he designed this home for building contractor H. H. George. (Valentine Museum)

Architects

Monument Avenue and West Franklin Street were the first residential streets in Richmond where architects designed a major portion of the houses. This testifies to the rise of the professional designer at the turn of the century and the disappearance of the master builder from the design profession. Great changes were occurring nationwide in the profession of architecture, and they were reflected in Richmond, where William Noland helped found the Virginia chapter of the American Institute of Architects in 1914 and became the state's first registered architect in 1920.[21] The designers who shaped Monument Avenue included many of Richmond's leading architects, as well as a select number of out-of-state professionals. The choice to employ either William Lawrence Bottomley or John Russell Pope meant that a client had more money than residents who worked with local architects and that his social aspirations needed the imprimatur of a leading New York designer. For the most part, however, Richmond architects were employed for Monument Avenue houses, which helped give the street its common themes.

Individual architects, and their biographies and work, will be treated below, but a few general observations are necessary. The Richmond architectural community was not especially large, and all the architects knew each other through clubs, employment, family connections, common clients, and professional associations. The general respect that they showed to each other's designs on Monument Avenue—through height of construction, materials utilized, and repetition of elements—suggests that the Richmond architectural community recognized the avenue as a showplace for its work and for the city as a whole. Some architects even lived on Monument Avenue; in 1930, for instance, the street was home to eight members of the profession.[22] In a sense, the architects who worked on Monument Avenue shared a common vision of the street, and whatever personal differences they may have had were less important than this vision they were realizing on Monument Avenue.

The architects who worked on Monument Avenue reflect a variety of backgrounds and approaches, but they can be divided roughly into two groups that might be termed "late Victorian" and "academic." The first, or late Victorian, group, represented by Albert Huntt and D. Wiley Anderson, tended to be slightly older and received their training as apprentices with architects who practiced in the high Victorian eclectic mode of the 1850s–70s. Consequently, Huntt and Anderson retained a spirit of bold picturesqueness and large overscaled details. In general they disdained academic correctness. The second, or academic, group—composed of John Kevan Peebles, William C. Noland, W. Duncan Lee, and the firm of Carneal and Johnston, along with the out-of-state architects William Lawrence Bottomley and John Russell Pope—prided themselves on the employment of more orthodox models and correctness in details. Finally, there were architects who straddled both groups, such as Claude K. Howell. Most of the academic architects either attended architecture school or apprenticed with architects who had an academic background. This meant the École des Beaux-Arts in Paris, or one of its American derivatives, in which classicism was the basis of design and accuracy with historical detail was considered very important. Their designs relied on restraint and fluency in traditional styles, with little of the exuberance that Huntt or Anderson could achieve. Like many architects of the period, they did not limit their repertoire to the Colonial Revival alone, but could also draw on Italian Renaissance and Medieval sources.

Albert F. Huntt (1868–1920) designed seven houses and one apartment building on Monument Avenue. He was a pioneer in Richmond with regard to the design of apartment houses, and he produced distinctive and original designs. The grandson of Otis Manson, one of Richmond's earliest architects, Huntt attended the Pennsylvania Military Academy in Chester, Pennsylvania, and then worked in Philadelphia for four years. He returned to Richmond in 1892, joining the firm of German-born architect Carl Ruehrmund. During Huntt's time in Philadelphia, the city's leading architect, Frank Furness, was designing a group of wildly original and eccentric bank buildings that challenged the orthodoxy of both the medieval and classical revivals. The freedom and imagination with which Huntt composed facades may result from observing Furness's buildings. Huntt combined an interest in Richmond's nineteenth-century classical tradition with an extraordinary inventiveness that sets his work apart from that of most of his contemporaries.[23]

Huntt used a rugged Romanesque style in his earliest works in Richmond, but in 1905, when he designed his first house for Monument Avenue—the George house, at 1831—he took a step toward the new Colonial Revival style. The building's large central dormer served as a reminder of Huntt's allegiance to the Romanesque, but its symmetry, jack arches, strong keystones, and widow's walk (now gone) looked toward the Colonial Revival. Since Huntt was experimenting, he built the front porch of granite and the cornice of molded brick, materials characteristic of the earlier style that valued fine stone carving.

TOP: *3117–31 Monument Avenue, 1928, Carl Lindner, architect. By the 1920s, many different styles had been explored, and Monument Avenue, like many streets across America, began to look like a collection of buildings from around the world.*

BOTTOM LEFT: *2502 Monument Avenue, 1926, Otis K. Asbury, architect. Asbury's design of this house for Henry S. Raab uses Mediterranean imagery.*

BOTTOM RIGHT: *2504 Monument Avenue, 1914, Asbury and Whitehurst, architects. This house for William C. Camp is one of several skillful houses in a variety of historical styles that architect Otis K. Asbury contributed to the avenue.*

2607 Monument Avenue, 1926, Otis K. Asbury, architect. Asbury's houses, this one with a half-timbered front gable, often appear to be cottages, belying their actual size.

By 1908, Huntt's American colonial forms developed an almost Baroque air at the Frank D. Beveridge house at 2500 Monument, where he incorporated triple windows on each side of an elaborate Doric porch and used stone lintels over the windows. These were typical elements of Richmond's Greek Revival, but Huntt transformed them in an eccentric manner. The doorway is particularly elaborate. The porches of Huntt's houses often demonstrate his inventiveness. They are complex, multilayered compositions that juxtapose elements in unorthodox ways. In the 1914 Sorg house at 2015 Monument, Huntt flanked a pair of small bay windows with a pair of Ionic columns and then surmounted the entire confection with a Baroque broken pediment—enough architectural elements for two normal houses. Huntt also practiced occasional restraint, however, as with the Francis D. Barksdale house at 2204 Monument, erected in 1909, and the Clifford Smith residence at 2300 Monument, built a year later. These houses have modest Doric porches and exceptionally elegant fanlight windows over the doors. The Smith house is of particular interest since it incorporated into the design traditional historical Richmond architectural elements, most notably a large stepped gable. Huntt's fine Stratford Court and Kenilworth Apartments at 2510 and 2512 Monument Avenue, built in 1917 and 1918, are discussed in Chapter 3.

Bascomb J. Rowlett (active 1909; died 1940), who appeared in Richmond about 1909

ABOVE LEFT: *2614 Monument Avenue, 1912, Albert F. Huntt, architect. The Dunlop house reveals Huntt's adventurous qualities. He mixed elements, like other late Victorian architects, even when using more modern details.*

ABOVE RIGHT: *2031 Monument Avenue, 1913, Albert F. Huntt, architect. Huntt's interpretation of the Tudor could be as distinctive as his interpretation of the colonial.*

RIGHT: *1831 Monument Avenue, 1905, Albert Huntt, architect. The George house was Huntt's first on Monument Avenue.*

ABOVE: *2320 Monument Avenue, 1927, William Lawrence Bottomley, architect. Bottomley's education at Columbia University, the American Academy in Rome, and the École des Beaux-Arts in Paris gave him an impeccable background in classical architecture. His designs always reflected his precise knowledge of historic styles.*

LEFT: *Front entrance, 2320 Monument Avenue.*

HOUSES, STYLES, AND ARCHITECTS

TOP LEFT: *2500 Monument Avenue, 1913, Albert Huntt, architect. This house recalls Greek Revival Richmond houses of the 1840s.*

TOP RIGHT: *Porch, 2500 Monument Avenue.*

ABOVE: *Entablature and balustrade, 2306 Monument Avenue.*

RIGHT: *2306 Monument Avenue, 1914, Albert Huntt, architect. The porch of the Lafferty house includes almost every classical element available.*

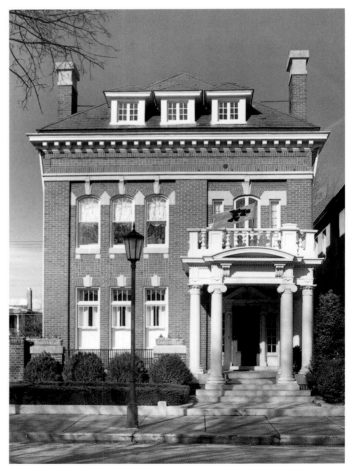

2015 Monument Avenue, 1915, Albert Huntt, architect. The composition of the Sorg house achieves a Baroque twist on Colonial Revival.

ABOVE: *2204 Monument Avenue, 1909, Albert Huntt, architect. Handsome white-painted trim, classical porches, and red brick make this house a conventional example of the Colonial Revival style.*

RIGHT: *2300 Monument Avenue, 1910, Albert Huntt, architect. Huntt borrowed details from early Richmond houses for the Smith house.*

ABOVE: *The Rixey Court, 2235 Monument Avenue, 1924, Bascom Rowlett, architect. Rowlett had worked with Albert Huntt, and the imaginative composition at the Rixey Court shows Huntt's influence.*

LEFT: *Detail, Rixey Court.*

and practiced there through 1935, had been an associate of Huntt's and picked up some of Huntt's inventiveness with facades.[24] In addition to working with Carl Lindner on St. John's United Church of Christ, Rowlett designed the luxurious Rixey Court Apartments at 2235 Monument Avenue (1924–25). Rowlett chose an Italian Renaissance idiom for Rixey Court, and the details are quite correct, but the massing is anything but conventional: two pavilions flank a recessed central tower and a three-sided bay, while an entrance loggia and balustraded walls push toward the street. The white stucco covering gives the apartments a vaguely Mediterranean air.

D. Wiley Anderson (1864–1940), one Richmond's most prolific and successful architects, designed nine houses on Monument Avenue. Born toward the end of the Civil War, in Scottsville, a small community on the James River, he was the son of a builder-carpenter. The Virginia Piedmont tradition of Thomas Jefferson and his workmen was in a sense Anderson's training ground, since he never attended college and learned through the apprenticeship method; he proudly referred to himself as self-educated. A relentless self-promoter, Anderson published catalogs of his work and placed advertisements in periodicals. His clients included many of Richmond's most notable German and Jewish families; he designed houses for Moses Binswanger, Arthur Straus, and William Schwarzschild.[25]

Anderson's earliest designs, like those of Huntt, were Gothic or Richardsonian Romanesque; by 1905 classical forms begin to make an appearance in his work, but with great boldness and imagination. His Monument Avenue houses are all large, but the architectural elements with which he adorned them are even larger. In 1908 Anderson designed one of his first houses on the avenue, a massive and imposing mansion of red brick and granite for Thomas T. Adams, a lumber dealer, at 1837 Monument. The broad, single-story porch and portico are supported by Roman Doric columns, which in turn sit on granite bases, separated by wrought iron balustrade panels. Three oversized dormers linked by a wrought iron and granite balustrade crown the house. Equally bold are Anderson's houses at 2024 Monument Avenue for James T. Walsh and 1612 for Ada Strause, both dating from 1910. Though the houses are nominally Colonial Revival, with red brick and white classical trim, Anderson placed a large bay window in the middle of each house's facade, definitely not a colonial touch.

Many of Anderson's clients were contractors or businessmen involved in the building trades, and he was known for integrating his clients' building materials into his designs so their houses would function as advertisements. Such was the case, for example, with the showplace of glass mentioned earlier that he designed for Moses I. Binswanger (1914) at 2230 Monument Avenue. In this house the elements seen in the Adams house are expanded and enlarged. The porch is grander, the dormers larger, and the window trim more substantial than in the earlier house. Anderson designed two similar houses in 1914 for Arthur Straus and William Schwarzschild, at 2708 and 2710 Monument respectively, that demonstrate his approach, unrestrained by academic concerns for correctness. The facade of the Straus house is crammed with elaborate architectural detail: a prominent porch, three different windows on the first two floors, and wild dormers. Next door, at the Schwarzschild house, Anderson undertook a difficult feat, to create a four-bay Colonial Revival house, where even the front porch is off-center. Anderson appears to have stopped his architectural practice with the beginning of World War I.

1837 Monument Avenue, 1908, D. Wiley Anderson, architect. Bold dormers and a strong porch define the house that Anderson designed for lumber dealer Thomas T. Adams.

Claude K. Howell (active 1904; died 1940) played a major role in the architectural development of Monument Avenue between 1906 and 1912; his designs reflected both late Victorian boldness and new academic sophistication. His background is unknown, but he lived in Richmond from 1904 to 1912, and then moved to Charlottesville, Savannah, Atlanta, Winchester, Martinsville, and Petersburg, before disappearing from the architectural scene about 1940. Howell formed a partnership with Francis W. Scarborough, an engineer, in 1909 that lasted until 1912. Howell's best-known work was movie theaters, including several in Richmond, such as the fine National Theater (1922) on Board Street, where Ferruccio Legnaioli provided the decorative sculpture.[26] Howell's ten buildings on Monument Avenue follow no definite stylistic idiom. In 1906 he designed an elegant limestone house, with a broad, gently bowed classical porch supported by paired Ionic columns, at 1822 Monument for engineer Edward Hoadley. Above the porch is a bay window, improbably bisected by a Corinthian column. The effect is odd and unexpected, but Howell produced similar two-part bays elsewhere on the street, such as in the Harry S. Binswanger house (1910) at 2220 Monument. Here a large bay window sits precariously on a rather delicate elliptical fanlight. The variety of architectural elements on the facade is remarkable,

1612 Monument Avenue, 1910, D. Wiley Anderson, architect. A slightly bowed porch and a central bay window ornament this classically detailed house.

with openings that are elliptical on the first floor, square on the second, and semicircular on the third.

Howell, as noted above, created the finest essay in the Arts and Crafts idiom on the street, the Laura Johnson house at 2023 Monument. Erected in 1908 for a widow from the Midwest, the exterior suggests the half-timbered Tudor style. Since all houses on the street were required to be brick, the half-timbered elements are applied to a brick bearing wall. The entrance opens into a narrow side hall that leads to a light-filled, internal stair hall. The handsome cantilevered stair boasts a railing similar to those employed by the English Arts and Crafts architect, C. F. A. Voysey. The narrow entrance hall allows maximum window area in the living room. Similar arrangements were used in the next decade by the sophisticated New York architect William Lawrence Bottomley.[27]

Howell and his partner Scarborough also designed a house for Monument Avenue's

Otway Allen at number 1631 (1910), which drew upon Boston Federal architecture from the time of Charles Bulfinch. This choice of a Yankee style for a Southern city may appear strange, but Howell had ample precedent. The Federal Revival had begun in Boston in the 1880s with a series of houses by the New York architectural firm of McKim, Mead and White, which then employed the style with great success in New York and Chicago.[28] Also, McKim, Mead and White had rebuilt the Rotunda at the University of Virginia after the fire of 1895 and added other buildings to the campus.[29] In the hands of these Yankee architects various colonial and Federal idioms became national and could be employed for successful businessmen in Richmond as well as elsewhere. Howell's house for Allen, with its fine red brick work and bow front, could have fit in on Boston's Beacon Hill, so skillful were its proportions and details. The one difference from what could be found on Beacon Hill—which was typical of McKim, Mead and White's work as well—is that the entablature and cornice balustrade were a little too rich and complicated for Boston tastes of the early 1800s.[30]

Typifying academic architects who employed more sophisticated models and details was John Kevan Peebles (1866–1934), perhaps the best-known Virginia-based architect of the period 1890 to 1930. His partner after 1917 was Finlay Forbes Ferguson (ca. 1875–1936). Operating from his base in Norfolk, Peebles designed hundreds of buildings across Virginia and in nearby states and was chairman of the architecture board for the Jamestown Ter-Centennial Exposition of 1907. His clients included universities, banks, and wealthy individuals, and he was one of the three architects of the additions to the Virginia State Capitol in 1902–6. At his death, he was involved in the design of the Virginia Museum of Fine Arts on the Boulevard. Peebles studied engineering at the University of Virginia (which did not have an architecture program until 1919) and then apprenticed with and became the partner of J. E. R. Carpenter in Norfolk, before setting up in business on his own in 1897.[31] Peebles designed two buildings for Monument Avenue. The first was Grace Covenant Church, which, as noted in Chapter 3, was a sophisticated English Perpendicular Gothic design. A few doors down from the church at number 1635, Peebles and Ferguson designed a red brick Colonial Revival house for Dr. David M. Mann. The lines and the scale of the dormers suggest that the architects were attempting to blend this house in with the similar house at number 1637 built three years earlier in 1925 for contractor Elmslie Higginbotham.

William C. Noland (1865–1951) and his partner Henry Baskervill (1867–1946) were nearly as respected as Peebles and provided sophisticated academic designs for Monument Avenue with their houses, St. James's Episcopal Church, and Temple Beth Ahabah on West Franklin Street. Noland and Baskervill were partners from 1897 to 1917. Then Noland went out on his own, and Baskervill formed a partnership with Alfred Garey Lambert (active 1916–38) and subsequently with his son, Coleman Baskerville (1905–69) in the firm Baskervill and Son, which continues today.[32] For well over a century, this firm has produced some of Richmond's most important buildings. In the original Noland and Baskervill firm, Henry Baskervill, who had a degree in electrical engineering from Cornell University, took care of the engineering and business half, while Noland operated as the designer. Noland was a native Virginian who studied at private schools but did not attend college and instead worked—and presumably apprenticed—with architects in New York, Philadelphia,

ABOVE: *2710 and 2708 Monument Avenue, both designed in 1914 by D. Wiley Anderson. These two houses repeat the bold dormers and porches of Anderson's earlier work.*

RIGHT: *Porch, 2708 Monument Avenue.*

ABOVE: *2910 Monument Avenue, 1912, architect unknown. Building contractor and real estate developer Samuel Meredith's house is asymmetrical and unbalanced.*

RIGHT: *2906 Monument Avenue, 1914, D. Wiley Anderson, architect. Though Anderson designed and Meredith owned this apartment building next door to Meredith's home, they chose not to relate the two buildings architecturally.*

ABOVE: *2340 Monument Avenue, 1910, and 2338 Monument Avenue, 1909, both by Scarborough and Howell, architects. Abraham McClellan, owner of the house at 2340, was the secretary-treasurer of the stockyard owned by his neighbor at 2338, Thomas Smyth.*

RIGHT: *2218 Monument Avenue, 1911, Claude K. Howell, architect. Howell's ability to jump from style to style and from townhouse to mansion attracted clients with different needs.*

OPPOSITE: *1815 Monument Avenue, 1905, Claude K. Howell, architect. The unusual window on the first floor of the Funsten house, a broken pediment within a segmental arch, has been copied elsewhere in the neighborhood.*

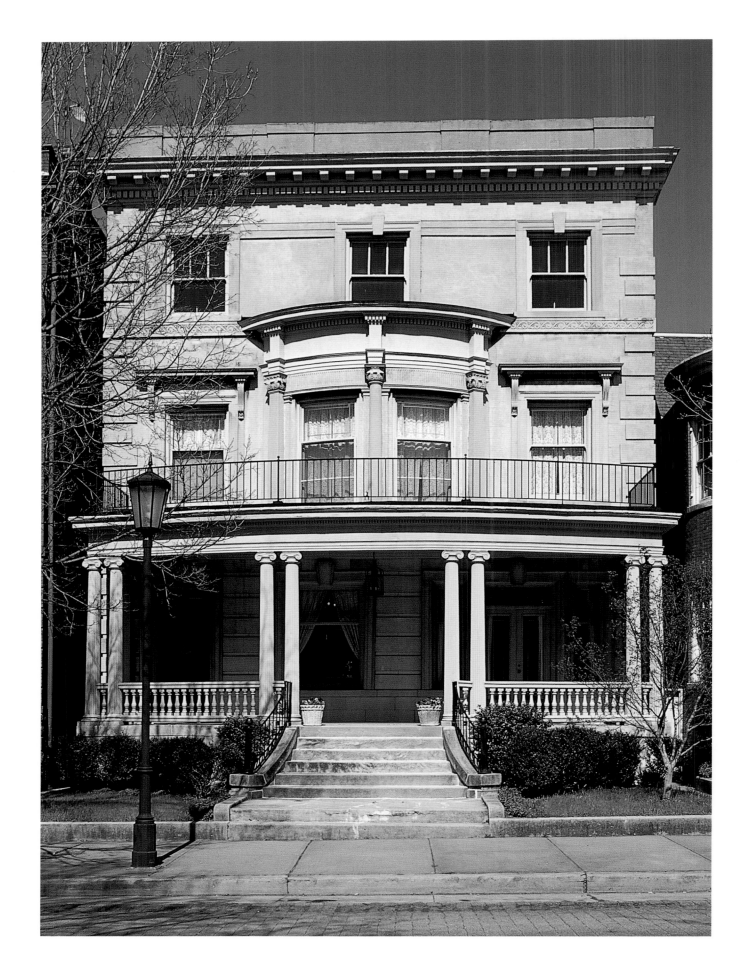

HOUSES, STYLES, AND ARCHITECTS

Roanoke, and Richmond. He also spent two years abroad. In Philadelphia, Noland worked for the firm of Cope and Stewardson, which specialized in sophisticated Neo-Gothic designs; and, while he seldom employed their idiom, he did adopt their method of a close study of original precedent. Noland was involved with Peebles on the Virginia State Capitol extensions and also the architectural setting of the Jefferson Davis Monument. He designed a spectacular Italian Renaissance mansion for Major James Dooley at Swannanoa, near Afton, Virginia, in the Blue Ridge. His work equaled that of architects who designed for Newport, Rhode Island, or Fifth Avenue in New York City.[33]

Noland and Baskervill's first house on Monument Avenue, designed for building contractor Wirt Chesterman at number 2020 in 1906 and built of crisply cut limestone, was perhaps the most elegant house built up to that point on the avenue. A rusticated base carries two elegantly detailed, three-bay upper floors and an attic. Stylistically it is eighteenth-century French. Similar in concept is the even more refined and simple Munce house at 2324 Monument. Originally built in 1914 for John S. Munce, it was sold in 1929, and the new owners of the house hired the Baskervill firm to redesign it. They removed the entire facade, added a few extra feet, and built an all-new front. The lush interior contrasts with the refined and almost austere simplicity of the exterior.

In 1924 Baskervill and Lambert created one of the most elegant houses on the street for Dr. Stuart McGuire, at 2304 Monument Avenue. Based on the well-known Mompesson House, which stands in the Cathedral Close in Salisbury, England, the McGuire house is simple, restrained, and refined—the stylistic opposite of the wild eccentricities of Huntt or Anderson. The owner is said to have been asked by his architect what kind of house he

OPPOSITE: *1822 Monument Avenue, 1906, Claude K. Howell, architect. Howell's complex composition for Edward M. Hoadley, a civil engineer, includes a bowed bay window over the porch.*

ABOVE LEFT: *2216 Monument Avenue, 1910, Scarborough and Howell, architects. Scarborough and Howell's second house for Alphonso W. Bennett on Monument is a variant of Howell's Funsten house at 1815 of five years earlier.*

ABOVE RIGHT: *2220 Monument Avenue, 1908, Claude K. Howell, architect. The large bay window on the second floor balances on an elliptical fanlight over the triple window on the lower level.*

RIGHT: *2023 Monument Avenue, 1908, Claude K. Howell, architect. With ivy and dark half-timbering, the Johnson house looked entirely different when it was built from how it looks today. (Valentine Museum)*

BELOW: *2023 Monument Avenue.*

OPPOSITE: *Stair hall, 2023 Monument Avenue. The light-filled interior stair hall is detailed with a unique Arts and Crafts–style railing.*

Living room, 2023 Monument Avenue. The low and broad proportions of the living room contrast with those of the stair hall. Originally, the woodwork was not painted.

ABOVE LEFT: *1631 Monument Avenue, 1911, Scarborough and Howell, architects. The Otway Allen house drew on Boston's Federal architecture, which had influenced Richmond in the early nineteenth century as well.*

ABOVE RIGHT: *2020 Monument Avenue, 1906, Noland and Baskervill, architects. Crisp limestone detailing distinguishes this French Renaissance house.*

LEFT: *2324 Monument Avenue, 1914, Marcellus Wright, 1929, Baskervill and Lambert, architects. The Wright-designed house of 1914 was all but completely rebuilt in the late 1920s when new owners had the Baskervill firm remove the facade, extend the house toward the street, and build a new front. The interior was also drastically altered.*

South side of the 1600
block of Monument
Avenue. Peebles and
Ferguson contributed
several buildings to this
block, starting with Grace
Covenant Presbyterian
Church and its Sunday
School and number 1635
(between the two houses
with porches), a Colonial
Revival house with two
gabled dormers.

would like. McGuire, who was a distinguished and well-known doctor, responded that he would never ask his patients for medical opinions and that he had hired the architect to make the architectural decisions.[34] The interior of the McGuire house contains elaborate paneling and plaster ceilings. A vaulted entrance hall leads to a circular stair, a close reproduction of the Wickham stair (circular stairs had been a prestigious element in Richmond houses ever since Alexander Parris used one at the Wickham House in 1812).

Baskervill and Lambert's design for Malcolm and Sallie Perkins at 2609 Monument Avenue (1925) is more a revival of Virginia's colonial past than many of the other Colonial Revival designs on the street. The house's five bays, Flemish-bond brick walls with glazed headers, and molded-brick door trim mimic mid-eighteenth-century Virginia detailing and indicates the growing influence of an out-of-state architect, William Lawrence Bottomley.

Bottomley (1883–1951), who designed seven houses and the Stuart Court Apartments on Monument Avenue, was one of the most prominent of the academic group of architects to work on the street. He was the favorite architect of the Virginia elite in the years between 1916 and 1940, receiving nearly fifty commissions in the state although he was a Northerner with his office in New York City. Born in New York and educated at Columbia University and in Paris, he exuded a cosmopolitan air that made him particularly attractive to Southerners who felt a need to combat their provincial reputation. He married Harriet Townsend, an architectural writer from Lexington, Virginia, and formed many strong

TOP: *The McGuire house, 2304 Monument Avenue, 1926, Baskervill and Lambert, architects. This sophisticated and elegant house is the Baskervill firm's finest residence on Monument Avenue. It is one of two houses based on Mompesson House, an English Georgian residence, that were built on the avenue in 1926.*

ABOVE: *Floor plans of 2304 Monument Avenue. (Historic American Buildings Survey)*

LEFT: *Front entrance of 2304 Monument Avenue.*

ABOVE: *Entrance hall, 2304 Monument Avenue. The vaulted ceiling in the hall is only one of several spectacular ceilings in the McGuire house. (Valentine Museum)*

RIGHT: *Stair, 2304 Monument Avenue. The stair closely resembles that at the 1812 neoclassical Wickham house in Richmond.*

friendships in Richmond, including a useful one with Herbert Claiborne, a principal in the construction firm Claiborne and Taylor. Claiborne's wife, Virginia Christian, was a power in the Garden Club of Virginia, and Bottomley received many of his commissions through this connection.[35] His strength as an architect was to create imaginative, livable, and clever houses in elegant and conventional garb. The houses mask their modernity behind Georgian Revival dress and detail. Locally, William Lawrence Bottomley is the most admired architect to have designed for Monument Avenue, and whereas many of the others are forgotten, the name Bottomley almost brings tears to some Richmonders' eyes.[36]

Unlike most Richmond architects (except Duncan Lee), Bottomley provided closets and bathrooms galore. He created houses that remained more livable than those of his contemporaries. He had little interest in the traditional elements of upper-class Richmond homes, such as great entrance halls and impressive porches. His entrance halls were narrow and often led to a central stair hall. The major rooms would pinwheel from this hall and provide a variety of spatial experiences. He often designed the outdoor spaces with the house and treated them as outdoor rooms. Bottomley selected the wall coverings and furniture to carry through with the design intent of the house. Some of his original wall-

ABOVE: *2609 Monument Avenue, 1925, Baskervill and Lambert, architects. This house refers to Virginia's architectural tradition.*

LEFT: *1832 Monument Avenue, 1907, Noland and Baskervill, architects. A handsome porch supported by paired Corinthian columns enhances this house.*

HOUSES, STYLES, AND ARCHITECTS   191

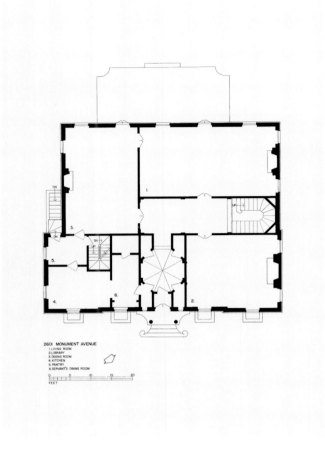

2601 MONUMENT AVENUE
1. LIVING ROOM
2. LIBRARY
3. DINING ROOM
4. KITCHEN
5. PANTRY
6. SERVANT'S DINING ROOM

ABOVE LEFT: *Stair hall, Parrish house, 2315 Monument Avenue, 1924, William Lawrence Bottomley, architect. Bottomley's interiors often include a spectacular stair hall such as this one, entered through a smaller entrance vestibule. The rich textures add to the impression of age. (Valentine Museum)*

ABOVE RIGHT: *Plan, 2601 Monument Avenue, 1926, William Lawrence Bottomley, architect. Bottomley's twist at the Cabell house is an octagonal entrance vestibule, with the stair to the right down a central hall. (Historic American Buildings Survey)*

LEFT: *William Lawrence Bottomley, the New York architect who designed seven houses and the Stuart Court Apartments on Monument Avenue. (Private collection)*

papers remain, and the original design quality of the houses is still apparent. The exteriors are richly textured, showing all of the widely used brick bonds, but they are simple compared with many earlier Monument Avenue houses. His architectural decoration is restrained, refined, and consistent.

Three houses illustrate the qualities of Bottomley's work especially well: the Golsan, Jeffress, and Parrish houses. His first house on the street, 2309 Monument, built for Mr. and Mrs. H. L. Golsan in 1916–18, combined his elegant detailing with imaginative planning. Instead of the traditional three or five bays, Bottomley created a four-bay facade with the entrance off center. The brick exterior was laid in an all-header bond that produced a particularly rich texture. This texture contrasted with a cast-stone broken pediment over the asymmetrical entrance, the only architectural ornamentation on the front, except for

ABOVE: *1800 Monument Avenue, 1931, William Lawrence Bottomley, architect. The Jeffress house was built late, on a quadrant lot with a pie shape.*

LEFT: *Dining room, 1800 Monument Avenue. The room's original wallpaper survives, attesting to Mrs. Jeffress's sense of style.*

ABOVE: *2309 Monument Avenue, 1916, William Lawrence Bottomley, architect. Bottomley enhanced a simple composition with rich textures and small balconies at the Golsan house.*

RIGHT: *Detail of the doorframe, 2309 Monument Avenue.*

OPPOSITE: *Stair hall, 2309 Monument Avenue. The wallpaper is a reproduction of the original.*

HOUSES, STYLES, AND ARCHITECTS

wrought iron balconies and railings. A narrow entrance hall leads into a spectacular internal stair hall. The unexpected narrowness of the hall followed by the expansiveness of the stair is dramatic. The cantilevered stair is richly ornamented, and the hall retains its original scenic wallpaper. Bottomley's wife, Harriet, often helped with interior design, and she took special care with the selection of the paper for his houses.

In contrast to the full-bodied Georgian Revival Golsan house, the house designed for Mr. and Mrs. Robert Jeffress at 1800 Monument Avenue in 1929 is late Georgian and almost Adam in character. The interior trim is quite delicate. The current owners have restored the living room wallpaper, but the dining room retains its original wallpaper. The basic form of the exterior of the house recalls Virginia plantation houses such as Westover, with a steep roof and tall windows. Bottomley used Greek Revival details on the exterior and incorporated a cast iron porch salvaged from New York on the side elevation. He recast a second porch to make the house symmetrical.

The J. Scott Parrish house designed in 1922 and built in 1924 at 2315 Monument Avenue illustrates a different aspect of Bottomley's architectural persona: it is a Mediterranean architectural fantasy. Bottomley had developed an expertise on Spanish architecture and would write several articles on houses and furniture from the Iberian peninsula as well as the book *Spanish Details* (1924).[37] He originally designed a Georgian Revival house for the Parrishes, but after they took a trip to the Mediterranean—possibly at his urging—they had the house redesigned.[38] The house's plan recalls Italian and Spanish prototypes. Massive gates lead to a side courtyard and then to the entrance. Each major room entered from the hall has a distinctive character established by its elaborately decorated ceiling. The rear courtyard is treated as a small streetscape, with false fronts on the kitchen and garage wings suggesting a village. Mrs. Parrish was an avid gardener, one of several members of the Garden Club of Virginia for whom Bottomley designed houses, and the garden space is focused on an ornamental pool. The space feels like a stage set, and the house seems more like the home of a silent screen star than a Richmond businessman and his wife.

Bottomley's 1924 design for the Stuart Court Apartments has a similar aspect of fantasy. At nine stories, with more than sixty apartments, Stuart Court is easily the largest apartment building in the historic area of Monument Avenue. The Mediterranean-style building is a reinforced concrete structure clad in stucco and ornamented with varied windows, quoins, string courses, balconies, and frescoes. The lively roofline includes concrete urns and capped chimneys, creating a small village, though the original cornice deteriorated and had to be removed. The building lends an air of exoticism to the intersection where it is located.

John Russell Pope (1874–1937) is the other major out-of-town architect whose work appears on Monument Avenue, at number 2501, with the John Kerr Branch house, designed and built between 1913 and 1917. Although Bottomley was a well-known and admired architect, Pope easily stood at the head of the profession, and it was a real coup for the Branches to lure him to design a house in Richmond. Trained in New York, Rome, and Paris and the heir in many ways of Charles McKim's classical mantle, he had an equal facility with medieval styles. Pope designed numerous large country and resort houses in Newport, on Long Island, and in New Jersey, utilizing both the Tudorbethan and the Colonial Revival idioms. As an architect of public buildings, Pope employed a severe classi-

TOP: *The Parrish house, 2315 Monument Avenue, 1924, William Lawrence Bottomley, architect. Bottomley originally designed a Georgian house for the Parrishes, but they changed their minds—and Bottomley created this design—after a trip to the Mediterranean. (Valentine Museum)*

ABOVE: *J. Scott Parrish, for whom the house at 2315 Monument Avenue was built. (Valentine Museum)*

LEFT: *Entrance, 2315 Monument Avenue. Bottomley gave the Parrish house a side entrance, approached though a gate at the sidewalk.*

ABOVE: *2301 Monument Avenue, 1925, William Lawrence Bottomley, architect. The Wortham house is one of the few on the avenue that remains in the hands of the same family that built it.*

LEFT: *Staircase, 2301 Monument Avenue.*

OPPOSITE, TOP: *Rear courtyard, 2315 Monument Avenue. Mrs. Parrish, an avid gardener, encouraged lush vegetation in the courtyard (left). Since the garden was completely replanted and overgrown by the time the current owners moved into the house, they chose to pave all but the edges of the courtyard (right), allowing them to indulge in their love for entertaining. (left, Valentine Museum; right, John O. Peters)*

OPPOSITE, BOTTOM LEFT: *Library ceiling, 2315 Monument Avenue. Great care was taken by the current owners to restore the colors and details in the house's decorative features.*

OPPOSITE, BOTTOM RIGHT: *Living room, 2315 Monument Avenue. Ceilings were used to differentiate the rooms at the Parrish house.*

Stuart Court Apartments, 1600 Monument Avenue, 1925, William Lawrence Bottomley, architect. Bottomley's apartments add another evocative style to the intersection at Stuart Circle.

cism, as can be seen in the National Gallery of Art, the National Archives building, and the Jefferson Memorial, all in Washington, D.C.

Concurrent with the Branch house, Pope's firm was designing Broad Street Station, two blocks away from Monument Avenue, in which John Kerr Branch was an investor. Apparently Pope himself had little interest in the Branch house, since family lore holds that he never came to see the finished house and the actual design came largely from the hand of Otto R. Eggers, Pope's leading designer, while the interiors were by Spencer Guidael, an Englishman who worked in Pope's office.[39] The Branch house is a Tudor concoction that borrowed heavily from Compton Wynyates, in Warwickshire, a venerable English house of the sixteenth century often visited by traveling Americans. Compton Wynyates's south elevation provided the general organization for the north facade of the Branch house. A bay window in the inner court at Compton Wynyates reappears on the south elevation of the Branch house. As is typical in American adaptations, the interior courtyard of Compton Wynyates was abandoned. Though the house is pushed up against Monument Avenue, large gardens stretched to the west and south. Pope's firm excelled at designing and specifying materials that looked old. The door surrounds, brickwork, and stone lintels for the exterior were weathered to evoke antiquity. The interior, while modern American in conveniences, is medieval in character. The long galleries and varied floor and ceiling heights imply that the house might have been constructed over centuries. The interior decoration followed suit, and to the requisite Tudor rooms (which contained Branch's collection of medieval furniture and tapestries) were added Georgian and Adam rooms. These reflected

TOP LEFT: *The Branch house, 2501 Monument Avenue, 1917–19, John Russell Pope, architect. The largest house on Monument Avenue is a sophisticated evocation of the late middle ages.*

TOP RIGHT: *John Russell Pope, architect of the Branch house at 2501 Monument Avenue. (Courtesy of Steven Bedford)*

BOTTOM: *Rear facade, the Branch house.*

HOUSES, STYLES, AND ARCHITECTS   201

ABOVE: *Living room, the Branch house. The various periods represented by the art and furniture in the Branch house create a convincing atmosphere of treasures acquired over time. (Valentine Museum)*

RIGHT: *Music room, the Branch house. The mezzanine above the screen allowed musicians to play above the room. (Valentine Museum)*

OPPOSITE: *The long hall, the Branch house.*

Mrs. Branch's tastes, and again suggested the passage of time. Various inscriptions on the house testified to the Branch family's arrival in Virginia in the seventeenth century, though, as noted in Chapter 3, James Branch Cabell indicated in his account of the family's origins that their beginnings were in more modest houses, not in mansions.

W. Duncan Lee (1888–1952), Richmond's most popular residential designer for two decades, was involved in at least fifteen buildings on Monument Avenue. Although Lee was known for his academic sophistication, his earliest work was more in the vein of the bold picturesque architects. His work included small cottages and substantial mansions, ranging from modernist experimentation to full-blown restorations and adaptations of older houses. Born in Ashland, Virginia, and educated in public schools, Lee received his architectural education with George R. Tolman, a partner in the established Richmond firm of Marion Dimmock in 1904–6. Tolman, an instructor at the Massachusetts Institute of Technology in the 1890s, probably gave Lee an education superior to the typical apprenticeship. In 1906 Tolman left the firm and the twenty-two-year-old Lee became Dimmock's partner. Lee established his own firm in 1908 after the death of Dimmock. Lee's first independent commission, probably the result of Dimmock's connections, was the 1906–8 expansion of the Governor's Mansion in Capitol Square. Lee successfully added an oval dining room, and this launched the young man on his career as a society architect.[40]

Lee's first building on Monument Avenue, designed while he was with Dimmock, was the Luther Jenkins house at number 1839. (It was one of only three houses on the street still inhabited by the descendants of the original owner at the end of the twentieth century.) Also with Dimmock, Lee designed the nearby Jefferson Club on Allen Street, a Jewish men's club similar in character to the prestigious Commonwealth and Westmoreland men's clubs. Later the building became the Elks Club. The Jenkins house, a full-scale Colonial Revival mansion, was symmetrical, with a pair of Palladian windows flanking the central entrance porch. It is similar to works by Albert Huntt or Scarborough and Howell.

Lee's next works, the Thomas A. Smyth house at 2336 Monument, built in 1913, and the James J. Pollard house at 2314, built in 1915, shift toward a calmer, more academic mode; the roofs are simple and massive, sheltering the houses. The Pollard house served as the inspiration for the house just west, 2320, the Cary house, designed by Bottomley in 1926. Mrs. Pollard's mother, Maria Cary, liked Lee's design so much she commissioned Bottomley to design a similar house right next door, quite a compliment for the local architect. Mrs. Cary asked Bottomley to make her house smaller and more formal; hence the yellow brick and green tile roof of the Pollard house are transformed into a Georgian red brick and slate composition.[41] Still more adventurous were the houses Lee designed for James Moncure at 1821 Monument in 1913–14 and Dr. Henry Stuart MacLean at 2307 in 1915. The buff brick and hipped tile roofs have an Arts and Crafts air, recalling several of Frank Lloyd Wright's early houses. Some classical detail remains, but it is reticent.

Retaining some of the restrained air, but far more extravagant, was Lee's 1914 Italian villa design for Jaquelin P. Taylor at 2325 Monument Avenue. Its construction cost of $45,000 was almost four times more than that of the Smyth house, located across the street. A three-story center block is flanked by two-story wings that give the house great bulk and presence. Exterior trim is minimal, except for the pedimented door surrounds and window hoods. With its gray stucco covering and jade green roof, the front is austere. Lee thought

TOP: *The Jenkins house, 1839 Monument Avenue, 1908, M. J. Dimmock and W. Duncan Lee. Lee designed several very large houses on Monument, of which the Jenkins house was his first.*

BOTTOM: *View through hall, 1839 Monument Avenue.*

Stair hall, 1839 Monument Avenue. The staircase at the Jenkins house is impressive and lighter than many contemporary designs. Architecturally unchanged since it was built, the color scheme is modern.

HOUSES, STYLES, AND ARCHITECTS

TOP: *1819 Monument Avenue, the Thornton house, 1905, architect unknown; 1821 Monument Avenue, the Moncure house, 1913, W. Duncan Lee, architect. The Moncure house shows Lee's skill at using minimal detail to create a rich composition.*

ABOVE: *2307 Monument Avenue, 1916, W. Duncan Lee, architect. The MacLean house's simple ornament and buff brick echo Lee's Moncure house at 1821.*

RIGHT: *Living room, 1821 Monument Avenue.*

that the simple doorway, with its wrought bronze grille, was his finest ornamental work. Restraint and simplicity are characteristic only of the public face of the house. The rear elevation is open and light. The Taylor family has preserved the interior of the house beautifully. The garden room particularly contrasts with the severe street front. Along with John Russell Pope's Branch house and Baskervill and Lambert's McGuire house, the Taylor house represents a high point of design on the street.

Lee built nothing on the street between 1915 and 1922, but designed eight more houses after that. The most striking of these later houses are the residence and office of Dr. Henry A. Bullock at 2017–19 Monument Avenue and the Gus M. Schwarzschild house at 3114 Monument Avenue, both designed and built in 1925–27. The Bullock house, Lee's only foray into the design of townhouses, combined a doctor's office on the ground floor with his home above. Paired doors on the lower level and a Palladian window on the first floor directly express the organizational scheme of the house. The richly textured brickwork, slate roof, and entrance piers are all attractive and distinguished. For the Schwarzschild house Lee drew upon Bottomley's Golsan scheme of four bays and placed the entrance to one side. A richly detailed sun porch with a Palladian window scheme extends from the opposite side. By this time Lee was an accomplished scholar of the American colonial idiom, and his treatment of the robust entrance detail, the brickwork, and the massive chimney display this knowledge. Within a few years he would be working on one of Virginia's most famous mansions, Carter's Grove outside Williamsburg.

Marcellus Wright (1881–1962), who founded a prominent Richmond architectural firm that is still in business, designed the Christian Science Church, an apartment block, and four houses on Monument Avenue. His best-known works are the John Marshall Hotel and the Mosque, now the Landmark Theater, which he designed with Charles M. Robinson. Wright graduated from the University of Pennsylvania. He worked for Noland and Baskervill and for Charles Robinson before starting his own firm in 1912.[42] Wright's first house on Monument Avenue, the Nuckols house at number 1614, designed in 1912, recalls the work of Anderson or Huntt with its bold asymmetry. This house was an office-residence for Dr. M. E. Nuckols. Many American doctors had their offices in their homes in the early twentieth century, and the double function was a challenge for an architect. The facade of the Nuckols house included all the standard Richmond townhouse features, and Wright tried to resolve the imbalance with the central projecting dormer. His apartment house at 2923 Monument Avenue (1922) betrays the same interest in asymmetry, with the strong central porch offset by the pedimented entry to one side. Wright confronted the same compositional puzzles in his last house on the street, the Lee Paschall house at 2716 Monument Avenue, where three dormers are centered above a five-bay second floor and a four-bay first level.

William Leigh Carneal Jr. (1881–1958) and James Markham Ambler Johnston (1885–1974) ran one of the largest architectural firms in the city. They had been educated in engineering at Virginia Military Institute and Virginia Polytechnic Institute respectively, and that practical background found its outlet in a specialization with commercial and industrial architecture such as the Richmond Dairy of 1913, with its huge twin milk bottles, and the French Renaissance–style Colonial Theater of 1922. While their residential work was limited, they did design three houses and two apartment buildings for Monument Avenue. They de-

ABOVE: *The Taylor house, 2325 Monument Avenue, 1915, W. Duncan Lee, architect. Although the Taylor house is one of the largest homes on Monument Avenue, its simple forms and detailing give it a serene ambience.*

RIGHT: *Rear elevation, the Taylor house. The garden elevation also resembles an Italian palazzo.*

ABOVE LEFT: *Sunroom,
the Taylor house. The
house remains in the
Taylor family today. The
interior spaces are de-
signed in various styles,
surprising the visitor
who may have expected
the entire house to be
Mediterranean.*

ABOVE RIGHT: *Library,
the Taylor house. Many
of the house's ceilings are
lightly ornamented in
plaster.*

LEFT: *2017–19 Monument
Avenue, 1927, W. Duncan
Lee, architect. This building provided an office
on the first floor and a
residence upstairs for a
doctor. The Palladian
window in the living
room indicates the piano
nobile.*

ABOVE: *3114 Monument Avenue, 1927, W. Duncan Lee, architect. Lee began his work on Monument Avenue as the street was first being built up, and he continued west of the Boulevard with suburban designs like this one for the Schwarzschild house.*

RIGHT: *3142 Monument Avenue, 1923, W. Duncan Lee, architect. The Lewis house is another of Lee's Georgian designs along the avenue.*

Pond with fountain (above) and garden bench with pergola (left), 3142 Monument Avenue. The Lewis house has the remains of a garden designed by Charles Gillette, who worked with many respected architects to create both natural-looking gardens with azaleas and woodland spaces, and formal gardens with terraces and boxwood hedges.

RIGHT: *2605 Monument Avenue, 1926, W. Duncan Lee, architect. The Bryan house is simple in form and richly textured.*

BELOW: *2712 Monument Avenue, 1916, W. Duncan Lee, architect.*

HOUSES, STYLES, AND ARCHITECTS

TOP: *1612–24 Monument Avenue, with the Nuckols house (second from right), 1913, Marcellus Wright, architect, at number 1614. The Nuckols house served as a doctor's office as well as residence for its owner. It was Wright's first house on Monument Avenue.*

BOTTOM: *The Southampton Apartments, 2923 Monument Avenue, 1922, Marcellus Wright, architect. These apartments offer the avenue's typical stacked porches, but in the center of the facade.*

signed the Isaac and Mary Held house, 3201 Monument, which later became the residence of James Branch Cabell. A difficult pie-shaped lot, the front is eighty feet long while the width of the house is thirty-five feet at its deepest and eight feet at its narrowest. With great skill, Carneal and Johnston treated the long facade as a pair of peaked roof pavilions sheltering a recessed center and a long Ionic columned porch. At the narrow end, the architects used a Mansard roof.

Reflecting Carneal and Johnston's talents as institutional architects are the two sophisticated apartments they produced for Monument Avenue: the Stafford and the Brooke at numbers 2007 and 2215 respectively. The Stafford Apartments (1909) housed three families in three flats and fits in harmoniously with the surrounding row of houses. Carneal and Johnston loaded the Colonial Revival facade with rich ornament and a unique two-story portico-porch. The Georgian Revival Brooke Apartments building (1912) is larger and features a limestone basement floor that carries red brick upper floors with elaborate window detailing. The building was put up by W. Creed Davis, a land speculator and also a partner in a building supply company in which William Carneal was a partner.

HOUSES, STYLES, AND ARCHITECTS   217

Carneal and Johnston's most important design for the avenue, number 2312, for Henry S. Wallerstein, a real estate developer, is one of the street's real eye-catchers. Its unique style and its flashy red brick and white terra cotta trim make it stand out. Stylistically, the Wallerstein house has been called everything from Tudor to Gothic, but what the architects had in mind was a form of English architecture known as Jacobean, or the architecture of James I (reigned 1603–25), in which classical detail was grafted onto essentially medieval forms.[43] Buildings such as Hatfield House, in Hertfordshire (ca. 1611), served as models for twentieth-century American eclectic architects. The result is a plethora of ornament and a picturesque outline. Wallerstein got just that, a spectacular design with a large entrance porch pushed up to the street front, and an elaborate house with a variety of roof forms and dormers.

Possibly the most complex of the business and familial relationships along Monument Avenue was that of Carl and Max E. Ruehrmund, Charles Phillips, and Carl Lindner, who were all related as well as sometime business partners in architecture, real estate speculation, and building. The specialization of this family lay in apartments and more modest houses. The time span of their work stretches from 1906 to the late 1920s and hence shows

2035 Monument Avenue, 1920, Carneal and Johnston, architects. Carneal and Johnston's ability to shift from one style to another is underlined in this charming cottage, the Norvell house.

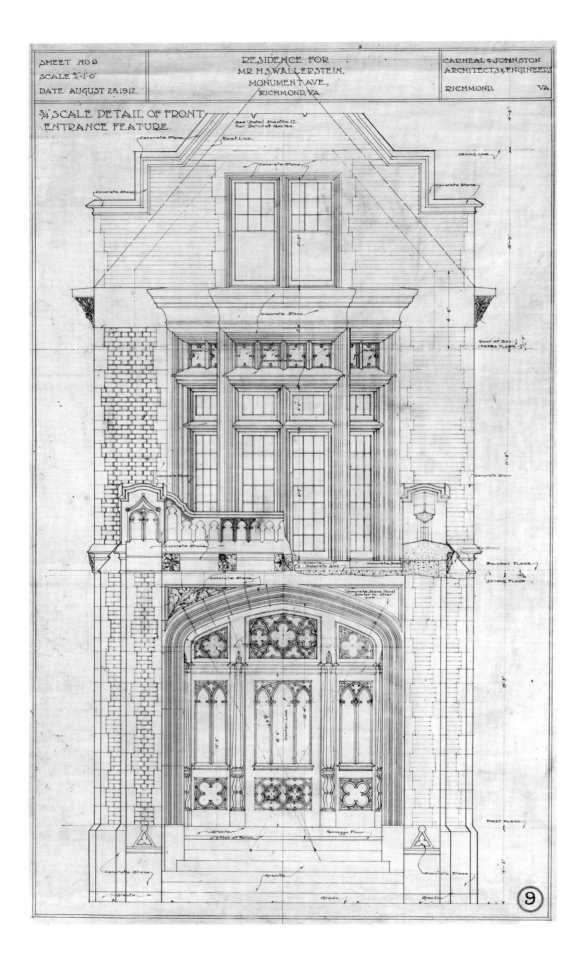

Elevation, 2312 Monument Avenue. (The Library of Virginia)

Library, 2312 Monument Avenue. The built-in bookcases survived the Wallerstein house's many years as a boarding house. (Valentine Museum)

the evolution from the late Victorian to the more academic approach and then to a new, though more restrained, picturesqueness.

Carl Ruehrmund (1855–1927), a German-born and -trained architect, arrived in Richmond in 1883 and designed numerous buildings throughout the city, including the six-story Shenandoah Apartments (1906) on Allen Avenue just north of the Lee Monument. The alternating square and three-sided bay windows of the Shenandoah may owe a debt to contemporary Chicago high-rise design. Carl Ruehrmund designed only one house on Monument Avenue, 1633, for Mrs. Otway Allen's sister, Jennie McDonald Wellford. Built in 1910, the house is a restrained example of the Colonial Revival, three stories high.

Carl's son, Max Ruehrmund (1891–1948), studied engineering at Virginia Military Institute and practiced with his father for three years, from 1916 to 1919, before taking over the firm. His finest buildings were the Anne-Frances Apartments at 2805 Monument and the Halifax Apartments at 3009, both built between 1919 and 1921. The Anne-Frances is among the most elegant buildings on the street, with its rusticated limestone base and vaguely French Renaissance detailing. The entrance porch is a hearty portico that serves as the base for two porches with exceptionally slender Corinthian columns. Max built a house for himself and his father at 3007 in 1920. A year later, he built the Majestic Apartments (later renamed the Halifax) next door at number 3009. The Majestic is a Colonial Revival building and makes use of columns to create a grand facade reminiscent of the popular version of Southern plantations, with their great porticos. Ruehrmund became more involved in managing his properties and largely dropped out of active architectural practice by the mid-1920s.

Max Ruehrmund's first cousin on his mother's side was Charles Phillips, who grew up

ABOVE: *The Shenandoah Apartments, Allen Avenue, 1906, Carl Ruehrmund, architect. In addition to the Shenandoah, Ruehrmund designed only one house on Monument, though his son, Max, made his own mark on the street west of the Boulevard.*

RIGHT: *1633 Monument Avenue, 1910, Carl Ruehrmund, architect. Ruehrmund designed this house for Otway Allen's sister-in-law, Jennie McDonald Wellford.*

ABOVE: *The Anne-Frances Apartments, 2805 Monument Avenue, 1920, Max Ruehrmund, architect. One of the most elegant buildings on Monument, the Anne-Frances helped define the apartments in the Sheppard section.*

LEFT: *The Halifax Apartments, 3009 Monument Avenue, 1921, Max Ruehrmund, architect. After his work on the Anne-Frances, Ruehrmund designed this handsome Colonial Revival apartment building.*

3007 Monument Avenue, 1920, Max Ruehrmund, architect. Ruehrmund designed this house for himself. In 1921 he built the Majestic Apartments —later renamed the Halifax Apartments— next door.

to become one of the most active real estate developers in Richmond in the 1920s. Carl Ruehrmund's sister Katherine married Maximilian Lindner, and their son Carl Max Lindner Sr. became an architect, too. Max Ruehrmund, Carl Lindner, and Charles Phillips were first cousins and were engaged in a complex series of architectural projects throughout the 1920s.[44]

Carl Max Lindner Sr. (1895–1973) worked for his uncle, Carl Ruehrmund, and attended the Virginia Mechanics Institute, a trade school in downtown Richmond. Lindner designed several impressive small stores on Grace Street in the Art Deco style.[45] His design for the Ritz Apartments on Grove Avenue is also modern. The building housing the Lord Fairfax Apartments (1923–24), 3101–15 Monument Avenue, is a simple truncated triangular shape, enlivened with a complex brick pattern, three entrance bays framed by richly carved limestone surrounds, and a heavy cornice. Stylistically, it reflects the new modernistic currents beginning to emanate from New York City. Next door to the Lord Fairfax, Lindner designed the row of cottages at 3117–31 in various popular styles of the period: Norman, Tudor, Cotswold, California Mission, and Colonial Revival. Lindner richly detailed each

ABOVE: *The Maury Monument, 1929, F. William Sievers, sculptor, and the Lord Fairfax Apartments, 1923, Carl Lindner, architect. The Lord Fairfax, built several years before the Maury Monument, is an elegant design on a potentially awkward lot.*

LEFT: *3117–33 Monument Avenue, 1928, Carl Lindner, architect. Lindner's skill as an architect was displayed all along the 3100 block—the Lord Fairfax Apartments filled one end and these picturesque cottages the other.*

house, with appropriately varied roof materials and walls of half-timbering, stucco, or brick.

In addition to those mentioned here, many other architects contributed to Monument Avenue. Although variations in training, approach, and skill existed among these different architects, they were united by a common vision for the street. Their designs, though not planned in unison or with any overall guidelines, contribute to the impression of harmony that makes Monument Avenue one of America's great streets.

INFLUENCE, DECLINE, AND REBIRTH

Influence

Monument Avenue thrived and captured Richmond's imagination in the first decades of the twentieth century. For many Richmonders it represented a coming of age, a triumph for the city. Ellen Glasgow caught this note of pride: when, in one of her novels, a businessman's report says, "Richmond was as progressive as Denver," his wife explains the reason, "There is not a street in the West that looks fresher or more beautiful than Monument Avenue. . . . It shows what the South can do when it tries."[1]

As a plan, Monument Avenue became a model that could be adapted to a variety of residential needs. While not every neighborhood could have a statue of its own, many subdivisions discovered the pleasures of a landscaped boulevard. Windsor Farms, a Richmond suburban development of the 1920s, incorporated some of the elements pioneered on Monument Avenue. Thomas C. Williams Jr. hired John Nolan and Allen J. Saville to create an exclusive suburban enclave with radial boulevards focusing on a central square. Architecturally, Windsor Farms followed Monument Avenue's lead with a mixture of the Tudorbethan and the red brick Georgian modes. The Carillon (1926–32), Virginia's memorial to the dead of World War I, by Cram and Ferguson of Boston in collaboration with Carneal, Johnston and Wright (Oscar P. Wright having been added as a partner in the firm of Carneal and Johnston), was intended as the formal focus of a residential development.

Several of Richmond's most attractive Monument Avenue–inspired neighborhoods were not grand at all. The Rosewood and Idlewood areas near Byrd Park and the Roseneath development at Monument contained smaller houses clustered along boulevards. Planted with trees that have matured, these more modest boulevard developments are intimate and charming. Developer/architects such as the Ruehrmund-Lindner group and the Davis Brothers democratized the boulevard form and made it available to a wide range of income groups.

Combining the grand architecture of Monument and the modest architecture of Roseneath are the comfortable upper- and middle-class areas of Richmond's north side. The lone monument over the grave of Confederate General A. P. Hill at Hermitage Road and

A clear line marks the western edge of dense development in this aerial view of Richmond from about 1930. Monument Avenue is delineated by the straight lines of trees, punctuated by the Lee Circle. (The Library of Virginia)

Laburnum Avenue became the centerpiece of a series of boulevards. Brook and Hermitage Roads and Laburnum, Wilmington, Palmyra, and Confederate Avenues formed spacious and handsome sites for homes ranging from mansions to modest cottages and bungalows. Throughout Richmond's pre–World War II neighborhoods, boulevards add distinction and character to what otherwise might have been ordinary subdivisions.

Decline

Most of the historic area of Monument Avenue had been built by the time the stock market crashed in 1929, so the lack of construction during the 1930s did not affect the continuity of the avenue. Some homeowners were devastated by the crash, however. Whitmell S. Forbes lost his empire and left his mansion at 3401 Monument Avenue.[2] Many other Monument Avenue residents also suffered but not as publicly. In spite of the hard times, Monument Avenue remained an affluent address throughout the 1930s.

The Great Depression undermined the architectural profession in Richmond in several ways and also brought into question many of the assumptions underlying developments such as Monument Avenue. The design of individual family houses was no longer the staple of an architect's practice. Architects seldom were offered the chance to plan expansively, to detail in fine materials, or to work in different architectural styles. William Bottomley and Duncan Lee faded from the architectural scene. Henry Baskervill turned to hospital construction: the Medical College of Virginia hospital of 1936 and 1941 was his firm's major work after the crash. Carneal and Johnston, their partnership now augmented by

Virginia War Memorial Carillon, 1922, Cram and Ferguson, architects, Carneal, Johnston and Wright, associate architects. Richmond continued erecting monuments other than those on Monument Avenue, and even planned the carillon as a memorial that would be the formal focus of a neighborhood.

Wright, had always been more of an institutional firm, and they turned almost exclusively to university work. The older generation was passing away. John Kevan Peebles and Finlay Forbes Ferguson died in 1934 and 1936 respectively. They were no longer designing houses, but their last work was, fittingly, the Virginia Museum of Fine Arts on the Boulevard. Simplicity, economy, and austerity were the demands of midcentury America, and these were qualities that had not played a role previously in the architecture of Monument Avenue.

The Maury Monument was being dedicated as John D. Rockefeller began his spectacular restoration of Colonial Williamsburg. When the first phase of Williamsburg's restoration and reconstruction was completed during the 1930s with the re-creations of the Capitol and Governor's Palace, the Colonial Revival style was again redefined with even more attention to archaeological accuracy. The comparative austerity and simplicity of Williamsburg's smaller houses were adapted by the restoration architects, Perry, Shaw and Hepburn

of Boston, as suburban house types and became the model for the tremendous suburban explosion that followed World War II.[3] Colonial Williamsburg also provided another post-war model: its Market Square became the prototype of innumerable shopping centers as the automobile became the new definer of urban form.

During the late 1940s and the 1950s, the few vacant lots left on Monument Avenue were filled in. Stylistically, the new buildings usually referred to the earlier Colonial Revival structures around them, but they seldom made a significant contribution to the street-scape. Stuart Circle Hospital added a wing in 1955–56. The larger houses that dominated the east end of the avenue began to seem too enormous for families that no longer had live-in staffs. The preference for an efficient, compact house plan, along with "family rooms," that came to dominate domestic architecture after World War II and the introduction of air-conditioning in the 1950s ended the spacious house plans of the first part of the century. The modest houses west of the Boulevard seemed more appealing as Richmond adapted to suburban ideals.

The 1950s and 1960s saw many of the larger single-family houses on the avenue trans-formed into apartment buildings, nursing homes, and doctors' offices. John Russell Pope's

ABOVE: *3309 Monument Avenue, 1950, architect unknown. Though the houses that filled in the empty lots in the 1940s and 1950s usually referred to the Colonial Revival style of the older houses, they seldom made a significant contribution to the street.*

LEFT: *3322 Monument Avenue, 1949, architect unknown. The postwar infill sometimes continued the apparent visual harmony of the avenue in scale, setback, and architectural details.*

Branch house became the headquarters for the United Way and later an insurance company, while Bottomley's Parrish house accommodated the American Lung Association. A nursing home occupied Duncan Lee's MacLean house. The transformations necessary for these business purposes appear kind compared to the more intrusive modifications needed for conversion to a rooming house or a doctor's office. Several of Claude K. Howell's houses suffered greatly in this regard. The Binswanger house at 2020 Monument had been divided into twelve to fifteen units before its rear kitchen wing burned in 1989. The Arts and Crafts–style Johnson house at 2023 Monument was subdivided into multiple units, and poor maintenance left it without a single functioning bathroom, while the rear of the building was in a state of collapse. At one time, before the house was rescued by its current owners, the half-timbering was painted. In some blocks, such at the 2300 block, the houses did remain largely in the hands of resident homeowners, but even there, at number 2307, a nursing home was installed until new owners restored the house in the 1970s.[4]

For ease of maintenance, suspended acoustical ceilings hid ornamental plaster cornices, and linoleum or wall-to-wall carpet covered parquet floors. A bathroom and closet were wedged into major rooms of many houses and still left enough room for a bed. At 2016, in 1955, a flat-roofed, steel-and-glass, single-story doctor's office was placed in the side yard next to a house built in 1915. It seemed that Monument Avenue, a street of oversized white elephants, had little future except to suffer decline and deterioration.

Luckily, much of this neglect was reversible, and architectural modernism caught on only in other parts of Richmond. It is often said that Richmond simply skipped modernism, but a quick glance downtown along the James River or in the suburbs indicates otherwise. Large corporations such as Reynolds Metals and Philip Morris erected fine monuments of modern architecture, but these had little effect on the city's older residential districts in the near west end.

In the 1960s most of the houses on Monument Avenue were only forty or fifty years old. The fine materials and craftsmanship of their construction ensured that they remained viable residential properties even with only sporadic maintenance. By 1960, property values on the street had plummeted, and one could buy a house of 6,000 square feet for $35,000 to $45,000. The 28,000-square-foot Branch house was offered for sale at a price of $100,000 in 1970. Fortunately there were some who recognized both a good house and a bargain.

Rebirth

Richmond's preservation community had formed early. The Association for the Preservation of Virginia Antiquities (APVA), established in 1889, had its first Richmond project in 1911, and in 1935 Mary Wingfield Scott, an architectural historian, persuaded some friends and relatives to join her in creating the William Byrd (Richmond) Branch of the APVA to concentrate on Richmond's historic structures. Scott's initiative in Richmond was in keeping with patterns elsewhere, as much of the American preservation movement has been led by women from the very beginning. Under the leadership of Scott, the Byrd Branch began by purchasing individual buildings, but its members realized that broader efforts were called for if they intended to preserve entire neighborhoods. In 1957 they created the His-

2016 Monument Avenue, 1955, Frederick Hyland, architect. The construction of this starkly modern, prosaic office building proved to be an inspiration for preservationists, who turned their attention to Monument Avenue.

toric Richmond Foundation to focus on the preservation of the neighborhood around St. John's Church in the area known as Church Hill. The APVA and the Historic Richmond Foundation lobbied the City of Richmond to create a special zoning designation to be called Old and Historic Districts and institute design controls for them. The area around St. John's Church on Church Hill was named the first such district in 1957, and Monument Avenue became the second major district in 1971. With the passage of the National Historic Preservation Act in 1966, states began surveying and registering significant properties and districts. Monument Avenue became one of the first districts entered on the National Register of Historic Places in 1969, and in 1998 it was designated a National Historic Landmark.

Various civic plans for Monument Avenue were floated during the 1960s, with seemingly conflicting goals. As more Richmonders moved to the suburbs, commuters, with the blessing of the city's traffic engineers, used Monument as a speedway to reach downtown offices. Some planners wanted to create a more efficient thoroughfare; widening the street, cutting down trees, and even moving monuments to spread them further apart and provide a smoother traffic flow were all proposed. Other plans seemed to honor the avenue's past. A *Richmond News Leader* article from 1965 detailed the dreams of city planners to move the Stuart Monument, to move the Davis Monument and add a reflecting pool in front of it, and to add as many as seven more monuments to the length of the avenue.[5]

A dramatic confrontation between an asphalt machine and Monument Avenue residents led by Helen Marie Taylor, owner of the Taylor house at 2325 Monument Avenue, in September of 1968 brought the issue of Monument Avenue's future to a head. Over the years a variety of paving materials, including brick, granite, and asphalt, had been laid on the street. In front of the Taylor home, a type of "Belgian" or "Hastings" paving block, which

Richmond mayor Timothy M. Kaine addressed celebrants on the occasion of Monument Avenue's being designated a National Historic Landmark in 1999.

has a distinctive visual pattern and hums when driven on, had been installed.[6] The City of Richmond had been covering or removing block paving in the city for years to avoid having to maintain it and to accommodate automobile traffic. Additionally, rumors were flying that the city intended to widen the avenue and remove the trees in the median. When a crew from the Department of Public Works appeared on the 2300 block, Taylor blocked their asphalt machine, threatening to lie down in the street to save the historic paving.

The confrontation generated a huge amount of publicity and focused public attention on the street. Taylor, and others who worked quietly with city officials, won the contest with the Department of Public Works and forced the city to quit treating the avenue as a speedway.[7] During the next decade the City of Richmond responded to citizens' interests with major efforts, restoring the paving, installing new sidewalks, and cleaning the statues. At the same time, protests of a different sort began to emerge, as the statues became targets for vandals who would paint them, sometimes tagging them as "racist."

Civic organizations joined preservation groups to help revitalize the area at an early date. In 1941, the West Avenue Improvement Society, the first neighborhood organization in Richmond, was founded. Fan District residents established the Fan District Association in 1961. These groups both promoted their neighborhoods and fought poor-quality renovations. Monument Avenue is included in the Fan District, but the avenue's residents established their own organization, the Monument Avenue Preservation Society (MAPS), in the

late 1960s to focus specifically on the street. These civic organizations became powerful forces for preservation. In 1976 they sponsored the creation of the Historic Monument Avenue and Fan District Foundation, which has played a role in saving badly deteriorated houses and sponsoring educational activities.

As a result of these organizations' work, the city rezoned the entire district from one of multifamily apartments to one of single-family attached houses in the early 1970s. This put an end to the subdividing of houses into apartments and adult homes. The civic groups also sponsored events focusing attention on the beauty and history of the area and its houses. Garden and house tours and Easter parades were typical of these efforts.

Garden and house tours have played a significant role in promoting preservation and rehabilitation in Richmond. The Garden Club of Virginia began springtime tours of historic Virginia gardens in 1927 to raise money for its preservation projects. By midcentury these garden tours were major tourist events. The Fan District Association established a Christmas house tour to raise money and promote the neighborhood, and a Fan District or Monument Avenue tour has been a recurring element in the spring Garden Week tours for two decades. These tours have been accompanied by lectures and exhibits that increase public awareness of the street, and they sometimes focus on the work of particular architects, such as William Lawrence Bottomley or Duncan Lee, and highlight a recent showplace restoration.

City engineers pointed out problems with the aging pavement on Monument Avenue for newspaper reporters in the 1960s. Apart from structural problems, the street hummed when cars drove down it; but residents defended the old pavers, citing history and fearing that their replacement could lead to a widening of the busy street. (Valentine Museum)

The inaugural Easter Parade, sponsored by the Monument Avenue Preservation Society in 1973, brought thousands of people to celebrate on Monument Avenue, beginning a tradition that continues today. (Courtesy Zayde Dotts)

Staid and proper Monument Avenue was the site for the first modern street fair held in Richmond, the Easter Parade. For the event, sponsored by MAPS, a crowd estimated at several thousand arrived on Easter Sunday afternoon in 1973 just to wander up and down the street. Of different backgrounds, races, and sexual preferences, the participants had a good time in the shadow of the statues of Confederate officers. Overdressed, underdressed, in costume, in leather, and in drag, they made that year's parade and other early events fun and liberating.

By the 1980s Monument Avenue had become quite different from the place it had been thirty years earlier. At the eastern end, in response to the growth of nearby Virginia Commonwealth University, many houses were still cut up into apartments. And of course the original apartment houses still stood on the avenue. But as one moved west from Stuart Circle, increasingly the majority of buildings were restored single-family homes. In contrast to many of the other grand avenues of turn-of-the-century America, Monument Avenue was still a residential street and a desired address.

Richmond resumed erecting monumental sculptures in the later decades of the century. In 1966, Salvador Dali discussed designing a monument to Sally Tompkins, a famous Confederate nurse who ran a hospital in Richmond, to be placed on the avenue. Tompkins was chosen as a representative of all the women of the Confederacy. Several prominent Richmonders were involved in the effort, but it never progressed to the fund-raising phase. Whether Dali thought this was a serious commission or an opportunity for a surrealist joke is not clear. The only illustration of what Dali had in mind for the work is a sketch by a Richmond commercial artist based on a telephone description; it shows Tompkins as a

ABOVE: *Ventures such as Christmas house tours, Garden Week, and the 1999 Richmond Symphony Decorator House at 2312 Monument, pictured here, have drawn attention to the beautiful restorations and renovations done on the avenue and encourage more homeowners to take on renewal projects. This view records the library at the Wallerstein house, which is also pictured in Chapter 4.*

LEFT: *This sketch represents one of Salvador Dali's 1966 concepts for a proposed monument to Captain Sally Tompkins on Monument Avenue. Dali described his idea over the phone to a Richmond artist, who then sketched this undeniably surreal twist on images of St. George and the Dragon. In Dali's version, Captain Tompkins attacks a germ, in the form of a dragon, on a stylized petri dish balanced on the tip of a finger. (Virginia Historical Society)*

RIGHT: *Easter, 1997.*

BELOW LEFT:
Easter, 1998.

BELOW RIGHT:
Easter, 1998.

INFLUENCE, DECLINE, AND REBIRTH

ABOVE: *The Richmond Marathon draws a crowd on Monument Avenue every year. Here runners pass the Davis Monument in 1996.*

LEFT: *2610 Monument Avenue, 1909, architect unknown. Holiday carolers enjoy visiting Monument Avenue at Christmas time when the decorations on the houses almost outshine the monuments.*

INFLUENCE, DECLINE, AND REBIRTH

latter-day St. George, slaying a germ-dragon atop a pedestal composed of a petri dish balanced on a finger. Not unexpectedly, Dali's proposal did not resonate in Richmond's philanthropic quarters, and the proposal is little more than a footnote to the history of the street.[8]

Elsewhere, a monument to African American dancer Bill "Bojangles" Robinson, a native Richmonder, was placed in the Jackson Ward area in 1973. Monuments to the ordinary working people who helped to make Richmond, such as Paul DiPasquale's *The Headman*, erected on an island in the James to commemorate the bateaumen who navigated the canal, began to appear in the 1980s.

During the discussions surrounding the Ashe Monument, Richmonders echoed the questions that had been heard about all of the monuments over the last century, citing complaints about the competition, or lack thereof, the quality of the sculpture, and the choice of sites. Was Monument Avenue a shrine to Confederate leaders, or a street honoring heroes distinguished for achievements in the face of adversity? The avenue, which was begun as an attempt to lead Richmond visually and economically into the future, had anchored the city firmly in the past in many people's eyes. Placing Arthur Ashe's statue on Monument broadened the street's appeal and constituency. Monument Avenue still provides the city's parade ground, its social arena, and its most spectacular residential boulevard, but now it also speaks for all the citizens of Richmond by honoring heroes who can be admired by its entire citizenry.

Certainly Otway Allen never anticipated that the street would be lined with large apartment houses. He planned for one statue—Lee. The street expanded and evolved. The Ashe Monument is the most recent step in the avenue's evolution. If the Lee Monument teaches about Richmond in the 1890s, the Ashe Monument does the same for the 1990s.

Monument Avenue still arouses passion and commitment. The mere thought of placing Arthur Ashe on Monument Avenue generated national attention. That level of concern is what inspires confrontations with asphalt machines and what brings hundreds of area residents to city council meetings to support or oppose proposals for the street. It impels families to undertake massive reconstruction and restoration projects, as well as the tedious and mundane tasks of everyday maintenance.

The Ashe debate confirmed the fact that Monument Avenue is still healthy, still growing, still evolving. Monument Avenue has not just maintained itself: its long-standing role as a residential neighborhood, as a site for civic celebrations, as a tribute to the great, and as a symbol of Richmond has not diminished—and will continue throughout its second century.

CONCLUSION

Monument Avenue gives an impression of unity, an image of orderly growth and architectural harmony. In reality, this order and harmony were created by a series of individual decisions that were not foreseen during the initial planning. Several factors contribute to this unusual combination of accord and variety.

The overall design of the street is simple, strong, and memorable. The basic plan, a central median with two lines of trees dividing four lanes of traffic, is unexceptional. The physical presence of the long, straight street and the canopy of trees provides an irresistible order that goes unchallenged by the buildings. Only the series of statues is on the main axis. They punctuate the composition, establishing a distinctive image of the street. The actual pavement, the landscaping, and the statues provide such a strong unifying framework for the avenue that individual buildings do not disrupt the overall image. The buildings within the historic district developed without consistent design covenants, and they include a rich mix of architectural styles. They remain compatible, nonetheless, because of the use of similar materials, cornice lines, setbacks, orientation, and other repetitive visual devices in their design and construction.

A clear hierarchical scheme, which places the houses as background structures, providing an appropriate setting for the monuments, reinforces the overall impression. Even the churches, major monumental buildings, do not disrupt the unity of the street. Each building and structure plays its assigned role.

While the overall plan is clear and strong, it is not obsessive. Nonconforming elements interrupt the pattern without distracting from the whole. Several streets do not intersect with the neighboring grid well, and thus accidental, nonaxial elements disrupt the regular aspect of the plan.

The addition of later statues has allowed the street to change. Otway Allen initially thought of his development as Lee Place—a static, cross-shaped space with a single focus, the Lee Monument. Before Allen's death in 1911, Stuart and Davis had joined Lee, and the avenue had been greatly extended. While the next honoree added to the street, Jackson, was clearly another Confederate hero, the one who followed, Maury, was only incidentally a Confederate. Ashe added a completely different set of interpretations to the street. As it stretched well into the countryside, Monument Avenue had the potential for many more monuments, and thus the potential to evolve.

ABOVE: *Aerial view of the north side of the 1800 block, Monument Avenue.*

RIGHT: *The avenue looked straight and fresh in 1907. (Valentine Museum)*

By 1926, *most of the lots at the east end of the avenue were filled, and the trees had matured. (Valentine Museum)*

The Washington Monument and the Statue of Liberty sit in isolation, well apart from the bustle and activities of the cities they embellish. Monument Avenue is fully integrated into Richmond's day-to-day life. The avenue is a clustering of statues *and* a residential neighborhood. To be successful the avenue's developers needed to inspire two hundred families to build impressive houses. Individual families not only participated in creating the street, they were essential to the street's success. The famous early photographs of the Lee Monument sitting in isolation, looking forlorn and stranded, illustrate the necessity of the residential setting. Without the houses, the statues are lost, their impact much diminished. The houses and the statues have a symbiotic relationship, mutually enhancing each other.

Monument Avenue is a private enterprise, created by individual developers and families. The developers took a risk. Not only did they succeed, the street has been able to attract new residents who were willing to invest in it and cherish the houses. The Jenkins, Taylor, and Wortham families alone, at the beginning of the twenty-first century, lived in houses built for their families. Every other house on the avenue has changed hands.

Monument Avenue has often been regarded as either hopelessly out of date or an amusing curiosity. It is everything city planners regarded for years as being undesirable in the modern city. Monument Avenue has a mixture of building types, and houses persons of greatly varied income levels. The sculptures are impediments to the easy flow of traffic, and traffic itself is unwelcome in residential areas. The population density of the area appalled city planners and was regarded as a feature that condemned the neighborhood to deterio-

Monument Avenue is a symbol and a tourist attraction, but it is also a neighborhood.

ration into slum condition. But the street has thrived. It is as well preserved as any century-old neighborhood in Virginia. It is a living street in a living neighborhood. Its ability to attract new residents, and, indeed, new monuments, testifies to its success. Monument Avenue is preserved by the vigor and energy of its residents and other citizens of Richmond.

The concept of a street of monuments dedicated to the men who lost a war was an unlikely formula for success, but succeed it did. It is equally improbable that at the end of a century dedicated to efficiency and technology, the "white elephant" houses that stretch for almost two miles would retain their appeal, but they do.

Monument Avenue is a beautiful street. It is a pleasure to drive down it, jog in the median, or walk on the sidewalk. It is orderly but not rigid, simple but not dull. It can accommodate the residents of small apartments and large mansions, students and millionaires, Arthur Ashe and Robert E. Lee. Built to reflect the hopes and attitudes of 1890 Richmond, it survives because it has adapted to the very different needs and changed worldview of Richmonders at the turn of the twenty-first century.

APPENDIX
THE BUILDINGS OF MONUMENT AVENUE

STREET ADDRESS	DATE	ORIGINAL OWNER	ARCHITECT/BUILDER
West Franklin St.			
1201 (now 1205)	1913	St. James's Episcopal Church	Noland & Baskervill
1205 (was 1201)	1889	Robert W. Powers	M. J. Dimmock
1206	1926	The Rosa Apartments, W. D. Selden	Max E. Ruehrmund
1207	1926	The Merlin Apartments	
1208 (and 1208A)	1925	Mrs. Louise B. Page & Mrs. Pattie B. Augustine	
1209 (was 1207?)	1913	Dr. W. Lowndes Peple	Marcellus Wright
1211	1914	Stafford H. Parker	
1212	1922	Edward L. Word	
1213 (was 1209?)	1913	Philip A. Fore	
1214–16	1926	The Gill Apartments, Max E. Ruehrmund	Max E. Ruehrmund
1215	1923	Lee Fergusson	
1217	1922	Samuel S. Dear	
1218	1926	Heath Lorton	
1219 (was 1215)	1900	Langbourne M. Williams	
1220	1925	Mrs. P. Armistead McCarty	Otis K. Asbury
1222	1922	Dr. Clifton M. Miller	
Stuart Circle			
413	1913	Stuart Circle Hospital	Charles M. Robinson
501		Richmond College president's house, Bennett Puryear	
503–7	1921, 1926–28	St. John's United Church of Christ	Lindner & Rowlett

Monument Avenue

STREET ADDRESS	DATE	ORIGINAL OWNER	ARCHITECT/BUILDER
1600	1924–25	Stuart Court Apartments	William L. Bottomley
1601	1894	Otway Warwick	
1603	1910	First English Lutheran Church	Charles M. Robinson
1605	1954	Scherer Building	
1611	1911	Dr. Edward J. Mosely Jr.	
1612	1910	Mrs. Ada Strause	D. Wiley Anderson
1614	1913	Dr. Marvin E. Nuckols	Marcellus Wright
1616	1903	Langhorne Putney	
1617 (was 1615)	1922	Helen Baker & Nadine Ward	H. Carl Messerschmidt
1618	1912	Isaac Lichtenstein	C. W. Davis & Brother
1619	1918	Collegiate School for Girls, Helen Baker	H. Carl Messerschmidt
1620	1903	Charles Cohen	
1622	1907	Emanuel & Rosa Belle Raab	
1624	1907	Isaac Hutzler	
1626	1903	Jacob Coleman	
1627	1920	Grace Covenant Presbyterian Church	Peebles & Ferguson
1628	1907	Roland D. Harlow	
1630–32	1926	E. D. Taylor (apts.)	
1631	1911	Mrs. Otway Allen (Mary McDonald Allen)	Scarborough & Howell
1633	1910	B. Randolph Wellford	Carl Ruehrmund
1634 (was 1632)	1903	Leon L. Strause	
1635	1928	Dr. David M. Mann	Peebles & Ferguson
1637 (was 1633)	1925	Elmslie G. Higginbotham	W. H. Pringle
1643	1910	John G. Farland	Scarborough & Howell

North Allen

STREET ADDRESS	DATE	ORIGINAL OWNER	ARCHITECT/BUILDER
413	1921	Randolph Watkins	

Monument Avenue

STREET ADDRESS	DATE	ORIGINAL OWNER	ARCHITECT/BUILDER
1800	1931	Robert M. Jeffress	William L. Bottomley
1805	1950	Lee Medical Building, Franklin A. Trice	
1808 (was 1800)	1926	Mrs. Martha A. Wise	Isaac T. Skinner
1810	1908	Julien H. Hill	
1811	1904	George J. Freedley	
1812	1905	Louis W. Pizzini	Claude K. Howell
1815	1905	O. Herbert Funsten	Claude K. Howell
1816	1908	Mrs. Carrie L. Waddey	
1817	1905	Bayard H. Ellington	

STREET ADDRESS	DATE	ORIGINAL OWNER	ARCHITECT/BUILDER
1819	1905	Robert G. Thornton & James Lewis Anderson	
1820	1907	Garrett B. Wall	
1821	1913	James A. Moncure	W. Duncan Lee
1822	1906	Edward M. Hoadley	Claude K. Howell
1824	1905	Isaac Thalhimer	
1825	1907	James B. Elam	
1826	1907	Joseph H. Estes	
1828	1907	Williamson Talley	Claude K. Howell
1830	1913	Henry Clarke	W. Duncan Lee
1831	1905	H. H. George Sr. & Jr.	Albert F. Huntt
1832	1907	William J. Whitehurst	Noland & Baskervill
1834	1908	Charles R. Guy	
1835	1905	Frederick Phillips	
1837	1908	Thomas Tunstall Adams	D. Wiley Anderson
1839	1908	Luther H. Jenkins	M. J. Dimmock & W. Duncan Lee
1840	1905	Bertha Binswanger	
1842	1902	George E. Guvernator	
2000	1902	John S. Harwood	
2001	1907	Henry G. Taylor Sr. & Jr.	
2003	1907	Samuel Bachrach	Noland & Baskervill
2004–6	1904	Oliver J. & Lucile R. Sands & Austin H. & Susan M. Burr	
2005	1904	Dr. H. Cabell Tabb	
2007	1909	The Stafford Apartments	Carneal & Johnston
2008	1906	Walter W. Marston	Claude K. Howell
2009	1919	Harvey C. Brown	
2010	1905	Leroy B. Stern	
2012	1908	Alphonso W. Bennett	Scarborough & Howell
2013	1905	David C. Richardson	
2015	1915	Joseph E. Sorg	Albert F. Huntt
2016	1955	Dr. S. Elmer Bear	Frederick Hyland
2017–19 (was 2019)	1927	Dr. Henry A. Bullock	W. Duncan Lee
2018	1915	The Lawrence Apartments, Mrs. Lawrence Sycle	L. C. Jenkins
2020	1906	Wirt A. Chesterman	Noland & Baskervill
2021	1908	Dr. H. Ward Randolph & Henry P. Randolph	
2022	1909	Elmslie G. Higginbotham	
2023	1908	Laura H. Johnson	Claude K. Howell
2024	1910	James F. Walsh	D. Wiley Anderson
2025	1922	Milton & Irving Straus & Joseph M. Rosenbaum	
2028	1909	Dr. H. Cabell Tabb	
2030	1907	Emanuel B. Ullman	
2031	1913	George F. Jones	Albert F. Huntt

STREET ADDRESS	DATE	ORIGINAL OWNER	ARCHITECT/BUILDER
2032	1911	Dr. Alex Bear	
2034	1907	Mrs. Elizabeth B. Jones	
2035	1920	M. Lee Norvell	Carneal & Johnston
2036	1915	E. & Isaac Hutzler	Asbury & Whitehurst
2037	1911	John T. Wilson	John Kevan Peebles
2038	1905	Samuel B. Dunstan	
2039	1908	Dr. Richard C. Walden	Albert F. Huntt
2200	1909	R. Henry Harwood	Scarborough & Howell
2201	1931	First Church of Christ Scientist	Marcellus Wright
2204	1909	Francis D. Barksdale	Albert F. Huntt
2205–7	1915	Harvey C. Brown	Isaac T. Skinner
2206	1910	John Bagby	Charles K. Bryant
2208 (was 2206)	1910	Emanuel H. Gunst	A. G. Higginbotham
2209	1910	Harvey C. Brown	
2211	1910	Harvey C. Brown	
2213	1909	Samuel Bendheim	Albert F. Huntt
2215 (was 2217)	1912	The Brooke Apartments, W. Creed Davis	Carneal & Johnston
2216	1910	Alphonso W. Bennett	Scarborough & Howell
2217 (and 2217A)	1917	Harvey C. Brown	Isaac T. Skinner
2218	1911	Leroy S. Cohen	Scarborough & Howell
2219	1918	Harvey C. Brown	Isaac T. Skinner
2220	1908	Harry S. Binswanger	Claude K. Howell
2221	1918	Harvey C. Brown	Isaac T. Skinner
2222	1908	Harry S. Binswanger	D. Wiley Anderson
2223	1918	Harvey C. Brown	Isaac T. Skinner
2225	1916	Harvey C. Brown	Isaac T. Skinner
2226 (was 2224)	1905	Philip C. Schloss & Frederick C. Brauer	
2227	1913	Harvey C. Brown	Isaac T. Skinner
2229	1913	Harvey C. Brown	Isaac T. Skinner
2230	1914	Moses I. Binswanger	D. Wiley Anderson
2231	1910	Harvey C. Brown	
2233	1910	Harvey C. Brown	
2234	1915	Charles B. Richardson	Asbury & Whitehurst
2235	1924–25	Rixey Court Apartments, Mrs. E. Hawes Lipscomb	Bascom Rowlett
2236	1910	The Addison Apartments	W. Leigh Carneal Jr.
2300	1910	Clifford Smith	Albert F. Huntt
2301	1925	Mary T. Wortham	William L. Bottomley
2304 (was 2302)	1926	Dr. Stuart McGuire	Baskervill & Lambert
2306	1914	Edgar R. Lafferty	Albert F. Huntt
2307	1916	Dr. H. Stuart MacLean	W. Duncan Lee
2309	1917	H. Logan Golsan	William L. Bottomley
2312	1915	Henry S. Wallerstein	Carneal & Johnston
2314	1915	James J. Pollard	W. Duncan Lee

STREET ADDRESS	DATE	ORIGINAL OWNER	ARCHITECT/BUILDER
2315	1924	J. Scott Parrish	William L. Bottomley
2319 (was 2321?)	1926	Dr. H. Stuart MacLean	Merrill C. Lee and Clifton Lee
2320	1927	Mrs. Maria A. Cary	William L. Bottomley
2324	1914	John S. Munce	Marcellus Wright, altered 1929 by Baskervill & Lambert
2325	1915	Jaquelin P. Taylor	W. Duncan Lee
2326	1914	Llewellyn W. McVeigh	
2327	1913	Lewis H. Blair	Walter Blair
2330	1913	Malcolm G. Bruce	Charles K. Bryant
2336	1913	Thomas A. Smyth	W. Duncan Lee
2338	1909	Thomas A. Smyth	Scarborough & Howell
2340	1910	Abraham L. McClellan	Scarborough & Howell
2500	1913	Frank D. Beveridge	Albert F. Huntt
2501	1917–19	John Kerr Branch	John Russell Pope
2502	1926	Henry S. Raab	Otis K. Asbury
2504	1914	William C. Camp	Asbury & Whitehurst
2510	1918	Kenilworth Apartments, Oscar Hooker	Albert F. Huntt, Bascom J. Rowlett, assoc.
2512	1917	Stratford Court Apartments, Oscar Hooker	Albert F. Huntt, Bascom J. Rowlett, assoc.
2514	1911	Joseph Weinstein	Carneal & Johnston
2516	1911	Hill Montague	D. Wiley Anderson
2600	1916	Clifford Smith	W. Duncan Lee
2601	1926	Mrs. Robert G. Cabell	William L. Bottomley
2602–6	1923	Belvin Apartments	Davis Brothers, Inc.
2605	1926	Mrs. Jonathan Bryan	W. Duncan Lee
2607	1926	Miss Julia B. Andrews & William B. Andrews	Otis K. Asbury
2608	1913	Arthur Levy	D. Wiley Anderson
2609	1925	Malcolm W. & Sallie S. Perkins	Baskervill & Lambert
2610	1909	Charles E. Straus & Allyn C. Straus	
2614	1912	James K. Dunlop	Albert F. Huntt
2616	1914	The Westover, E. D. Hobbs	E. D. Hobbs
2625	1915	T. Garnett Tabb	Marcus Hallett
2700	1908	Moses L. Hofheimer	William C. West
2702	1910	Edward N. Calisch	Charles K. Bryant
2704	1912	William J. Whitehurst	Asbury & Whitehurst
2708	1914	Arthur L. Straus	D. Wiley Anderson
2709	1929	First Baptist Church	Herbert L. Cain
2710	1914	William H. Schwarzschild	D. Wiley Anderson
2712	1916	John J. Ballou Jr.	W. Duncan Lee

STREET ADDRESS	DATE	ORIGINAL OWNER	ARCHITECT/BUILDER
2714	1929	Anna B. Boykin & Ellen T. Boykin	William L. Bottomley
2716	1926	Lee Paschall	Marcellus Wright
2800	1917	The Monument Apartments	E. D. Hobbs
2805	1920	The Anne-Frances Apartments, Columbus K. Lassiter	Max E. Ruehrmund
2806	1919	The Jackson Apartments	
2810 (was 2808)	1919	The Greenwood Apartments, Davis Brothers, Inc.	Davis Brothers, Inc.
2812 (was 2810)	1919	The Seminole Apartments, Davis Brothers, Inc.	Davis Brothers, Inc.
2816	1925	W. E. Purcell Jr.	W. E. Purcell Jr.
2820	1924	Davis Brothers, Inc.	Davis Brothers, Inc.
2822	1924	Davis Brothers, Inc.	Davis Brothers, Inc.
2824	1924	Davis Brothers, Inc.	Davis Brothers, Inc.
2826 (was 2910)	1919	The Versailles Apartments, Robert Powell	Max E. Ruehrmund
2828	1912	The Rosemary Apartments	Carneal & Johnston
2830	1928	Rosa B. Hexter	W. Duncan Lee
2832–34	1926	The Montclair Apartments, M. R. Palmore	Bascom J. Rowlett
2900 (was 3000)	1922	The Flavius Apartments	W. E. Purcell Jr.
2902–4 (was 3004–8)	1921	Sulgrave Manor Apartments, Meyer Greentree	Davis Brothers, Inc.
2903	1916	The Galt Apartments	Davis Brothers, Inc.
2905	1916	Asher & Nathan Simon & Leon M. Nelson	W. Duncan Lee
2906 (was 3012–14)	1914	The Meredith Apartments	D. Wiley Anderson
2907	1960	Lacy Jeffries	
2910 (was 3016)	1913	Samuel G. Meredith	
2911	1916	Carter B. Snow	Carneal & Johnston
2914	1926	Mrs. Rosa L. Bruner	F. B. Walker
2915	1921	Edgar Allen Jr.	Otis K. Asbury
2916 (was 3018)	1925	Flavius B. Walker	F. B. Walker
2917	1921	Edgar Allen Jr.	Otis K. Asbury
2923–25	1922	The Southampton Apartments, Robert M. Bryant	Marcellus Wright
3000–3002	1927	O. J. E. Gray (apts.)	F. B. Walker
3001	1919	W. Creed Davis & E. Leonard Delaney	
3004 (was 3004–6)	1927	Maury Apartments	W. E. Purcell Jr.
3005	1917	The Ardelle Apartments	Davis Brothers, Inc.
3006	1927	Charles H. Phillips	Lindner & Phillips
3007	1920	Max E. Ruehrmund, Carl A. Ruehrmund, & Charles R. Ruehrmund	Max E. Ruehrmund

STREET ADDRESS	DATE	ORIGINAL OWNER	ARCHITECT/BUILDER
3009 (was 3009–11)	1921	The Halifax Apartments (was the Majestic Apartments)	Max E. Ruehrmund
3011	1924	Steadman S. Sloan	
3012	1927	C. L. Massie (apts.)	Bascom J. Rowlett
3013	1924	Manley L. Hubbard	
3015	1921	Joseph Kass	Max E. Ruehrmund
3019	1961	Mrs. Harriet M. Moore	
3021 (was 3023)	1922	William B. Nelson & Howell R. Weisiger	R. M. Anderson & Co.
3025	1954	Abbey Court Apartments, Nathan & Bernard Webber	
3029 (was 3035–37)	1926	The Frankmont Apartments	Davis Brothers, Inc.
3039	1912	Thomas H. E. O'Keefe	
3100	1926	Merrill E. Raab	W. Duncan Lee
3101–15	1923	Lord Fairfax Apartments, Willis Co., Inc. [Norfolk?]	Lindner & Phillips
3102	1931	Irving & Elsie Greentree	Carl Lindner
3104	1928	Harold E. Calisch	Davis Brothers, Inc.
3114	1927	Gus M. Schwarzschild	W. Duncan Lee
3117 (was 3109)	1928	B. Sidney & A. James	Carl Lindner
3119 (was 3111)	1928	Harry F. Byrd	Carl Lindner
3121 (was 3113)	1928	Melville H. Wells	Carl Lindner
3123 (was 3115)	1928	Ernest W. Lemay	Carl Lindner
3125 (was 3117)	1928	C. Custer Robinson	Carl Lindner
3127 (was 3119)	1928	William A. Crowder	Carl Lindner
3129 (was 3121)	1928	Mrs. Joseph C. Herbert	Carl Lindner
3131 (was 3123)	1928	Channing F. MacNeil	Carl Lindner
3133 (was 3125)	1928	Herman F. McDaniel	Carl Lindner
3142	1923	Mrs. J. E. Lewis	W. Duncan Lee
3170	1922	M. McGregor Anderson	W. Duncan Lee
3200	1923	Mrs. Robert F. Sycle	W. Duncan Lee
3201	1911	Mary & Isaac Held	Carneal & Johnston
3202	1926	Real Estate Holding Corp.	Carl Lindner
3203	1918	E. Craig Pelouze	
3205	1919	Hugh G. Russell & Richard C. Walden	
3206 (was 3204)	1927	Arthur L. Straus	Otis K. Asbury
3207	1919	H. Vance Godbold	
3208	1928	Charles H. Phillips	
3209	1922	Charles Rose	R. M. Anderson & Co.
3212	1922	Jonathan H. Frischkorn	G. Herbert French
3213	1964	Mr. & Mrs. R. P. Howell	
3215 (was 3211)	1920	Harry D. Lipford	Davis Brothers, Inc.
3216 (was 3220)	1925	Misses Van Vort	
3217 (was 3213)	1920	Walter R. Taylor	Davis Brothers, Inc.
3218	1928	Charles H. Phillips	

STREET ADDRESS	DATE	ORIGINAL OWNER	ARCHITECT/BUILDER
3219 (was 3215)	1920	Harry D. Lipford	Davis Brothers, Inc.
3220	1926	Charles Greenebaum	Bascom J. Rowlett
3221 (was 3217)	1920	Samuel W. Morris	Davis Brothers, Inc.
3223 (was 3219)	1924	G. J. Jackson	Davis Brothers, Inc.
3224	1928	Nannie E. Willingham & Edward V. Willingham	
3225 (was 3221)	1924	E. I. Parrish	Davis Brothers, Inc.
3300	1929	Charles H. Phillips	Carl Lindner
3301	1921	Mrs. Ora E. Garner	Otis K. Asbury
3302	1929	Charles H. Phillips	Carl Lindner
3303	1925	Hon. H. Lester Hooker	Davis Brothers, Inc.
3304	1959	Amy K. O'Flaherty	
3305 (duplex)	1963	Harry Stein	
3306	1922	P. Albert Smith	
3309 (duplex)	1950	Mrs. Myrtis W. Blackburn	
3310	1936	Mr. & Mrs. Charles E. Straus	A. L. Kidwell
3312	1928	William W. LaPrade	A. W. Harman
3314 (duplex)	1953	Bent? M. Saslaw	
3317	1922	Warren M. Goddard	Davis Brothers, Inc.
3318	1930	Mrs. Nancy Allen Cann & Lawrence B. Cann	
3319 (duplex)	1947	Lee A. Whitlock & Keene Marks	
3322	1949	Julius Novick	
3324 (duplex)	1940	H. C. & F. W. Brauer	
3401	1914	Whitmell S. Forbes	

Note: The appendix in this second printing (2002) contains new information about some of the buildings on Monument Avenue. Many of the new attributions and dates come from the City of Richmond building Permits and Drawings Collection: Blueprints, 1907–1940, in the archives at the Library of Virginia. These drawings are currently being catalogued by Selden Richardson, who kindly made the entries available to us for this second printing.

NOTES

Chapter One

1. For the history of Richmond, see Marie Tyler McGraw, *At the Falls: Richmond, Virginia, and Its People* (Chapel Hill: University of North Carolina Press, 1994); Christopher Silver, *Twentieth-Century Richmond: Planning, Politics, and Race* (Knoxville: University of Tennessee Press, 1984); Michael Chesson, *Richmond after the War, 1865–1890* (Richmond: Virginia State Library, 1981); and Virginius Dabney, *Richmond: The Story of a City* (Garden City, N.Y.: Doubleday and Co., 1976).

2. *Richmond Whig and Advertiser*, April 4, 1876, quoted in C. Vann Woodward, *Origins of the New South, 1877–1913* (Baton Rouge: Louisiana State University Press, 1951), 151.

3. The term "New South" comes from Henry Grady, the editor of the *Atlanta Constitution*, who used it in the 1880s; see Henry Grady, *The New South: Writings and Speeches of Henry Grady* (Savannah: Beehive Press, 1971). The classic study of the New South is Woodward, *Origins of the New South*. See also Edward L. Ayers, *The Promise of the New South: Life after Reconstruction* (New York: Oxford University Press, 1992).

4. For Richmond's West End, an invaluable source is Drew St. J. Carneal, *Richmond's Fan District*. (Richmond: Council of the Historic Richmond Foundation, 1996). For the creation of Western Square, see Richmond City Council Minutes, p. 521, July 21, 1851, Archives, Library of Virginia, Richmond.

5. Bainbridge Bunting, *Houses of Boston's Back Bay* (Cambridge: Harvard University Press, 1967); Walter Muir Whitehill, *Boston: A Topographic History* (Cambridge: Harvard University Press, 1959); and Boston Museum of Fine Arts, *Back Bay Boston: The City as a Work of Art* (Boston: Museum of Fine Arts, 1969).

6. Thomas B. Brumbaugh, "The Evolution of Crawford's Washington," *Virginia Magazine of History and Biography* 70 (January 1962): 3–29.

7. Wayne Craven, *Sculpture in America* (New York: Crowell, 1968), 235.

8. Among the few studies of Civil War statuary, see Catherine W. Bishir, "Landmarks of Power: Building a Southern Past, 1855–1915," *Southern Cultures* 1 (1993): 5–45; Wayne Craven, *The Sculptures at Gettysburg* (n.p., 1982); Kathryn Allamong Jacob, *Testament to Union: Civil War Monuments in Washington, D.C.* (Baltimore: Johns Hopkins University Press, 1998); and Kirk Savage, *Standing Soldiers, Kneeling Slaves: Race, War, and Monument in Nineteenth-Century America* (Princeton: Princeton University Press, 1997).

9. On the Confederate monuments, see Stephen Davis, "Empty Eyes, Marble Hand: The Confederate Monument and the South," *Journal of Popular Culture* 16 (Winter 1982): 2–21; and John J. Winberry, "Lest We Forget: The Confederate Monument and the Southern Townscape," *Southern Geographer* 23 (November 1983): 107–21. See also W. Asbury Christian, *Richmond: Her Past and Present* (1912; Spartanburg, S.C.: The Reprint Company, 1973), 348–49.

10. [Pamela H. Simpson], *American Sculpture in Lexington* (Lexington, Va.: Washington and Lee University 1977), 33.

11. Brooklyn Museum, *The American Renaissance, 1876–1917* (Brooklyn and New York: Brooklyn Museum and Pantheon Press, 1979).

12. *Richmond Dispatch*, October 29, 1887, 1.

13. Charles R. Wilson, *Baptized in Blood: The Religion of the Lost Cause, 1865–1920* (Athens: University of Georgia Press, 1980); Gaines M. Foster, *Ghosts of the Confederacy: Defeat, the Lost Cause, and the Emergence of the New South, 1865–1913* (New York: Oxford University Press, 1987); and Martha E. Kinney, "'If Vanquished I am Victorious': Religious and Cultural Symbolism in Virginia's Confederate Memorial Day Celebrations, 1866–1930," *Virginia Magazine of History and Biography* 106 (Summer 1998): 237–66.

14. Thomas L. Connelly, *The Marble Man: Robert E. Lee and His Image in American Society* (New York: Knopf, 1977).

15. "The Monument to General Robert E. Lee," *Southern Historical Society Papers* 17 (1889): 189.

16. *Richmond State*, June 30, 1886, quoted in Jay Killiam Bowman Williams, *Changed Views and Unforeseen Prosperity: Richmond of 1890 Gets a Monument to Lee* (Richmond: privately printed, 1969), 10.

17. *Richmond Dispatch*, June 19, 1886, 1.

18. Ibid., March 28, 1886, 5.

19. Ibid.

20. Ibid.

21. Emily J. Williams, "'A Home for the Old Boys: The Robert E. Lee Camp Confederate Soldiers' Home," *Virginia Cavalcade* 29 (Summer 1979): 40; and R. B. Rosenburg, *Living Monuments: Confederate Soldiers' Homes in the New South* (Chapel Hill: University of North Carolina Press, 1993).

22. *Richmond Dispatch*, June 19, 1886, 1.

23. "Statue and Sculpture," *Richmond Dispatch*, May 29, 1890, 2.

24. Robert H. Gudmestad, "Baseball, The Lost Cause and the New South in Richmond, Virginia, 1883–1890," *Virginia Magazine of History and Biography* 106 (Summer 1998): 267–300.

25. *Richmond Dispatch*, March 28, 1886, 5.

26. City of Richmond, *Common Council Journal*, 1890–1894, 262, Archives, Library of Virginia, Richmond. See also *Richmond Dispatch*, October 12, 1886, 1.

27. City of Richmond, *Common Council Journal*, 1890–1894, 262; and Williams, *Changed Views*, 41.

28. Allen Deed, June 18, 1887, Lee Monument Association Papers, State Treasurer's Office, Miscellaneous Papers, Library of Virginia, Richmond, quoted in Williams, *Changed Views*, 39.

29. Ibid. Burgwyn's obituaries are in the *Richmond Virginian*, February 24, 1915, 1; and the *Richmond Times-Dispatch*, February 24, 1915, 1, 5.

30. Williams, *Changed Views*, 34; *Richmond Dispatch*, October 28, 1887, 1; *Richmond Dispatch*, April 28, 1889, 5; Ann Hunter McLean, "Unveiling the Lost Cause" (Ph.D. diss., University of Virginia, 1998), 83.

31. Williams, *Changed Views*, 34–35, notes several complaints. See also *Richmond Whig*, September 22, 1887, 4; and various letters, such as Elizabeth Byrd Nicholas to Col. Archer Anderson, undated [probably late 1887], and Sarah Randolph to Col. Archer Anderson, November 11, 1887, Lee Monument Association Papers, State Treasurer's Office, Miscellaneous Papers, Library of Virginia, Richmond.

Chapter Two

1. Considerations of the Lee Monument are in Joseph T. Knox, "Le general Lee," *Virginia Cavalcade* 38 (Autumn 1988): 76–85; Ulrich Troubetzkoy, "The Lee Monument," *Virginia Cavalcade* 11

(Spring 1962): 5–10; Kirk Savage, *Standing Soldiers, Kneeling Slaves: Race, War, and Monument in Nineteenth-Century America* (Princeton: Princeton University Press 1997), chap. 5; and Ann Hunter McLean, "Unveiling the Lost Cause" (Ph.D. diss., University of Virginia, 1998), 59–78.

2. Colonel G. T. Fry to Samuel Basset French, November 10, 1877, Lee Monument Association Papers, State Treasurer's Office, Miscellaneous Papers, Library of Virginia, Richmond; also cited in Savage, *Standing Soldiers*, 142.

3. "Trash in the Library," *Richmond State*, November 17, 1877, 1.

4. Sarah Nichols Randolph to Fitzhugh Lee, April 16, 1886, Executive Papers, Fitzhugh Lee, Archives Division, Virginia State Library, Richmond, cited in Savage, *Standing Soldiers*, 139.

5. Undated clipping, Lee Monument File, Valentine Museum, Richmond, Va.

6. "Equestrian Monuments—XLIV," *American Architect and Building News* 34 (November 14, 1891): 104.

7. Ibid., and Lida Rose McCabe, "Mercie Talks about Lee," *Richmond Dispatch*, May 25, 1890, 1.

8. "Equestrian Monuments—XLIV," 103.

9. Joseph T. Knox, *Antonin Mercié: Sculptor of the Lee Monument*, exhibition catalogue (Richmond: French Institute, St. Christopher's School, 1990); Christiane Vogt, "Mercié (Marius-Jean-) Antonin," *Dictionary of Art*, ed. Jane Turner, 34 vols. (London and New York: Grove's Dictionaries, 1996), 21:147.

10. Savage, *Standing Soldiers*, 146, argues this point. On Saint-Gaudens and Mercié, see Homer Saint-Gaudens, ed., *Reminiscences of Augustus Saint-Gaudens*, 2 vols. (London: A. Melrose, 1913), 1:74–78, 110.

11. *Richmond Times*, October 28, 1887, 2, quoted in Jay Killiam Bowman Williams, *Changed Views and Unforeseen Prosperity: Richmond of 1890 Gets a Monument to Lee* (Richmond: privately printed, 1969), 19, n. 22.

12. "Viewing the Model," *Richmond Dispatch*, August 22, 1888, and *Richmond Daily Times*, August 22, 1888, clippings in Lee Monument File, Valentine Museum, Richmond, Va.; C. H. M., "The Lee Monument," *Richmond Dispatch*, April 28, 1889, 5.

13. G. J. D., "The Monument to Lee," *Richmond Times*, May 25, 1890, 6.

14. McCabe, "Mercie Talks about Lee," 1.

15. C. H. M., "The Lee Monument," 5.

16. "The Statue Is Here," *Richmond Dispatch*, May 6, 1890, 1.

17. "Equestrian Monuments—XLIV," 104.

18. "The Monument to General Robert E. Lee," *Southern Historical Society Papers* 17 (1889): 202–3.

19. "Praise by Paris," *Richmond Dispatch*, [ca. March 20, 1890], clipping, Lee Monument File, Valentine Museum, Richmond, Va. See also "The Lee Monument," *Richmond Times*, February 28, 1890, clipping, ibid.

20. "The Statue Is Here."

21. Ibid.

22. The accuracy of the 1857 legend is questioned in Thomas B. Brumbaugh, "The Evolution of Crawford's Washington," *Virginia Magazine of History and Biography* 70 (January 1962): 21, though it is reported in contemporary newspapers.

23. "Patriotic Pullers," *Richmond Dispatch*, May 8, 1890, 1; "Monument Complete," *Richmond Dispatch*, May 25, 1890, 1.

24. *Richmond Planet*, May 10, 1890, 2.

25. "What It Means," *Richmond Planet*, May 31, 1890, 4.

26. *Richmond Planet*, June 7, 1890, 2.

27. Ibid.

28. Savage, *Standing Soldiers*, 152.

29. Marie Tyler McGraw, *At the Falls: Richmond, Virginia, and Its People* (Chapel Hill: University of North Carolina Press, 1994), 225–27.

30. Colonel Archer Anderson, "Robert Edward Lee, An Address," *Southern Historical Society Papers* 17 (1889–90): 312–35.

31. "Unveiled," *Richmond Dispatch*, May 30, 1890, 1.

32. Undated and unidentified clippings; *Richmond State*, May 30, 1890; reprint of *New York Mail and Express*, Lee Monument File, Valentine Museum, Richmond, Va.

33. *New York Times*, May 30, 1890, 4.

34. "Memory of Our Dead," *Richmond Dispatch*, June 30, 1896, 9; see also "Richmond's Confederate Monuments," *Richmond Times*, June 30, 1896, 6.

35. Henry James, *The American Scene* (1907; New York: Horizon Press, 1967), 393; James originally published the Richmond section in the *Fortnightly Review* 86 (1906): 870.

36. The Stuart statue is covered in Ulrich Troubetzkoy, "The Best Picture of General Stuart," *Virginia Cavalcade* 12 (Winter 1962–63): 40–47; and McLean, "Unveiling the Lost Cause," 86–92.

37. "Memory of Stuart," *Richmond Dispatch*, May 24, 1896, 1; "Equestrian Statue to Major-General J. E. B. Stuart," *Richmond Times*, July 2, 1896, 6.

38. "J. E. B. Stuart Statue," *Richmond Dispatch*, November 16, 1902, 1.

39. Frederick Moynihan to Edward Valentine, October 7, 1896, Edward V. Valentine Papers, Valentine Museum, Richmond, Va.

40. Barbara Groseclose, *British Sculpture and the Company Raj* (Newark: University of Delaware Press, 1995), 17–18; Mark Stocker, "Foley, John Henry," Turner, *Dictionary of Art*, 11:237–39.

41. Frederick Moynihan to E. V. Valentine, n.d., marked "confidential," Edward V. Valentine Papers, Valentine Museum, Richmond, Va.

42. Letter, Frederick Moynihan to E. V. Valentine, November 28, 1895, ibid.

43. "Moynihan Design for Statue Is Accepted," *Richmond News-Leader*, May 11, 1904, 1.

44. "Mr. Montague Protests," *Richmond Times-Dispatch*, May 12, 1904, 2.

45. "The Stuart Monument," *Richmond News-Leader*, May 13, 1904, 4; "The Stuart Monument," ibid., May 24, 1904, 4.

46. "Lee Prompt in His Reply," *Richmond Times-Dispatch*, May 13, 1904, 2.

47. Troubetzkoy, "The Best Picture of General Stuart," 47.

48. *Richmond Times-Dispatch*, December 6, 1904, clipping, Lee Monument File, Valentine Museum, Richmond, Va.

49. *Richmond News-Leader*, May 11, 1904, 1.

50. Carden C. McGehee Jr., "The Planning, Sculpture, and Architecture of Monument Avenue, Richmond, Virginia" (M.A. thesis, University of Virginia, 1980), 94 and n. 25, cites *Board of Aldermen Journal*, City of Richmond, 1911–1914, p. 236.

51. *Richmond Times-Dispatch*, December 6, 1904, clipping, Stuart Monument File, Valentine Museum, Richmond, Va.

52. The Davis Monument is covered in John H. Moore, "The Jefferson Davis Monument," *Virginia Cavalcade* 10 (Spring 1961): 29–34; and McLean, "Unveiling the Lost Cause," 92–102.

53. Gaines M. Foster, *Ghosts of the Confederacy: Defeat, the Lost Cause, and the Emergence of the New South* (Baton Rouge: Louisiana State University Press, 1987), 89, 95–98.

54. Quoted in Moore, "The Jefferson Davis Monument," 30.

55. *Richmond News-Leader*, May 19, 1896, 3.

56. Illustrated in "Davis Monument Design," *Richmond Times*, June 30, 1896, 17; and *Richmond Dispatch*, June 30, 1896, 17. See also, "Have Many Designs," *Dispatch*, May 22, 1896, 8.

57. "The Davis Monument," *Richmond Times*, July 1, 1896, 1, 13; "Oratory, Prayer and Song," *Richmond Times*, July 3, 1896, 1–3; "The Stone Was Laid," *Richmond Dispatch*, July 3, 1896, 1, 7.

58. "Many Models for the Davis Arch," *Richmond Times*, May 25, 1902, 1; see also the following articles in the *Richmond Times*: "Mrs. Davis Willing for Memorial Arch," May 28, 1902, 1–2; "An Attack on Davis Arch," May 31, 1902, 1–2; "Well-Known Artists Have Submitted Models," June 1, 1902, 1, 6; "May Not Build Arch to Mr. Davis' Memory," June 3, 1902, 1–2; "Enemies of Davis Arch Gaining

Courage," June 4, 1902, 1; "Mrs. Davis Withdraws Opposition to Arch," June 5, 1902, 1–9; "Accepted Design for the Davis Memorial Arch," June 6, 1902, 1; "Davis Memorial Arch to Adorn Monroe Park," June 7, 1902, 1; "Design a Growth in Artist's Mind," June 8, 1902, 1, 14.

59. "Splendid Memorial," *Richmond Times-Dispatch*, November 15, 1903, 9, 1. Edward Virginius Valentine, *Dawn to Twilight: The Work of Edward V. Valentine*, ed. Elizabeth G. Valentine (Richmond: William Byrd Press, 1929), 140.

60. Board of Aldermen Journal, 1901–1904, 464, Archives, Library of Virginia, Richmond.

61. Kathy Edwards, Esme Howard, and Toni Prawl, *Monument Avenue: History and Architecture* (Washington, D.C.: Historic American Buildings Survey, 1992), 38, n. 97; Richmond City Council resolution of October 14, 1904, Richmond City Council Journals, Archives, Library of Virginia, Richmond; and Richmond Deed Book 187, A:2, Archives, Library of Virginia, Richmond.

62. Valentine, *Dawn to Twilight*, 139. See also L. Moody Simms, "A Virginia Sculptor," *Virginia Cavalcade* (Summer 1970): 20–27.

63. Charles E. Brownell, Calder Loth, William M. S. Rasmussen, and Richard Guy Wilson, *The Making of Virginia Architecture* (Richmond and Charlottesville: Virginia Museum of Fine Arts and the University Press of Virginia, 1992), 342, 330. The Virginia State Capitol extension was designed in conjunction with two other firms.

64. "Davis Monument Is Almost Ready," *Richmond News-Leader*, April 17, 1907, 1; "A Gentle Tribute to the Memory of Jefferson Davis," *Harper's Weekly*, May 4, 1907, 656.

65. *Richmond Times-Dispatch*, May 30, 1907, 1.

66. "Entire South Pays Tribute to Memory of Davis," *Richmond Times-Dispatch*, June 3, 1907, 1.

67. "Monument Is Unveiled," *Richmond News-Leader*, June 3, 1907, 5.

68. "Entire South Pays Tribute to Memory of Davis," 1.

69. "Monument Is Unveiled," 1.

70. *Richmond News-Leader*, October 11, 1919, 1.

71. *Richmond Times-Dispatch*, June 4, 1915, 8.

72. *Richmond News-Leader*, March 18, 1916, 4.

73. A multiple property listing for the National Register of Historic Places, probably the most detailed research article that has been done on the Jackson Monument in Charlottesville, gives no indication that Keck had already designed a model for a Jackson Monument for Richmond when he was commissioned to do another in 1919. See Betsy Gohdes-Baten, "Four Monumental Figurative Outdoor Sculptures donated by Paul Goodloe McIntire to the City of Charlottesville, Virginia and to the University of Virginia," April 13, 1996, Archives, Department of Historic Resources, Richmond, Va.

74. "Coppini, Pompeo," entry in Inventory of American Sculpture, Museum of American Art, Smithsonian Institution, Washington, D.C.

75. *Richmond News-Leader*, May 25, 1916, 5.

76. *Richmond Times-Dispatch*, October 12, 1919, 1.

77. Richmond Traffic Order No. 963, June 15, 1946, Richmond City Office of Traffic Engineering. In an article about Sievers, Troubetzkoy details the discussion. See Ulrich Troubetzkoy, "F. William Sievers, Sculptor," *Virginia Cavalcade* 12 (Autumn): 9. Also, in the National Register nomination for the Charlottesville monument, Gohdes-Baten notes a situation that illustrates the confusion. As the Jackson sculpture in Charlottesville was being installed, those present realized that it might look better if it faced north, "not from sentiment, but on account of the lay of the land." The benefactor decided to leave it facing south, but did not elaborate on his reasons. Gohdes-Baten, "Four Monumental Figurative Outdoor Sculptures," sec. 8, p. 7.

78. R. B. Munford Jr., "Dream of Maury Memorial True after Years of Toil," *Richmond News-Leader*, November 9, 1929, 9. Troubetzkoy, "F. William Sievers, Sculptor," is a biographical sketch of the sculptor of the Maury Monument. A wealth of information about the process through which the Maury Monument was created exists in the Maury Association Papers at the Virginia Historical Society, Richmond.

79. William Underwood, "Elvira Worth Jackson Walker Moffitt," *Dictionary of North Carolina Biography*, ed. William S. Powell, 6 vols. (Chapel Hill: University of North Carolina Press, 1979–96), 4:284–85.

80. Frances Leigh Williams, *Matthew Fontaine Maury: Scientist of the Sea* (New Brunswick, N.J.: Rutgers University Press, 1963); "Matthew Fontaine Maury," *Dictionary of American Biography*, 22 vols. (New York: Scribner's, 1928–58).

81. "Governor Eulogizes 'Pathfinder of the Seas,'" *Richmond Times-Dispatch*, June 23, 1922, 1.

82. Douglas Hall, "Armistice Day Celebration to Pay Tribute to 'Pathfinder of the Seas,'" *Richmond Times-Dispatch*, November 10, 1929, 5.

83. R. B. Munford Jr., "Sievers Finishes His Final Model for Maury Monument," *Richmond News-Leader*, March 9, 1929, 1. See also Sievers Papers, Virginia Historical Society, Richmond.

84. Sievers describes the Maury Monument and its iconography several times in the Maury Monument Association Papers and the Sievers Papers at the Virginia Historical Society, Richmond. Leslie A. Przybylek compares Sievers's Virginia Memorial at Gettysburg to his Maury Monument in detail, exploring the Maury Monument as Sievers's classical approach to modernism in "Soldiers to Science: Changing Commemorative Ideals in the Public Sculpture of Frederick William Sievers" (M.A. thesis, University of Delaware, 1995).

85. Arthur Ashe and Arnold Rampersad, *Days of Grace: A Memoir* (New York: Knopf, 1993), 283.

86. Ashe and Rampersad, *Days of Grace*, 267.

87. Arthur Ashe Jr., *A Hard Road to Glory: A History of the African-American Athlete since 1945* (New York: Warner Books, 1988).

88. Paul DiPasquale, personal communication with Richard Guy Wilson, January 27, 1999.

89. Jeanne Moutoussamy-Ashe to Paul DiPasquale, May 25, 1993, copy in possession of DiPasquale.

90. "Richmonders of the Year: Monumental Effort," *Style Weekly* 15 (January 7, 1997): 11.

91. Benjamin Forgey, "Richmond's Happy Median," *Washington Post*, December 1, 1996, G4.

92. "Arthur Ashe Monument Site Selection Process, Chronology, June 1995," typescript by Paul DiPasquale, in his possession.

93. *Richmond Times-Dispatch*, July 18, 1995, A1.

94. Gordon Hickey, "Sculptor Makes Changes," *Richmond Times-Dispatch*, December 28, 1995, A1.

95. Quoted in Peter Baker, "Richmond Is Still Not at Peace With Its Monumental Past," *Washington Post*, December 8, 1994, B7.

96. Tony Horwitz, *Confederates in the Attic* (New York: Pantheon Books, 1998), 249–52.

97. "Race-Tinged Furor Stalls Arthur Ashe Memorial," *New York Times*, July 9, 1995, 1, 20.

98. Gordon Hickey, "Ashe Statue Will Go on Monument," *Richmond Times-Dispatch*, July 18, 1995, A1, A10.

99. Michael Paul Williams, "National Embarrassment Avoided in 'Our Finest Hour,'" *Richmond Times-Dispatch*, July 18, 1995, A1, A10; Hickey, "Ashe Statue Will Go on Monument."

100. "Breaking Fertile Ground," *Roanoke Times and World News*, August 16, 1995, C1; "Council Again Gives OK to Ashe Statue Site," *Richmond Times-Dispatch*, February 27, 1996, B1.

101. "Ashe Statue Joins Those of Confederates," *New York Times*, July 11, 1996, A17.

102. Richmond Plat Book 6:176, Archives, Library of Virginia, Richmond; and City Council Resolution, February 12, 1925, Archives, Library of Virginia, Richmond.

103. Paul DiPasquale, personal communication with Richard Guy Wilson, January 27, 1999.

104. Among the many later commentaries are Richard T. Hines, "Free for All [letters to the editor]," *Washington Post*, July 27, 1996, A21; Edward Smith, "A Statue Lacking Stature," *Richmond Times-Dispatch*, January 18, 1997, A9; Cynthia Abramson, "Hero among Confederates," *Public Art Review* 8 (Fall/Winter 1996): 23, 25; Richard Foster, "Return of the Native," *Style Magazine*, September 17, 1997, 20; and Bill McKelway, "Love at First Site?," *Richmond-Times Dispatch*, July 16, 1996, D1, D3.

1. Ellen Glasgow, *Life and Gabriella: The Story of a Woman's Courage* (1916; New York: Charles Scribner's Sons, 1938), 501.

2. For the historical background, see Marie Tyler McGraw, *At the Falls: Richmond, Virginia, and Its People* (Chapel Hill: University of North Carolina Press, 1994), and Christopher Silver, *Twentieth-Century Richmond: Planning, Politics, and Race* (Knoxville: University of Tennessee Press, 1984).

3. Drew St. J. Carneal, *Richmond's Fan District* (Richmond: Council of the Historic Richmond Foundation, 1996). Carneal provides meticulously researched information on the Fan District and its development, as well as its architects, builders, and contractors.

4. Kathy Edwards, Esme Howard, and Toni Prawl, *Monument Avenue: History and Architecture* (Washington, D.C.: Historic American Buildings Survey, 1992), provides a detailed discussion of the development of Monument Avenue, from which much in this chapter is derived. Additional information has been provided by a catalogue of buildings assembled by students of Robert P. Winthrop at Virginia Commonwealth University and obtained from the City of Richmond, Building Permits and Drawings Collection, Library of Virginia, Richmond.

5. James Branch Cabell, *Branchiana, Being A Partial Account of the Branch Family in Virginia* (Richmond: Whittet & Shepperson, [1907]), 9. See also Edgar MacDonald, *James Branch Cabell and Richmond-in-Virginia* (Jackson: University Press of Mississippi, 1993).

6. Throughout this chapter and the appendix, the dates of houses and the professions of residents are taken from Edwards, Howard, and Prawl, *Monument Avenue*, apps. A and B; the Winthrop students' catalogue; and the City of Richmond, Building Permits and Drawings Collection, Library of Virginia, Richmond. The dates have been derived from several sources, including building permits, city directories, and insurance maps. There may be a variation of a year or two between the date of a permit and the date when a house appears as occupied in the city directory. In such instances, the more likely of the dates has been chosen, but the differences in the dates are usually minimal. Several buildings were built over a long period of time. For those, beginning and end dates are shown.

7. Permits number 1289 and 1290, City of Richmond, Building Permits and Drawings Collection, Library of Virginia, Richmond.

8. Payne lost some of his properties in a foreclosure, a common occurrence for those who tried to develop upper-class housing as a speculative venture. Richmonders preferred individual designs for expensive dwellings.

9. John E. Wells and Robert E. Dalton, *The Virginia Architects, 1835–1955: A Biographical Dictionary* (Richmond: New South Architectural Press, 1997), 107–11; and Carneal, *Richmond's Fan District*, 209–12.

10. Edwards, Howard, and Prawl, *Monument Avenue*, 210–11.

11. Edith Wharton, *The Age of Innocence* (New York: D. Appleton & Co., 1920), 29.

12. On the history of American apartment houses, see Robert A. M. Stern, Gregory Gilmartin, and John Massengale, *New York 1900* (New York: Rizzoli, 1983), 279–305; James M. Goode, *Best Addresses: A Century of Washington's Distinguished Apartment Houses* (Washington, D.C.: Smithsonian Institution Press, 1988); Paul Baker, *Richard Morris Hunt* (Cambridge: MIT Press, 1980), 204–10; Elizabeth C. Cromley, *Alone Together: A History of New York's Early Apartments* (Ithaca: Cornell University Press, 1990); and Elizabeth Hawes, *New York, New York: How the Apartment House Transformed the Life of the City (1869–1930)* (New York: Knopf, 1993).

13. Myron Berman, *Richmond's Jewry, 1769–1976* (Charlottesville: University Press of Virginia, 1979), 246–49, 254.

14. Conversation between Robert P. Winthrop and M. Greentree, son of Meyer Greentree, 1983.

15. There is not an adequate study of American religious architecture; for background, see Peter W. Williams, *Houses of God: Region, Religion, and Architecture in the United States* (Urbana and Chicago:

University of Illinois Press, 1997); and Roger G. Kennedy, *American Churches* (New York: Stewart, Tabori & Chang, 1982).

16. Mary Grace Scherer Taylor, *Saints Alive!* (Richmond: Dietz Press, 1976).

17. Richard A. Cheek, *Through One and One Quarter Centuries: An Historical Booklet Published for the Quasquicentennial Anniversary of St. John's United Church of Christ, 1843–1968* (Richmond: Dietz Press, 1968).

Chapter Four

1. Thorstein Veblen, *Theory of the Leisure Class* (1899; Boston: Houghton Mifflin Co., 1973), 60.

2. Brooklyn Museum, *The American Renaissance, 1876–1917* (Brooklyn and New York: Brooklyn Museum and Pantheon Press, 1979).

3. Ellen Glasgow, *Life and Gabriella* (1916; New York: Charles Scribner's Sons, 1938), 402.

4. Harry Desmond and Herbert Croly, *Stately Homes in America* (New York: D. Appleton, 1903), 279, 287. Although there are many individual studies of the homes of wealthy Americans in the period 1880–1930, an overall study—and in particular a study of the newly wealthy's houses—is lacking. A partial exception is James T. Maher, *The Twilight of Splendor: Chronicles of the Age of American Palaces* (Boston: Little Brown and Co., 1975). See also J. Mordaunt Crook, *The Rise of the Nouveaux Riches: Style and Status in Victorian and Edwardian Architecture* (North Pomfret, Vt.: John Murray/ Trafalgar Square, 1999), which is devoted to England.

5. Ellen Glasgow, *The Woman Within* (New York: Hill and Wang, 1980 [1944]), 217–18.

6. Ibid., 217.

7. Ellen Glasgow, *They Stooped to Folly* (New York: Doubleday, Doran & Co., 1929), 28–29.

8. Edith Wharton and Ogden Codman, *The Decoration of Houses* (New York: Charles Scribner's Sons, 1897; subsequent editions, 1901, 1907, and 1917—and there have been more recent reprints as well). Elsie de Wolfe, *The House in Good Taste* (New York: Century Co., 1913; subsequent editions, 1914, 1920).

9. There is no adequate study of "traditional" American interiors of the twentieth century. Books that contain some discussion of the subject are Pauline Metcalf, ed., *Ogden Codman and the Decoration of Houses* (Boston: Boston Athenaeum and David R. Godine, 1988); and Stephen Calloway, *Twentieth-Century Decoration* (New York: Rizzoli, 1988), which is British oriented.

10. Eben Howard Gay, *A Chippendale Romance* (New York: Longmans, Green and Co., 1915); and Walter Alden Dyer, *The Lure of the Antique* (New York: Century Co., 1910).

11. Henry Beck, *Building Code, City of Richmond* (Richmond: Clyde W. Saunders, 1912).

12. A discussion of building codes is found in Kathy Edwards, Esme Howard, and Toni Prawl, *Monument Avenue: History and Architecture* (Washington, D.C.: Historic American Buildings Survey, 1992), 48–49. Portions of this chapter draw upon this study.

13. William Herbert [Montgomery Schuyler], *Houses for Town or Country* (New York: Duffield & Co., 1907), 10. See also Alan Gowans, *The Comfortable House: North American Suburban Architecture, 1890–1930* (Cambridge: MIT Press, 1986).

14. Mint Museum of Art, *Southern Arts and Crafts* (Charlotte, N.C.: Mint Museum of Art, 1996).

15. Allen W. Jackson, "The Half-timber House," in Henry H. Saylor, ed., *Architectural Styles for Country Houses* (New York: McBride, 1919), 77–88.

16. The literature on the Colonial Revival is vast; see Alan Axelrod, ed., *The Colonial Revival in America* (New York: W. W. Norton, 1985); and Richard Guy Wilson, "Building on the Foundations," in Charles E. Brownell, Calder Loth, William M. S. Rasmussen, and Richard Guy Wilson, *The Making of Virginia Architecture* (Richmond and Charlottesville: Virginia Museum of Fine Arts and the University Press of Virginia, 1992), 83–131.

17. Joseph Everett Chandler, *The Colonial House* (New York: McBride, 1916), 252.

18. Vincent Scully, *The Shingle Style* (New Haven: Yale University Press, 1955).

19. Glenn Brown, "Old Colonial Work in Virginia and Maryland," *American Architect and Building News* 22 (October 22, November 19, 26, 1887): 198–99, 242–43, 254; reprinted in *The Georgian Period*, pts. 1–2 (New York: American Architect and Building News, 1898–1901), pls. 9–10.

20. Gavin Townsend, "The Tudor House in America, 1890–1940" (Ph.D. diss., University of California at Santa Barbara, 1986).

21. "The Virginia Chapter, AIA: A History," in *Virginia Architect's Handbook* (Richmond: Virginia Chapter, American Institute of Architects, 1968), 19–23; Turpin C. Bannister, ed., *The Architect at Mid-Century: Evolution and Achievement*, 2 vols. (New York: Reinhold, 1954), 1:357; and Mary N. Woods, *From Craft to Profession: The Practice of Architecture in Nineteenth-Century America* (Berkeley: University of California Press, 1999).

22. Edwards, Howard, and Prawl, *Monument Avenue*, 76.

23. For a list of Huntt's works, as well as those of any of the other architects mentioned, see John E. Wells and Robert E. Dalton, *The Virginia Architects, 1835–1955: A Biographical Dictionary* (Richmond: New South Architectural Press, 1997), an invaluable resource; Huntt's works are listed on pp. 218–20. A good discussion of Huntt's work in the Fan District is Drew St. J. Carneal, *Richmond's Fan District* (Richmond: Council of the Historic Richmond Foundation, 1996), 188–91. His downtown Richmond work is described in Robert P. Winthrop, *Architecture in Downtown Richmond* (Richmond: Historic Richmond Foundation, 1982).

24. Wells and Dalton, *The Virginia Architects*, 391–92.

25. Ibid., and "David Wiley Anderson," in *Dictionary of Virginia Biography*, ed. John T. Kneebone, J. Jefferson Looney, Brent Tarter, and Sandra Gioia Treadway (Richmond: Library of Virginia, 1998), vol. 1.

26. Wells and Dalton, *The Virginia Architects*, 207–9. Howell's Richmond theaters are discussed in Winthrop, *Architecture in Downtown Richmond*, 60.

27. Laura Johnson lived in Richmond for just a few years. She died in the West, and the house was inherited by her daughter, Mary Scarborough. It is not known if Mary Scarborough was related to Howell's partner.

28. Richard Guy Wilson, *McKim, Mead & White, Architects* (New York: Rizzoli, 1983); and Leland Roth, *McKim, Mead & White, Architects* (New York: Harper, 1983).

29. Richard Guy Wilson, *"Arise and Build!": A Centennial Commemoration of the 1895 Rotunda Fire* (Charlottesville: University of Virginia Library, 1995), 17.

30. Allen's house had been credited previously to John Kevan Peebles, but Selden Richardson has pointed out detailed drawings and specifications for the Allen house by Claude K. Howell in the City of Richmond, Building Permits and Drawings Collection at the Library of Virginia, Richmond. As Richardson continues to catalogue and describe this collection, more new information about Monument Avenue may come to light.

31. Wells and Dalton, *The Virginia Architects*, 345–50. Peebles's work is discussed and illustrated in Winthrop, *Architecture in Downtown Richmond*.

32. Coleman Baskerville added the final "e" to his name. The firm has reverted to Henry Baskervill's "e"-less spelling.

33. Wells and Dalton, *The Virginia Architects*, 23–25, 328–31; Elizabeth Drake Updike, "Henry Eugene Baskerville and William Churchill Noland: Richmond's Response to the American Renaissance," (Master of Architectural History thesis, University of Virginia, 1987).

34. Edwards, Howard, and Prawl, *Monument Avenue*, 177.

35. This connection was pointed out by Davyd Foard Hood.

36. William B. O'Neal and Christopher Week, *The Work of William Lawrence Bottomley in Richmond* (Charlottesville: University Press of Virginia, 1985); and Davyd Foard Hood, "William Lawrence Bottomley in Virginia: The 'Neo-Georgian' Houses in Richmond" (Master of Architectural History thesis, University of Virginia, 1975).

37. William Lawrence Bottomley, "Small Italian and Spanish Houses as a Basis for Design," *Archi-*

tectural Forum 44 (March 1926): 185–90, and "Spanish Furniture of the XVI and XVII Centuries . . . ," *Arts and Decoration* 23 (November 1925): 42–43, 80.

38. Edith Sheerin, granddaughter of Mr. and Mrs. J. Scott Parrish, to Susan Eckis, March 1999, in Eckis's possession.

39. Steven McLeod Bedford, *John Russell Pope: Architect of Empire* (New York: Rizzoli, 1998); we are indebted to Bedford for information on the Branch house. Also, for the interior, see Allen W. Jackson, "The Englishman and His Country Home," *Country Life* 34 (October 1918): 38.

40. Wells and Dalton, *The Virginia Architects*, 252–55. Carneal, *Richmond's Fan District*, 195–96.

41. Sarah Shields Driggs interview with Jane Cecil, the Pollards' daughter, February 20, 1998.

42. Wells and Dalton, *The Virginia Architects*, 490–92.

43. John Summerson, *Architecture in Britain, 1530–1830*, 5th ed. (Harmondsworth, Eng.: Pelican, 1970), chap. 5.

44. James Ruehrmund (grandson of Carl Ruehrmund), in personal conversation with Robert P. Winthrop, explained these relationships and provided insight into the family's working arrangements. More details were discussed by Ruehrmund March 6, 2000, with Sarah Shields Driggs.

45. Wells and Dalton, *The Virginia Architects*, 261–63.

Chapter Five

1. Ellen Glasgow, *Life and Gabriella* (1916; New York: Charles Scribner's Sons, 1938), 395.

2. Sam Richardson, quoted in Neil November, "I Remember When . . . ," *Richmond Times-Dispatch*, May 29, 1949.

3. *House & Garden* 72 (November 1937) devoted the entire issue to Williamsburg and published three house designs by the restoration architects (pp. 69–80).

4. Kathy Edwards, Esme Howard, and Toni Prawl, *Monument Avenue: History and Architecture* (Washington, D.C.: Historic American Buildings Survey, 1992), 99.

5. "Mayor Supports Plan for More Monuments," *Richmond News-Leader*, November 17, 1965.

6. The paving blocks on Monument are commonly referred to as "Belgian Blocks." They are actually Hastings Blocks, an American-made paver. The Hastings Company still operates and produced new pavers for the restoration of the paving in the 1970s.

7. James Davis, "City Council Grants Delay in Paving Monument Avenue," *Richmond Times-Dispatch*, July 24, 1969; see also the "Monument Avenue" vertical file, Valentine Museum, Richmond, Va.

8. Karen Schultz, "Dali Statue of Nurse Suggested," *Richmond News-Leader*, March 17, 1966, 1; Harry Kollatz Jr., "Richmond As It Never Was," *Richmond* 3, no. 5 (May 1995): 47–49; Kevin Concannon, "Dali in Virginia," unpublished typescript, December 10, 1996, Virginia Historical Society, Richmond.

INDEX

HISTORIC MONUMENT AVENUE AND FAN DISTRICT FOUNDATION DONORS

The Lee Circle: Individuals, $2,500+

Ceci Amrhein-Gallasch and Bill Gallasch
Zayde R. Dotts
Bruce B. Gray
Cabell and Patti Harris
Mr. and Mrs. Thomas M. Horton
Mr. and Mrs. C. Todd Peyton Jenkins
Judge and Mrs. Thomas O. Jones
Richard and Sylvia Summers
Helen Marie Taylor
Keith Kissee and David E. Tolman, M.D.
Molly and Mike Wray

The Lee Circle: Foundations and Corporations, $2,500+

Elmwood Fund, Inc.
Martha Moore Trust
A Private Richmond Foundation
Roller-Bottimore Foundation
Windsor Foundation

Individuals, $1,000–2,499

Mr. and Mrs. James C. Ambler Jr.
Dr. and Mrs. Wyatt S. Beazley III
Roy E. Burgess II
Doug and Carole Conner
Michael T. Dan
Mr. and Mrs. Gregory A. Forman
Marjorie Richardson Goodall
Frances A. Lewis
Calder Loth
Stella H. and Hugh C. Miller

Janice and Steve Nuckolls
Mary and Jack Spain

Organizations, $1,000–2,499

Bon Secours–Stuart Circle Hospital
Fan District Association
Monument Avenue Preservation Society

Individuals, $250–999

Pat and Jordan Ball
Dr. and Mrs. Joseph Battista Jr.
John and Judy Beardsworth
Janet F. Brown
Stewart Bryan
Dr. and Mrs. Francis F. Carr Jr.
Elisabeth Reed Carter
Mr. and Mrs. James C. Cherry
Pat Daniels and Mike Rohde
Joni and Mark Dray
Mr. and Mrs. Marshall H. Earl Jr.
Warren Fry and Tina Bachas
Pat and Jim Glave
James W. Gunnard and Joseph Ross Hill
Mr. and Mrs. William G. Hancock
Walter and Mary Anne Hooker
Mr. and Mrs. Thomas Jefferson III
Frank and Elinor Kuhn
Mark and Georgia Kukoski
Al and Bev Lacy
Sue and David Nagle
Mr. and Mrs. H. J. Parry Jr.
William H. Poarch

Jacquelyn and Bob Pogue
Mr. and Mrs. W. Taylor Reveley III
Dr. and Mrs. Thomas L. Shortt
Doug and Bonnie Stanard
Barbara and Roy Sutton
Mr. and Mrs. William S. Tate
Gary and Robyn Tyer
Mr. and Mrs. George A. Warthen II
Susan Weeks
Mr. and Mrs. George B. Wickham
Mr. and Mrs. David G. Wilson Jr.
Marshall and Stevie Wishnack

Mr. and Mrs. David A. Wofford
Dr. and Mrs. H. S. Zfass
Gail F. Zwirner and Paul M. Feine

Foundations and Corporations, $250–999

John Stewart Bryan Memorial Foundation, Inc.
The Fan Woman's Club
Historic Richmond Foundation
Liberty Mortgage Corporation
Virginia Foundation for Architecture
West of the Boulevard Civic Association